Praise for *Thirty Da*

From revi

"Mariani is a revealer . . . An engagingly and earnestly told story."
—*The Washington Post Book World*

"The lessons Mariani has learned prove compelling . . . Mariani's journey is a courageous act, and even an inspiring one."
—*San Francisco Chronicle*

"Mariani is a gifted poet, a mature writer, whose control of his material is beautiful to witness. For so talented an artist, everything is grist for his craft . . . *Thirty Days* is a glimpse of the effects of grace in a man who tries, through silence and prayer, to come closer to God."
—*America*

"[Readers] will be introduced to the heady *Spiritual Exercises* in an accessible way. Engaging, informative, and inspiring."
—*Library Journal*

"Gracious and courageous . . . with some wonderfully tender moments."
—*Publishers Weekly*

"[A] graceful memoir . . . a worthy addition."
—*Chicago Tribune*

. . . and from writers . . .

"Not since Henri Nouwen's *Genesee Diary* has a writer managed to wrestle (or dance) the elusive experience of a religious search into such a winning narrative. This is a big-hearted book, a treasure from a gifted poet whose 'retreat' is a revelation of reaching out.
—Patricia Hampl, author of *A Romantic Education* and *Virgin Time*

"Paul Mariani has gifted us with his finest book yet in these privileged insights into the vexations, joys, and mysteries of a passionate soul that is ever alert and responsive to the quiet promptings of God. *Thirty Days* is a stunning, moving, uplifting book.
—Ron Hansen, author of *Mariette in Ecstasy* and *A Stay Against Confusion*

"*Thirty Days* is a daring and courageous book, an intimate tour of a life of prayer and a vigorous life of the mind that leaves little unnoticed."
—Barry Moser, designer of *The Holy Bible: King James Version*

"In this groundbreaking new book, Paul Mariani, a layperson, invites the reader to accompany him on a spiritual journey that countless believers point to as the most important of their lives . . . *Thirty Days* is a classic in contemporary spiritual literature."

—James Martin, S.J., *America* magazine and author of *In Good Company*

and from readers.

"Thank you for writing *Thirty Days*—for the courage it took to be so honest and vulnerable. I have directed many thirty-day retreats. You have been able to express—eloquently—what can go on if a person is willing to let 'the Creator deal directly' with him or her. Congratulations and thank you!" —Fr. William A. Barry, former Provincial of the New England Province of the Society of Jesus

"I just finished reading *Thirty Days* and found it moving, down to earth, and vivid on every page. It was the human honesty of the book that made me hungry to pick it up again every time I had to put it down."

—Mark Jarman, poet

"*Thirty Days* has been a true source of inspiration and I want to write you sincere words of gratitude. You wield a mighty pen that portrays an even mightier heart."

—Eugene Linehan, S.J. Georgetown Preg, North Bethesda, Maryland

"I just finished reading your work, *Thirty Days,* and wanted to tell you how it has benefited me. More than anything else, I think I appreciated the emerging sense of gratitude that began to inform and permeate your experience. I do believe that the stance of thankfulness is fundamental to any spiritual life, and it was a pleasure to see how it emerged over the course of the Exercises."

—Rev. Justin DuVall, O.S.B., Saint Meinrad School of Theology

"Thank you for your deep honesty in writing about your experience, and your willingness to share it with the rest of us."

—Amy L. Cavender, CSC

THIRTY DAYS

Paul Mariani, an award–winning poet, critic, essayist, and biographer of William Carlos Williams, Hart Crane, John Berryman, and Robert Lowell, holds a chair in English at Boston College. A former professor of English at the University of Massachusetts, he has lectured widely across the country and lives in Montague, Massachusetts.

THIRTY DAYS

On Retreat with the
Exercises of St. Ignatius

PAUL MARIANI

PENGUIN COMPASS

PENGUIN COMPASS
Published by the Penguin Group
Penguin Putnam Inc., 375 Hudson Street, New York, New York 10014, U.S.A.
Penguin Books Ltd, 80 Strand, London WC2R 0RL, England
Penguin Books Australia Ltd, 250 Camberwell Road, Camberwell, Victoria 3124, Australia
Penguin Books Canada Ltd, 10 Alcorn Avenue, Toronto, Ontario, Canada M4V 3B2
Penguin Books India (P) Ltd, 11 Community Centre, Panchsheel Park,
New Delhi – 110 017, India
Penguin Books (N.Z.) Ltd, Cnr Rosedale and Airborne Roads,
Albany, Auckland, New Zealand
Penguin Books (South Africa) (Pty) Ltd, 24 Sturdee Avenue, Rosebank,
Johannesburg 2196, South Africa

Penguin Books Ltd, Registered Offices:
Harmondsworth, Middlesex, England

First published in the United States of America by Viking Compass,
a member of Penguin Putnam Inc. 2002
Published in Penguin Compass 2003

10 9 8 7 6 5 4 3 2 1

THE LIBRARY OF CONGRESS HAS CATALOGED THE HARDCOVER EDITION AS FOLLOWS:
Mariani, Paul L.
Thirty days : on retreat with the Exercises of St. Ignatius / Paul Mariani.
p. cm.
ISBN 0-670-89455-9 (hc.)
ISBN 0 14 21.9615 0 (pbk.)
1. Ignatius, of Loyola, Saint, 1491–1556. Exercita spiritualia. 2. Spiritual exercises.
3. Spiritual retreats. I. Title.
BX2179.L8 M334 2002
248.3—dc21 2001045432

Printed in the United States of America
Set in Garamond Three with Novarese display and Caslon ornaments
Designed by Carla Bolte

For Paul Philip and the Company of Jesus

Deep calls to deep . . .

—PSALM 42

CONTENTS

THIRTY DAYS

PROLOGUE

By the term "Spiritual Exercises" we mean every method of examination of conscience, meditation, contemplation, vocal or mental prayer, and other spiritual activities, such as will be mentioned later. For just as taking a walk, traveling on foot, and running are physical exercise, so is the name of spiritual exercises given to any means of preparing and disposing our soul to rid itself of all its disordered affections and then, after their removal, of seeking and finding God's will in the ordering of our life for the salvation of our soul.

—St. Ignatius of Loyola, *Spiritual Exercises*

TUESDAY, JANUARY 4, 2000

4:00 P.M. An ordering, as in a set of directions for getting there. And so, finally, by map, northeast of Boston and east of Gloucester, to a room (call it a cell) facing the North Atlantic. Beginning to settle in—whatever that means—here at Gonzaga Retreat House on Eastern Point, a place run by the New England Jesuits, preparing for a Thirty-Day silent directed retreat. Oh boy!

Drizzle and fog all afternoon, inside as well as out. Damn hard leaving Eileen. I could see she was keeping herself busy cleaning shelves, doing laundry, writing notes. *Anything* to keep her mind off the fact that in a short while her husband would walk out the door for five weeks, with two half-day visits only, and those on the eleventh and twenty-first days of the retreat. I too dithered about as long as I could, and then—at a quarter to one—kissed her good-bye and drove east along Route 2, past Gardner, Fitchburg, and Lexington, then onto Interstate 95 heading north around Boston, then east, and so to Gloucester. One hundred and fifteen miles. A two-hour-plus trip.

In the hours before I left, everything took on added significance. It was almost as if I'd been going off to war, or to a hospital from which I might not be returning. The truth is you can no more rehearse separation than you can death. I packed—casual stuff, for there will be no formalities here, no grand dinners, no events. Just the daily round of silence and prayer and meetings with a spiritual director. And at this point I don't even know if my director is a man or a woman, though I hope it's a Jesuit.

The place is officially called Gonzaga, after Aloysius Gonzaga, a Jesuit saint—an Italian nobleman of the illustrious Gonzagas—who died at the age of twenty-three caring for plague victims. The place took his name because he was young and this was once a Jesuit retreat house for high-school boys before being turned into a general retreat house some forty years ago. Everywhere a faded glory still hangs about the place: in the fine wood paneling and molded ceiling decorations, all dating back to the early 1920s, when the main house, built in a combination English Tudor and French country-estate style, was still a private residence with a commanding view of the Atlantic. These jerrybuilt, ugly aluminum windows and doors and the added wing that once served as a dorm for students on retreat, and which now houses other retreatants, look to have been added in the '50s, perhaps the worst decade ever in American architectural history.

A mix of rubbed splendor and practicality: like the Jesuits themselves. Good real estate turned to practical ends, rather like Napoleon's troops turning the Prado into stables for their horses. A place had to be found for retreats, and the Jesuits found it, here at Eastern Point. Still, one has all the luxury of living on an estate: walks along the Atlantic, three squares a day, heat, a roof over one's head, a room of one's own. Plus a spiritual director for the care and feeding of the soul. All this for thirty dollars a day, plus my undivided attention. Not bad. The only downside is living alone, in unbroken silence, praying every day for hours on end, and no movies, no TV, no radio, and one or two newspapers on a table for all of us to share. Still, I need this time, as the Psalmist says, as much as the thirsty deer that pants for water.

Only the flowers in the jars and vases in the Main Hall, where the altar table is, suggest a woman's hand. There are two here on the staff: a sister on loan, Mary Boretti, the one who answered my queries over the phone, and a laywoman who took her training at the Weston Jesuit School of Theology in Cambridge whose name is Dixie Burden. Otherwise, there seems to be a military cast about the place, a Spartan quality, as there is, of course, about the Jesuits themselves, a certain something that goes back to Ignatius, the founder of the Order and the only begetter of the *Spiritual Exercises.* A strong-willed bantam of a Basque fighter who refused to surrender to the French at Pamplona in one of those internecine border clashes back in the early sixteenth century and who had his legs shattered by a ricocheting cannonball for his troubles. A man who spent eleven months learning how to make the first thirty-day retreat based on his *Exercises.*

For twenty-five years now I've told myself I'd take this time out to go into the desert and meet my God face-to-face. And of course something always intervened: raising a family, the impossibility of being away too long from my teaching or writing. If truth be told, the willingness to find almost any excuse rather than actually undertake what Christ calls the one thing necessary: time—lots of it—spent with Him.

And why Gloucester? After all, I've never been taught by the Jesuits, at least in a classroom setting. Nuns did that in catechism classes for years. And then the Marianists at Chaminade High in Mineola, the town thirty miles out on Long Island where I lived—except for my one year in the Marianist seminary in Beacon—from the time I was thirteen until the day I got married. After the Marianists, it was the Christian Brothers at Manhattan College up in the Bronx. Over the years I've tried meditation—*Zazen*—and Franciscan pilgrimages to the Holy Land and Benedictine retreats, listening to the sound of the monks breaking the early spring darkness with plainchant in the church, then walking back down the hill to my bed in the predawn dark. And yet, looking back now, I see I've been following the Ignatian way for years, first in retreats on Staten Island with my father-in-law, then in the dark, lonely halls of the old Jesuit theology buildings in Weston, Massachusetts, where the elderly and infirm Jesuits find excellent care in their last years.

Then, too, there's my long literary association—positive and negative—with the Jesuits via Donne, Flannery O'Connor, Brian Moore, and that guilt-ridden Irishman Joyce. Especially there's my lifelong love of Gerard Manley Hopkins, the Jesuit whose poems I've taught and written about now for thirty-five years, and whom I have come to love like my own life. Throw in the brilliance and force of the early Jesuits, from Ignatius's companion, Francis Xavier, in India and Japan, to Matteo Ricci in China, the Jesuit who became a white-robed Confucian to gain the Emperor's confidence. Or the raw courage of the French Black Robes in Canada among the Iroquois and Hurons—Isaac Jogues and Jean de Brébeuf and the others in the flint-backed snows, fording the rapids into the interior of a brave new world. Or the Spanish Jesuits in Paraguay and Brazil, murdered by Portuguese soldiers for protecting the Indians there. Then, too, there's my oldest son, my namesake, who will be ordained a Jesuit priest in two and a half years.

So it made sense, I guess, to bite the bullet finally and do the Long Retreat Ignatius handed down as a way of coming in closer contact with God. In any case, I'm here for the long haul. This isn't the annual Eight-Day Jesuit retreat I've made half a dozen times over the past thirty years, or one of the Cursillo three-day retreats I've made in Holyoke for the past twenty-five. No, this is the big one: two days of prep, followed by thirty of almost total silence, with two half days off for socializing built into the structure, and finally two days of debriefing. It used to be that you had lunch on the thirtieth day and then walked out of here to rejoin the larger world. Like soldiers being moved to a new assignment. But they've added on these last two days by way of a debriefing, I guess. At least with the prep days I'll get to talk to some of the men and women who are about to go on the same journey I'll be making over the next month.

The question right now of course is, can I really do this? "Thirty days of silence," a friend said to me. "Hell, I couldn't keep silence for thirty minutes." It all made such eminent good sense back in November, when I applied for a spot here, filling out the long forms and getting letters of support to prove I wasn't crazy, and that I could actually see this retreat through. You might have thought I was going to the moon. Now I'm not so sure I really can make it through these next five weeks. How could I leave Eileen like this, four days into the New Year, the new century, the new millennium? It's hard enough being away from her overnight, especially in these last ten years or so. No matter. I have to believe He has led me here. "Eighty and six years have I been his servant," the Church Father St. Polycarp told his tormentors as he faced his own martyrdom, "and He has done me no harm. How can I blaspheme my King who saved me?" That was before they burned him alive in the amphitheater in Smyrna. Make it fifty-nine years for me, His servant at least part of that time.

The guidelines I was sent last month—once I'd been approved for the Thirty-Day Retreat—stipulated that I bring only two books with me and leave the others home. One is *The Jerusalem Bible*. The other is a copy of St. Ignatius Loyola's *Spiritual Exercises,* translated and with a commentary by Fr. George Ganss, S.J. It's a small book, the *Exercises.* A hundred and twenty pages with supplements. But how much is packed in there. Ganss says there have been 450 translations of the *Exercises* in the past 480 years. How many millions of retreatants since then have wound their way through them?

In addition, I've brought Ron Hansen's essay on the life of Loyola, as well as my *Magnificat* paperback, which slips easily into my pocket, and which I carry with me everywhere these days. I think of it as my layman's breviary, with the order and readings for Mass each day, as well as morning and evening prayers, and a daily meditation by a surprising range of saints, Church Fathers, and modern theologians and poets, women and men. I've also brought a collection of pens and pencils, as well as several blank blue-backed journals to keep notes in. Eileen and I both opted against my bringing my spiffy, state-of-the-art new laptop she gave me for Christmas. Too high tech for what I'm going to be doing here. Besides, I want the feel of my pen and wrist against the surface of the page. I want something more elemental, more physical, something more in keeping with the *Exercises* and the way generations of retreatants have made them.

The first (and last) time I was here was back in November 1984. It was the week Ronald Reagan was reelected to a second term. Ironically, I too had an election to make: leave my wife and family (and commit spiritual suicide) or learn how to behave. No wonder Eileen and I had such powerful if unspoken feelings when I left home today. I remember Fr. Rich Meehan, my spiritual director back then, a parish priest who'd been trained in the *Exercises,* telling me that the week I'd spent here had probably saved my marriage (to say nothing of my life), but that I should consider returning some day, when my life wasn't under siege. He was right. The sad part is that it has taken fifteen years to get back here.

The first law of spiritual psychodynamics seems to be this: if something can go wrong at the starting point, it will. The first indication that things were not going to go as planned was missing the turn-off to Eastern Point Boulevard. A yellow school bus had parked in front of the gates blocking the road and the street marker, with the result that, fifteen minutes later, I had looped my way back into Gloucester, angry and frustrated for getting lost at the very outset. I, who had equipped myself with written directions and two maps. Finally, admitting to myself that I didn't have the foggiest idea where the hell I was, I pulled over onto the gravel driveway of a roadside diner and got out to ask directions. The place was deserted. A woman in her fifties—businesslike, kindly, but looking tired—took one glance at me and asked if I was looking for the Eastern Point Retreat House. How many others over the years had wound up here to ask for directions?

How could I have lost my way, I stammered, embarrassed?

"We all get lost sometimes, honey," she offered quietly, without condescension. Then she pointed to where I was on the map and showed me how I'd gone wrong.

We all get lost sometimes. My first sign, and I've barely left home. Is this how it's going to be, Lord, with the signs waiting to be plucked out of air, thin air?

It was half past three when I pulled my Sable into a delicious spot just off the main circle, got out, walked past the Main House and in through the storm door leading to the dining hall. Sister Mary Boretti, the soft-spoken administrator with whom I'd spoken on the phone, smiled and welcomed me into the office just off the entrance, where she gave me my room assignment. There are no keys, though there is a door bolt once you're inside your room. They've given me No. 10 on the second floor of the Main House, and not one of those characterless rooms tacked on to the west wing fifty years ago. This alone, in a minimalist world, already makes me something of a small-time poobah.

Even so, the place is little more than a monk's cell. I can almost touch both walls with my arms stretched out. A single window overlooks the Atlantic. What else is here? A cold bed, a much-put-upon all-utility green rug covering the floor, an imitation-leather chair facing the window, and another—a pinewood affair in which I'm sitting now, while I write at this small desk with its beige Formica top. A foot behind me: a sink with a towel rack and a makeshift wooden shelf with room for a razor and toothbrush. At the foot of the bed there's a small closet with an old dresser stuffed in there, some hooks and hangers, and a shelf to store things on.

Over the bed there's a woodland scene. A river with rapids, towering mountains, the whole image dark and amateurish. On the wall above the desk there's a crucifix. This one's at least half a century old, the corpus with its extended arms and too-short feet reminding me of a hawk descending. The walls are painted what Joyce would call a snot green. So: this is home for the next five weeks. Yippee. It's getting late. Time to join the others downstairs.

11:00 P.M. At five I made my grand entrance into the dining room and was met by my own photo on a bulletin board off to the left of the entrance: a five-by-seven book shot I'd sent off and which glared back at me now in dramatic black and white. It loomed several times larger than the color snapshots the other retreatants had provided, some standing alone, but most in small groups, or with grandchildren or pets. Casual shots, the faces smiling or trying to smile. And then Mr. Hollywood, Mr. Professional Writer and Teacher, in the center under the *M*s, like some strange force field completely out of place. God forgive me.

Another surprise. Among the assembled staff milling about the tables was my spiritual director, who turns out to be Fr. John J. Bresnahan, S.J., of the Holyoke Bresnahans, a family I've known for the past thirty years. JJ they call him here. Not "Father Bresnahan" or even "Fr. John." Just JJ. Given my sixty-year penchant for authority figures, calling a priest JJ is going to take some getting used to. He's in his early seventies, has a gray beard, which I notice he strokes whenever he's thinking, dresses in regular clothes, Kmart variety, and wears glasses. I'll meet with him each morning—one-on-one—for forty-five minutes, going over a segment of the *Spiritual Exercises,* which he will guide me through. It promises to be like those annual Eight-Day retreats I've made over the years with the Jesuits, highlighting those areas the director feels I'll need or am ready for in terms of my spiritual journey. Each day I'll be given two short passages from the Bible—all of which my director will choose. I'll meditate on these passages several times a day, repeating the pattern over and over, each morning talking with my director about what I've gleaned between one day and the next. By the end, we will have gone through the Four Weeks of the *Exercises* and God knows what else.

Over the years, Abe and Marge Collamore have told me about Marge's brother, JJ, especially these past ten years since Paul has been a Jesuit. *When's Paul going to be a priest?* I get that question all the time. Ten, eleven, twelve years, between the time one enters the Jesuits and the time one is ordained. Think of it as a life sentence, Paul quipped once, with more than a tinge of truth. But then, haven't we all been given life sentences to try and make sense of it all? And here's JJ, at the other end of the spectrum, forty years a priest now, most of that time spent in Jamaica doing retreat work. Which is why, until today, I never met him. A few years ago he returned to the States. And now here he is and here I am. It strikes me that by the time the month is over, he's going to know me about as well as anybody, including Eileen. God help us all.

At half past seven tonight we met in the Fireplace Room, where the director, Fr. Bill Devine, introduced himself. He's a heavyset man, rather distinguished looking. He walks in a flatfooted way, with no little effort and apparently with some pain. He has a sly sense of humor, make no mistake about it. He let it be known, for instance, that though he and JJ were born on the same day, same year, it is *he,* thank you, and not JJ, who is in charge. He told us during his introductory remarks that, before coming to Eastern Point a dozen years ago, he'd been a professor of economics at Fairfield University. That means he must have replaced Fr. Duffy, who was my retreat director here in '84. It struck me once more how the great work goes on, year in and year out, this care and feeding of souls.

Four rows of comfortable chairs have been set up on each side of the room facing each other across a ten-foot divide. The retreat directors and staff on the opposite side introduced themselves, then the directors behind me did the same. Then each of the Thirty-Day retreatants. JJ will be directing two of us, plus several of the Eight-Day retreatants scheduled to begin arriving tomorrow. The other person he's directing for the long haul is Marcie Springer, a Sister of St. Joseph from Philadelphia. In her early fifties, I'd guess. One of those lean, strong women who can do it all, quietly, efficiently. She's even led spiritual retreats herself.

We met with JJ in his office after the meeting tonight. When he asked us when we wanted to meet, we settled that I would take the spot after breakfast, from 8:30 until 9:15, with Marcie following immediately after. The talk was all business, low-keyed, and JJ gave Marcie and me three Scripture passages to meditate on over the next thirty-six hours: Wisdom 9:9–11, John 7:37–38, and Isaiah 55:1–5. They're like little riddles, these readings, and you wonder what they will all have in common. I've been through this particular drill many times on my Eight-Day retreats.

There's very little of the personal in any of this at first. Even the Scripture passages seem isolated and discrete, though sooner or later they begin forming patterns for reflection. Usually one of them turns out to speak to something deep within you as you come back to it in prayer. Scripture reading at this level is unusually dynamic, resonating more and more as you allow it to work on you. After all, what you look hard at, Fr. Hopkins said, looks back hard at you. This is especially true of the Word of God.

JJ's office is small—a desk, two chairs facing each other with an eight-foot space between, a stand with a box of Kleenex on it, some posters of Jamaican schoolchildren smiling, and a few family photos. I noticed as I got up to leave a black-and-white framed photo of JJ's mother and father (both dead now), his two sisters and their husbands, and his brother, all of whom I've known, but never when they were this young. The photo was taken forty years ago, JJ tells me. He looks younger than Paul looks now, which tells me where *I'll* be in another forty years. His office is just off the foyer to the Main Hall, as one enters through the imposing Spanish colonial central doors of the Main House. Few of us will use this entrance. Instead we'll use the more practical doors off the dining hall, or—for those in the west wing, as I was when I was here fifteen years ago—enter through the corridor that leads into the Fireplace Room.

I can see heavy rain spattering off the edge of the roof, backlit by the outside arc lights as I sit here in my room. Just beyond is the tireless, eternal sea groaning out there somewhere in the dark. Strange. I've been here seven hours, and already how happy I am. For the past several weeks, preparing for this retreat, I've been going over Ignatius's short *Autobiography,* trying to get a firmer grip on the man who wrote the *Exercises.* He was born in 1491, the year before Columbus discovered this New World. Iñigo they called him then, the last of thirteen children, the runt of the litter, born in northern Spain, in Basque country, in the family castle of Loyola. He only took the name Ignatius in his mid-forties, when he finally became a priest. He lost his mother early, then his father when he was sixteen. Service in the courts and in the army. A small man. Hot-tempered, ready at a moment's notice to draw his sword if he thought his honor impugned. A vain romantic, a dandy who let his hair grow down to his shoulders and sported fine clothes. A courtier on the field and in the boudoir. Quite different from the close-cropped, bearded administrator in black soutane we see in the late portrait in Rome.

And yet how modern he seems, even now, after five hundred years. A corporate administrator, out to succeed in the ways of the world. At thirty, caught up in a border dispute with France over territories in the southern Pyrenees, he finds himself defending a small citadel in Pamplona with a handful of men against a well-trained force of French soldiers equipped with siege cannon. The citizens of Pamplona beg him to surrender, but Iñigo convinces the magistrate not to besmirch Spain's honor by doing so. And so, on

May 20, 1521, the French open fire and a cannonball, ricocheting off a wall, smashes Iñigo's legs, ripping his left calf to shreds and breaking his right shin. With their leader balled up in agony, the garrison loses no time in surrendering. The victorious French can afford to be gallant now and order their physicians to set his leg (badly, it turns out), and then send him on his way home. Courtesy or mockery? What were the French thinking, as Iñigo was strapped to a makeshift litter and bounced the forty miles back to Loyola? So much for worldly honor, worldly fame.

Back home, Iñigo's leg has to be rebroken and reset, without benefit of anesthetics. Even then the bone protrudes at an angle, so he insists on having the bone spur hacksawed off, only to find that his right leg is now shorter than his left. Worried how he will look in courtier's tights, he tries stretching the leg with weights, but that, too, fails. Everything fails. A fever nearly kills him. But he holds on somehow, and, after six weeks, on the Eve of the Feast of Saints Peter and Paul, the fever inexplicably breaks. What guts the man had, what unbelievable courage.

As he lays in bed, recovering, he asks to be supplied with novels about chivalry and high military deeds, the same kind of stories that, a century later, will turn an aging don into the gallant but addled Don Quixote de la Mancha. But there are no such stories to be found in that Spartan household. All they can find are a four-volume life of Christ and some dime lives of the saints. Out of necessity and boredom, Iñigo begins perusing these, reading them in the same spirit in which he has approached the lives of knight errants in the past: with a kind of one-upmanship. If this saint fasted, so, he imagines, can he, only longer and harder. Mortifications and pilgrimages ditto. A fierce competitor, one of those little guys who just won't back down.

Lying there, his leg in traction, he thinks back on the exploits of knights, of service to fair ladies and of the lacy favors that come with such service. Sweet, bountiful caresses to the ego. But the man is too smart, finally, to be taken in by his own fantasies, a glut of images that leave him feeling spiritually dry and dissatisfied, the spent spirit that has fed on the narcissism of pornography. On the other hand, whenever he thinks of the selfless example of Christ and the saints, he finds himself full of peace and a quiet joy.

What's behind this? Is it that romantic fantasies are fictions, false idealizations, ego-driven phantasmagorias, without real substance? Following such dreams, hadn't Iñigo wound up here on what might have been his deathbed, at the age of thirty, emaciated, exhausted, and crippled? And for what? A puff of empty glory? On the other hand, the consolations, he saw now, had come from God, and they made him feel happy and at peace. One night, he saw the Blessed Mother holding her infant son. The image was so sweet and lasted so long that afterward he could only feel loathing for his own sexual transgressions. So deep did this vision penetrate, he would say many years later, that it seemed to burn away all subsequent carnal images from his imagination.

I'm not altogether sure what's involved here, but I certainly get the gist: no more sexual preoccupations, no more expense of spirit in a waste of shame. In any case, from this point on, his family couldn't help noticing a profound change in him. He spoke now only of spiritual things. His elder brother, pragmatist that he was, believed Iñigo had merely replaced one fever with another and begged him not to do anything rash in the name of God that might compromise the Loyolas. Little did he know that this same brother would soon begin composing, by way of spiritual notes, the western classic we call the *Spiritual Exercises,* a book that has profoundly shaped the lives of millions, including my own.

WEDNESDAY, JANUARY 5

1:00 P.M. Up at six in almost total darkness. Slipped on some pants—brand-new ones, in fact—to go down to the bathroom and noticed ink stains on my right pocket. The cover of one of my new pens had come loose and now my goddamn pants are ruined. So much for thoughtful, efficient packing. *When you go, do not bring an extra cloak or sandals or money.* Thus Jesus, speaking to his disciples as he sent them out on their first mission. What's done is done. Let it go. But, damn it, it *is* a big deal. Everything feels like a big deal. *And peace to you, too, friend.* What a way to begin a retreat!

Went back to bed and woke again at nine, bright January sunlight streaming into the room. How quiet the place is, even now, ten hours before the official silence begins. I dressed and walked about the grounds, November-brown and lovely and without a trace of snow, looking for the room where the washers and dryers are located so I could wash my pants. Then a breakfast of English muffin, juice, and coffee. Five novices from Chicago were sitting in front of the picture windows looking out at the ocean. Several might be longshoremen's sons. It makes me think of my own son in Berkeley, facing another ocean. Young men just setting out, and here I am, with thirty years on them, my life as a husband, father, and teacher in the gap between.

And yet is not my own life at a crossroads, one largely of my own making, my thirty-two years at the University of Massachusetts/Amherst probably coming to an end, my time at Boston College about to begin? A major turnaround, and all because of an Eight-Day retreat at Campion nine months ago. "Can you turn everything over to Him?" Fr. Corcoran asked me then, catching me completely off guard.

"How can I?" I asked myself, climbing the dark stairs as I returned to my room down the massive dark hall, the only retreatant around. And then, like that, I found the grace somehow to say yes. "Why the hell not," I remember saying to myself. "Can I do any better than Him?" And then, suddenly, out of nowhere, the gentle command, *Go to BC.* Oddly, I've been following that directive ever since. The command was not, of course, what I'd been expecting, knowing no one at BC except a priest friend from the old days. In fact I'd never even seen the campus.

But there it was, the voice. *Go to BC*. After all these years at UMass, only to begin all over again at a Jesuit school. Why, I don't fully understand, but every time I have tried to shake the order off, something has steadied me. *This is what I want of you, Paul,* the voice seems to say, as it spoke to the prophets and to Christ. *It is enough for you to go. The rest will be made clear in due time. Do not be anxious or worried.* Well, isn't that what the Lord does, continually surprising us if we will but leave listening room? And what if BC should turn out to have stood not for Boston College but Bard or—worse—British Columbia? I don't understand the full import here and keep thinking of the long trip from Montague to Chestnut Hill. Eighty-seven miles each way. And the long New England winters. I wonder if the prophets had a sense of humor. I know God must.

At ten this morning I went for a walk along the rocks and tide pools of the North Atlantic to pray and meditate. Cold, blustery, and clear, in the twenties, the waves rolling in and crashing against the boulders. Gulls drifted in the wind, searching. Then Mass at 11:15. First the Liturgy of the Word in the Fireplace Room: a reading from the Old Testament, a Responsorial Psalm, then a passage from St. Mark. Then into the Main Hall for Eucharist: the bread and wine, Body and Blood. Then back again to the Fireplace Room for reflection. This will be the shape of the movements of the Mass each day, except that normally we will celebrate liturgy at five in the evening.

Today Fr. Bill Devine said Mass. He spoke of an older generation of Jesuits who used to give mission retreats in parish churches, a practice that died out in the '60s, with Vatican II. He recalled one old Jesuit telling his nephew, a young Jesuit just going out to give the *Exercises* for the first time, to give them straight. "None of this love stuff," he told him. "Give 'em hell."

"Well," Bill added, "it *is* love stuff God offers His children, as the old priest—for all his exterior gruff—knew well enough." Bill was my age when the call came to leave teaching and come to Eastern Point and direct retreats. He knew well enough that, having made his decision, there could be no turning back.

5:45 P.M. Napped for a long hour after lunch. This always happens with me on retreats, finding this old dogsbody more tired than I thought. Stresses sloughing off. Then in Gloucester for a look-around. A down-on-its-luck sort of place, much of it frozen still in the 1950s, when they fished the ocean here dry of everything but bottom feeders. Several lobster boats were coming in or going out through the channel, the pleasure boats in dry-dock. Passed a dozen fish processing plants along the water, ugly rectangular buildings in among the older Victorian houses, and pulled into the parking lot at Walgreens. Walked up Main and Rogers Streets in the long shadows of the short winter afternoon, stopping to examine an imposing brick edifice (1810) where Winslow Homer stayed when he came here to paint this ocean in the summer of 1873. No doubt Homer's waves will now be foremost in my mind whenever the sky darkens and the Atlantic comes crashing in against the rocks at Eastern Point.

Then over to the Unitarian-Universalist Church with its long dirt walkway and red-topped tower. In the square adjacent I caught sight of a massive bronze dray horse with a female figure in armor astride it, her right hand holding aloft a terrifying sword. Some fifty-odd names of the dead were inscribed on the pedestal: those from Gloucester who had perished in the Great War. Walking around the base of the statue with the sun setting, the maiden's face seemed to change slowly into a death's head.

On my way back to the car, I stopped in Walgreens for some cold medicine and Kleenex tissues—the last chance I'll have for some time—and caught the face of a woman in her late thirties. She looked tired and scarred. Many here look like her. What is it the sea does to these people? I suppose *The Perfect Storm,* set here and which I hear they're filming, tells part of the story, but you don't have to go out far or in deep to feel the human misery. I must have passed this kind of event—a woman walking the aisles of a store—a thousand times before without really seeing the person involved. No doubt about it. One thing a retreat does is force you to see with a new kind of clarity, without the scrim of our daily preoccupations. It rinses the soul, prayer does.

Saw three birds, metal feathers stiff as knives, facing into the bitter wind as I neared the retreat house. They clung tenaciously to the bare branches of a small black tree that swayed under their weight, bird and tree bleeding into one as the sun set behind Niles Beach.

The first batch of Eight-Day retreatants has begun arriving. About thirty of them, doubling our size. Lost my prime parking spot, and then, looking through the second-story window in the hallway outside my room, saw the spot vacant again and hurried down to reclaim it. How hard the old territorial imperative dies. But then how hard anything about us changes.

8:30 P.M. At dinner tonight I talked with Devon, a young black Jamaican who wants to be a Jesuit brother. He has an infectious laugh, all six foot four of him. He tells me he worked the nightshift in a mortuary for five years in West Kingston, following Christ's rather straightforward injunction to bury the dead. Earlier he'd joined a Jamaican religious order, made up mostly of Indians from the subcontinent: men who worked with the poor and the homeless. But he'd had to wear a long white robe on the streets as he made his rounds, the result being that the locals began mocking him for looking like a lady. Men, he tells me, have been shot dead for less in Kingston, charity work or no. He lasted three months with the Order, before quitting to work in a supermarket. Then he fell in with the Jesuits. And now here he is, making the Long Retreat alongside myself.

After dinner, Kathleen Keating, a Sister of St. Joseph and president of Our Lady of the Elms College in Chicopee—a spry, capable woman in her early seventies, and here for her annual Eight-Day retreat—came up to me at table and we talked. I happened to mention Fr. Duffy, the Jesuit who had been my director here in '84, and told her how, making my annual retreat at Weston these past several years, I had found his headstone in the cemetery there where the New England Jesuits are buried. Each has an identical white headstone with the familiar IHS—the first three letters of Jesus' name in Greek—across the top of the stone, with the name of the Jesuit chiseled beneath it in Latin. Each year the number of headstones increases by another fifteen or twenty. Sr. Kathleen told me that one of the last things Fr. Duffy did before he died was to be there for her when her father passed away. Hidden signatures of grace. As we stood up to leave, I noticed that everyone else had already left the hall. I walked out through the glass doors and into the Main House, suddenly aware that the long silence had begun.

Only now, in the hush of the evening and back here in my room, have I begun meditating on the three Scripture passages for my first meeting with JJ tomorrow morning. The first is from Wisdom, chapter 9, verses 9 to 11. *Wisdom . . . knows your works,* the passage begins:

> *she who was present when you made the world;*
> *she understands what is pleasing in your eyes*
> *and what agrees with your commandments.*

So: a passage on the original order of things as God intended, before everything unraveled with "Man's first disobedience and the Fall." My prayer now is that God might bestow His Wisdom on me that I might know His will. Ignatius knew—like every great spiritual visionary—that we suffer from a skewed, self-centered vision of things. Now it's time to try and put things back in order for myself. But that means understanding my own radical disorder, and then trying to align my will with God's. The funny thing is that others could spot my ludicrous failings in a heartbeat. It's only me who thinks everything I think and do should be up for an Oscar.

The second meditation is based on Isaiah, chapter 55, verses 1 to 5. It's a beautiful passage, a balm to the soul, and my tired heart lifted as I began to read it:

Oh, come to the water all you who are thirsty;
though you have no money, come!
Buy and eat; come, buy wine and milk
without money, free!
Why spend money on what cannot nourish
and your wages on what fails to satisfy?
Listen carefully to me, and you will have good things to eat
and rich food to enjoy.
Pay attention, come to me;
listen, and you will live.

It's like an oasis in a parched desert, this passage. All those daily worries that distract me from what's really important. Poof, gone like that. Hasn't He cared for me all these years? From my mother's womb? Food there for the asking. Manna in the desert. Give Him room to move in, and see what happens. But can I let go long enough to let Him do this?

And then this from John's Gospel, chapter 7, verses 37 to 38:

On the last day, the great day of the festival, Jesus stood and cried out:
'Let anyone who is thirsty come to me!
Let anyone who believes in me come and drink!'

Though the passage focuses on Christ as the Living Water, and so links to the previous passages from Wisdom and Isaiah, John centers on the rejection of Jesus' authority. I'm not sure this is exactly what JJ was after in giving me this passage, but it's what has forcibly struck me. John is describing the Jewish Feast of Booths, an eight-day annual festival held at the end of September and the beginning of October, after the harvest was in. Jesus, who has been preaching in Galilee, prepares to go up to Jerusalem for the holy days. But now he holds back, knowing the religious authorities want him silenced. He hesitates, and then tells the others to go on ahead without him. But later, alone, he does go up to Jerusalem. It's as if something in him will not let him stay away from the Temple and his Father, no matter how great the danger to himself.

Once there, he can't stop himself from preaching once more to the crowds. But how can this Jesus be the Messiah? the people ask. He lacks the right pedigree. He's from Nazareth, a miserable cow town up north, whereas Scripture says the Messiah, the Christ, is to come from Bethlehem, David's place of origin. Besides, they *know* who Jesus' father was: a small-town carpenter, some poor day laborer. But instead of answering them point for point, Jesus warns them that time is running out. After all, with his death will go their own best hope for freedom, not from servitude to the Romans but from something worse: slavery to their own self-bent sins.

For the last day of the festival, prayers for rain for the fall growing season were prescribed, which included the transference of water from the Pool of Siloam to the Temple. This was done in remembrance of Moses' striking the rock in the desert, from which had once sprung the living water that had saved the people in the desert. Watching the ritual now, Jesus tells the crowd that *he* is the Living Water, there for the asking. An open invitation, though many must have thought him just another half-crazed pseudo prophet shouting in the Temple precincts. But the invitation is addressed to me as well. And how shall I respond? But there's something more about the passage that seems to be troubling me. Jesus says he has come to do the Father's will. When they ask him who his Father is, he tells them that the Father is right here with him, because he and the Father are one. But do I really believe this? Who *is* this Jesus? That is, who do *I* say he is?

9:40 P.M. Downstairs through the Fireplace Room and out into the cold corridor to call Eileen. I haven't O.K.'d this yet with JJ, but will. For fifteen years now, I've always called her once a day when I'm on the road or she's away. A quick call, just to hear her voice and know she's O.K. It helps with the loneliness, and the fact of my leaving her in mid-winter for so long. She sounded good and is getting ready to head down to the high-rise apartment in Rockaway Beach Friday morning to see her parents. She'll take them to see an old friend, widowed now and nearly blind, and then drive into Manhattan to see her eighty-five-year-old uncle, who's been failing ever since his stroke a year ago. Then she'll take her aunt back to Montague for a visit. It's the only time I'll break the silence, with these short calls to her. But I have to know she's O.K. How many wives, after all, would let their husbands go away for five weeks, even for a retreat?

Afterward, I walked back into the Fireplace Room, where a fire was blazing beautifully: high-tiered, cuneiform. Several sat near the fire, reading by its light or quietly staring into the flames, thinking. This, it turns out, is the communal heart of the place. Unlike my monk's cell, it's a place to be warmed by human presence. English Tudor wood paneling covering the walls. Wideboard floors, varnished and darkened by time. Three-quarter-length recessed windows, with short tapestry curtains across the tops. Rows of hymnals sit in bookshelves opposite the fireplace. There's a small Baldwin piano and a guitar off in the corner, and a bas-relief of the Holy Family over the fireplace. Seasoned wood is brought in each evening and piled to one side. Except for the dining hall and the small Reading Room, this is the only place we have to congregate, even if from now on we'll be communicating only through nods and smiles. And even those are mostly avoided so as not to intrude on another's solitude.

I'm still thinking about that passage from John. It's a hook that won't let me go. *Why* did Jesus feel compelled to tell the people he was the Way? Why these metaphors? *Why* did he call himself the Living Water, the only one who could quench their thirst? In effect, wasn't he telling them he was one with God, and therefore somehow God? He existed before Abraham, he told them, and was the same great I AM who had spoken to Moses in the Burning

Bush. But then *why* should he stoop to us, this Wisdom, this Being, when other religions and philosophies go the other way, telling us how difficult it is to approach the Truth? Why should he hunger after the likes of us? But then Yahweh, too, was like this. Like Father, like Son, I suppose.

The thing about this Truth that Jesus and Isaiah speak of is that it fairly shouts its greeting, and seems willing to meet us more than halfway. God and His Son seem eager to embrace us and in turn be embraced by us. And yet Jesus knows we will kill him for his troubles, just as Herod had tried to kill him as an infant, for no other reason than that he was in the way. Always, it seems, this discordant note to ruin the great song of praise. How dark it is. The whole world seems just now to end here at my window.

And who was this Ignatius, who has shaped so many lives, including my son's and my own? What drove him? And is there a lesson in there for me? Go to BC. Go to Jerusalem. I will be propitious. When he left home in the spring of 1522 following his convalescence, Ignatius was thirty, and had no idea just *what* he was going to do with his life, other than that he knew that everything had been changed forever. He was still, of course, Iñigo, and so the zeal he had once exhibited for court intrigue and military exploit would now be employed in undertaking long penances for his past sins. And so he set off for sacred ground: the monastery of Our Lady of Montserrat, where he spent three days examining his sins in minute detail. Afterward, he made a general confession (such as I'll be making at the end of this First Week), detailing all he could remember in the way of personal failure: sins committed, good acts left undone. Then, like St. Francis centuries before, he gave away his fine clothes—doublet, cape, cap, all of it—to the poor milling about the place and donned rough sack cloth. On the eve of the Feast of the Annunciation—March 24—in imitation of knights who had sworn fealty to Our Lady, he placed his sword and dagger before the altar of the Madonna and spent the night there in prayer. Next morning, after Mass and Communion, he left the monastery, ready to be led wherever the Spirit wished to take him.

"Why is it that Jesuits find it necessary to try to discern what God's will for them should be," the abbot at the Benedictine abbey asked me once in a half-musing way, "when we already know what God wants of us? It's one of the great differences between our traditions, where we follow Benedict's exhortation to work and to pray, and where that is enough." But Ignatius seems to have thought otherwise. He comes at the dawn of the Modern mind—restless, seeking, forever exploring, with no set hours of prayer, and no great round of hours spent in choir at Matins and Terce and None and Vespers. Those routines, beautiful in themselves, demand stability, the staying in one place, a rooting down like a great beech tree, while the Jesuits have always taken pride in being ready to go where they are needed, like soldiers with orders to move out at a moment's notice.

And so down to Barcelona Iñigo went, set on leaving at once for the Holy Land, only to be thwarted by the presence of hostile Muslim Turks in the Holy Land. Thwarted—or led—he returned to Manresa, where he lived sometimes in a cave and sometimes in a cell at a nearby monastery, begging for the little he needed, and spending his days and nights in prayer, fasting, and contemplation, looking for some deeper peace. What he found instead was misery. He—who prided himself on his fastidiousness in dress—let his hair and fingernails grow long and dirty. He ate almost nothing. He kept tracing over his sins, picking at them until they bled. Had he confessed them correctly? Had he knowingly held anything back? Had he tried to make himself look better than he really was?

As week bled into week, his scrupulousness increased, and he began thinking of taking his own life. Finally, seeing what he was doing to himself, he vowed to stop eating and drinking altogether until the peace he so desperately wanted returned to him. A week into his total fast, his confessor stepped in and forbade him from continuing. Then—mercifully—the fever of self-loathing broke. Having met the obstacles to grace thrown in his way, he felt peace palpably return. At last he found what he had come to Manresa to find.

It was during this time that he began making notes of his spiritual trials, trying to make sense of them for himself and as an aid for others who had begun coming to him in their own search for God. Thus began the *Spiritual Exercises,* the little book he would expand upon and amend many times over the next twenty-five years as he directed hundreds of retreats and advised hundreds of others who would in turn give retreats based on his *Exercises.* How consoling that—hard as he was on himself—he should be a model of prudence when it came to advising others.

But he still wanted to go to the Holy Land and literally follow in the footsteps of his Master, in the process converting as many non-Christians as he could, and bringing lapsed Christians back to the Way. Finally, at the beginning of 1523, he set off from Barcelona on the arduous journey by sea. He took nothing with him, preferring to travel as Christ had said His followers were to travel, with only the barest necessities. The journey turned out to hold one hardship after another, both at sea and on land. Much of the time he was ill and hungry. More than once he was robbed of the little he had. Several times in Jerusalem and elsewhere he was beaten because he had nothing to offer those who held him at knifepoint. Each time the once-proud Basque, who would have gladly run a sword through a man for an insult, turned the other cheek. What exquisite patience and forbearance the man showed. How did he do it?

Finally, it was the Franciscans in charge of the holy places in Jerusalem who ordered Iñigo to leave. At first he refused. Here is where he had set his heart on living, he told them. If necessary, he would die here. Why should he return to Spain? Because, they explained, too many Christians had been forcibly seized and held until the papal authorities and others paid out huge ransoms for their safe return. To halt this practice, the pope himself had written

Bulls—documents with his seal, his *bullae*—giving the Franciscans authority to send Christians out of the country.

Hearing that it was the pope's wish, Iñigo at once obeyed and returned by sea to Barcelona. God, it appeared, had other plans for him. But that need for historically grounding Jesus in a geography and a time and so recapturing a living presence, a tactic so characteristic of Ignatius, had already begun to find its way into the *Exercises.* It is one of the things that so deeply attracts me to the *Exercises:* their sacramental sense of time and place, of God operating in our everyday world. After all, is it not He who lifts everything we do to new significance? How consoling to know that, no matter how small we may think we are against the backdrop of eternity, we do count in the cosmic scheme of things.

THE FIRST WEEK

The Loss of God's First Kingdom

DAY 1: THURSDAY, JANUARY 6

2:00 A.M. Awoke from some vague erotic dream to find my sheets scrambled into knots. What's going on here? I thought I was leaving this world behind.

Ah, but did you really think you could leave yourself behind?

Made my bed again—this narrow, coffin-sized thing, and put away one of my two blankets. Then I opened the outer aluminum storm window, on which the release spring is gone, and wedged the storm pane open with a small can of aerosol shaving cream.

Feels like fifteen degrees or so outside. In any event, clear, cold, and very dark. I can hear the surf pounding softly, insistently. Less than four hours of sleep and here I am, wide awake. I caught the detail from Perugino's fifteenth-century *Baptism of Christ* on the cover of this month's *Magnificat.* It shows Christ as a young man, the sinless one, the Lamb of God, taking on our sinfulness. St. John the Baptist knew who this one was when Jesus approached him at the edge of the Jordan River, where he was baptizing his fellow Jews. He had his work to do, as Jesus had his, and he thought himself unworthy of even loosening the sandal of Jesus, a duty usually reserved for slaves. But even John, the last of the old-line prophets, worried about Jesus and his way of working: his gentle, forgiving ways, his mingling with sinners. How unlike John's own sterner, more confrontational manner.

Was Jesus the expected Messiah? Even John seems to have expected someone different, someone more in the Essene tradition, perhaps the kind of person who would have lived in the Jewish community at Qumran, which had fled Jerusalem two centuries earlier to live as the Jews under Moses had lived: in the desert. After all, what would John have been expecting? A cross between a High Priest (though uncorrupted and so not a puppet like Herod) and a king in the Davidic line? Later, after he was thrown into prison, and sensing the end was near, John would send two of his followers to Jesus to ask him point blank if he was in fact the one the Israelites had been expecting. So even the Baptist—his own cousin—seems to have had second thoughts in the weeks before he was executed. *Who am I,* Jesus asks, as here at Eastern Point he asks again: *Who do* you *say I am?*

Go and tell John what you see, Jesus tells John's disciples in reply to their question. *The sick are cured, the dead are raised, the blind see, the deaf hear, the Good News is taught to them.* Jesus answers the prophet's question with a prophet's answer by echoing Isaiah, who described what the messianic era would bring. It would arrive, Isaiah had promised, not by way of violence and retributive justice but as a shower of mercy. And so with Jesus, so different from the more fiery, Old Testament John. Thus Jesus brings to a close the Old Covenant even as he issues in the New. And still—Jesus sees—the leaders go on rejecting the Father's advances, whether by refusing to celebrate the coming of the new dispensation (like Jesus, eating and drinking with sinners and tax collectors) or by fasting and penitence, like his ascetic cousin, John. Nothing, it appears, will convince us that God is among us in a very special way: neither John's stern words of impending doom nor Jesus' gentle invitation to follow him.

10:30 A.M. Wonderful to wake up this morning with the new dawn. Went down to the dining hall and caught the sun rising off to the southeast over the ocean. Through binoculars I watched something floating, unable to make out what I was seeing. A man in a kayak? In January? A dab of white and red, a long pole dipping. A bob to locate a lobster trap? The restless mind, that wants to name everything, to make something knowable in order to have power over it. So Moses, standing before the voice in the Burning Bush: *Who are you? Who shall I say sent me?* But can God ever be possessed by the names we give Him? And do I know what I'm looking at even when I'm looking at it?

After breakfast I had my first meeting with JJ. He sat opposite me, like some therapist or rabbi, mostly listening. The meeting itself turned out to be more emotional than I had anticipated, and I found myself grabbing for the Kleenex box several times. Even the most straightforward statements seemed capable of bringing me to tears. What is going on here? I told JJ what I'd gleaned from my readings. Pretty basic stuff, I would have thought, about God's wisdom in caring for me, His infinite attention to His children, Christ as the Living Water. But I found myself coming back again to the passage from John, wondering who this Jesus was who could make such extravagant claims, as to be the Son of God. I thought I believed this, so what's the difficulty here? Except that it's one thing to make an act of faith—like a marriage vow—and another to realize the full import of the promises one is making.

When I came away from the meeting, I found myself dwelling on God's thirst for us, and of my lifelong thirst for Him. Why is it, in spite of all my defiances, that He has never abandoned me? And why this fear of abandonment? *Why* should God care so much about us as to pursue us down the ways? *Look,* He seems to say, *I have given you life and breath. And yet there is so much more to give you.* At fifty-nine, one begins to think of cutting back, of doing less, and then of retirement. Why then do I keep feeling not as if I were about to close up shop but—like old Sarah in the Book of *Genesis*—as if I were on the verge of some great surprise?

JJ gave me two new passages to reflect on: Psalms 139 and 8. So, after my meeting, I went down to Chapel, sat on two pillows on the floor, and began reading. The lines from Psalm 139 seemed especially to speak to me:

Yahweh, you examine me and know me,
you know when I sit, when I rise. . . .
You created my inmost self,
Knit me together in my mother's womb. . . .

Test me, the final lines of the Psalm say:

Make sure that I am not on my way to ruin,
And guide me on the road to eternity.

And these lines from Psalm 8:

how majestic is your name throughout the world! . . .
what are human beings that you spare a thought for them . . .
Yet you have made him little less than a god,
you have crowned him with glory and beauty,
made him lord of the works of your hands,
put all things under his feet.

Minutely, minute by minute, from my mother's womb, when all I could fathom were fish thoughts, He already loved me. Is this possible? How can this be?

11:15 A.M. Time seems to be speeding up. Doing the wash this morning felt good, even if it wasn't really necessary. Still, it was something like work. In fact, I think I will look for some kind of manual labor to do while I'm here. After I put away the wash, I put on my sweatshirt and black ski cap and walked off the property. Gulls and ducks drifted on Niles Pond. A Cessna droned overhead, low, its right light blinking. It turned in a lazy loop and headed south. Gloucester's church and town towers shone brilliantly in the distance.

A male jogger in a red jacket and blue pants with a white stripe down one side ran by, overtaking me, then ran ahead. Four fat black ravens on a wide lawn majestically gallumphed about: Leonard Baskin's eagle-taloned Crows, meat-eaters, strutting across the grass looking for brunch. Ice patches on the road said how cold it was, though the walking kept me warm. To the south I caught sight of Boston's Prudential Building and a few other high-rises making thin vertical lines on some invisible stock market chart. Then back to Eastern Point. Five gulls—four white, one a shaggy, mottled tan—stood on the rocks, twisting their necks as I came across the broken boulders toward them, until they flapped off toward Brace Rock. It's the main landmark visible from the house, this rock outcrop, and forms its own island at high tide. I could walk out there and talk with God, much as I did fifteen years ago, and I know He would listen.

4:30 P.M. At meals everyone sits facing the water and eats in silence. A music tape—instrumental, always classical—is played: Mozart, Handel, Vivaldi, Schubert. There's a salad bar with five kinds of dressing (including oil and vinegar), two kinds of soup, usually some leftovers from the night before (ham and creamed potatoes today), a platter of cold cuts (ham, baloney, salami, turkey breast), and three kinds of cheeses: provolone, Swiss, American. There are pickles, green and black olives, cold vegetables. There's also an aluminum bowl filled with tuna salad and another with egg salad. Of such details are our lives here made up.

After lunch I rested, glanced at a newspaper, then read up again on the *Exercises*. What are they exactly? On page 21 of Fr. Ganss's translation I find this: "Any means of preparing and disposing our soul to rid itself of all disordered affections, and then—after their removal—of seeking and finding God's will in the ordering of our life for the salvation of our soul."

So: two major steps. A *via purgativa,* or emptying of the self of whatever static is keeping us from getting a clearer picture of what is essential. And then a *via positiva:* a filling of the self with what is necessary for our spiritual health: the being again on the right track. My old friend, the novelist Ron Hansen, offers a useful summary. The *Exercises,* he explains in "The Pilgrim: Saint Ignatius of Loyola," "fashioned for the first time what is now popularly known as a retreat." He did this by offering "spiritual directors a practical and systematic method of having retreatants meditate, in silence and solitude over an intensive four-week span, on God's plan in His creation of human beings, humanity's fall from grace through sin [Week I], the gifts of humility and poverty [interspersed], and the glory of the life [Week II], passion [Week III], and resurrection of Jesus [Week IV]." That says it about as succinctly as it can be said. Still, it's only a roadmap that I'm going to have to follow step by tentative step.

And here's Ignatius, in a passage addressed to the spiritual director: "The director should accurately narrate the history contained in the contemplation or meditation [for the day]. It should be a summary explanation, meant to help the exercitant [that's me] in finding a better understanding or more personalized concept of history, either through one's own reasoning and imagining or through God's grace [both, if possible]." So what I should be looking for as a retreatant is an understanding of the underlying spiritual reality of a particular human situation and then savoring that spiritual reality at the heart of the experience. Also this: "to give each other [retreatant and director] the benefit of the doubt and to cast each other's comments in the most favorable light."

And so begins the First Day of the First Week, opening with Ignatius's famous *Principle and Foundation:* what we're here for, what our purpose in life is. That assumes, of course, that one believes there *is* a purpose to existence, that there is a providential Creator who cares, and that we have a way of connecting with that Creator. As Judaism and Christianity have been teaching now for millennia, and as Ignatius understood, "we are created to praise, reverence and serve God our Lord, and by means of doing this to save our souls."

Also this: "Other things on the face of the earth are created for human beings, to help them in pursuit of the end for which they were created."

And this: "We must learn to use things as they help us, and free ourselves of them as they hinder us from praise, reverence, and service of God. Where free will is involved, we must be indifferent to all created things."

And this: "We must learn to desire and choose only what is more conducive to our proper end."

This, then, is at the heart of what I will be doing for the next four weeks. *Capisce?*

9:30 P.M. I wrote Eileen this afternoon, telling her how much I missed her. A real love letter, something I haven't had the opportunity of doing for years. Then a letter to Fr. Corcoran at the Campion Center to tell him I was here, and thanking him for his work with me last year, when so much about where I was going with my life was quietly decided. I wonder if he knows how much of what he said then has led to my being here now. And who knows where else in the coming months?

At Mass this evening in the Fireplace Room I got up and read from the lectern from the First Letter of St. John (4:19–5:4). "Let us love, then," St. John writes, "because he first loved us." God, then, is the initiator, and it is up to us to follow as we can. After the homily, we filed into the Main Hall for the Eucharist, standing in a semicircle facing the oak table that serves as altar. There were fifty-five of us there—the Eight-Dayers and the Thirty-Dayers and the staff—all joining in the responses as the bread and wine were consecrated, as they have been the world over for the past two thousand years.

Then dinner at six. The dining hall is lit mostly with candles, and we eat in silence. It's all buffet style, the food brought in from the kitchen off to the left and laid in aluminum bins. We eat in no particular order, six to ten of us at a table, though most prefer to sit facing the ocean, at least when it's light out. Tonight it was spaghetti and meatballs. At the opposite end of the hall, closest to the door, there's a counter with two large bowls of tossed green salad ingredients. Also several tubs of ice cream to choose from. There's coffee, hot water for tea (regular or herbal) and hot chocolate. Afterward I helped clean off several tables.

Called home at eight. Eileen was just getting off the phone with our son, Mark. She told me he'd had a successful first day teaching at Stoneleigh-Burnham, up in Greenfield. He seemed happy and relieved. Six years on that unpublished novel of his, slogging it out day after day, leaving his earlier teaching job to take whatever work he could find. Now, *there's* monklike dedication. But a job. A real job. Hoorah!

Ignatius. There's another who slogged it out. Thirty-two, just about Mark's age, and now back in Barcelona, his trip to the Holy Land ending in apparent failure. A failed soldier with a limp, a penitent roughed up in Jerusalem, without money or even a high school education. If he was ever going to be taken seriously, if he was ever going to spread the Gospel, he knew he was going to have to get himself an education. Strange to think of St. Francis, who didn't want his Little Brothers to even own a book. But Ignatius wasn't relinquishing power. No, he would use it for the Greater Glory of God. And an education in the classics, in philosophy, in theology, in the sciences, would give him a way to reach the educated and the power shakers.

It was an important decision, for it would shape the lives of countless Jesuits after him. It is, in fact, what makes him so attractive to me. Thirty-two when he made his decision, he would spend the next eleven years of his life pursuing his studies. First he would have to learn the ABCs of Latin, the language of the schools, and he would have to do this by sitting in a schoolroom with boys twenty years younger than himself, memorizing words and parsing sentences. Then, the rudiments once learned, he would go on for his bachelor's, his master's, even reaching out for his doctorate, before sickness stopped him.

He was careful to make sure that he grew in his spiritual life as well, for the one without the other would mean ending up with a kind of dry intellectual sterility, quibbling over nonessentials, divorced from the people. He watched out for others, was there to help. Once he barred a group of rakes from invading a convent in Barcelona where young men on the prowl had once been welcomed. That was before Ignatius helped turn the convent around, bringing it back to its purpose as a house of prayer. For his troubles, the frat boys nearly beat him to death. A friend who tried to help him was in fact killed. There are no shortcuts to holiness, it appears.

When, in early 1526, he at last left Barcelona to study philosophy at the University of Alcalá, he ran into difficulties with the Inquisition almost at once and was thrown into prison. The following year he transferred to the University of Salamanca, only to be jailed again by the religious authorities. A year later, in June of 1528, he transferred to the Sorbonne in Paris, the Harvard of its day, walking the entire seven hundred miles to enroll there. Six years later he earned his master's in theology, and the following year another in philosophy. He had hopes of going on for the doctorate in theology, but a bad stomach forced him to end his studies. The real key to what he learned in his university years was how to combine a life of prayer with the rigorous life of the mind.

Four times during these years he was censured by the Inquisition. At first he humbly acquiesced in the censure, but, when he realized that it was his orthodoxy that was being impugned, he began to fight back, demanding either a trial or insisting on calling on the Church authorities to intervene. Each time the Inquisitors backed down. Wherever he went he drew others by his example. His first disciples fell away, but the group he formed in Paris remained faithful to a man. Among them was one who would later be recognized by the Church as a blessed—Peter Faber (Pierre

Favre), from the Savoy region of France—and another canonized a saint: Francis Xavier (Francisco Javier), a Basque like Iñigo himself. Three others of the original group were also Spaniards, one a Portuguese. Over the next few years, three more would join the young Company.

At first Iñigo instructed them in the way he himself had gone: by self-denial, frequent fasting, begging, going barefoot. Eventually, however, he realized that, while such a way of life might go unnoticed in the Spanish countryside, it was sure to attract unwanted attention from the Church authorities in the cities. In Paris, therefore, he instructed his followers to dress like other Parisians. He even cut back on the habit of fasting, which was ruining his health, concentrating instead on his studies and the *Exercises.* He spent much of his time securing alms for his followers so that they could get on with their schooling.

There was as yet no Society, no Order. Just a small group of men drawn by Iñigo's holiness and charism, and ready like him to go out to the Holy Land and model themselves after Christ. Then, on August 15, 1534, the Company made three vows in the crypt chapel of St. Denis atop Montmartre: vows of poverty, chastity, and—in place of obedience—a vow to go to the Holy Land in two years' time, when their studies would be completed. At Easter 1535, Iñigo assumed the name Ignatius. At the beginning of 1537, their studies now completed, the Companions caught up with Ignatius in Venice and prepared at long last to sail for the Holy Land. But Venice was at war with the Turks, who had closed off the Holy Land. The men decided to wait a year, after which, if they could still not sail, they promised to place themselves at the pope's disposal to be sent where the pope deemed they were needed.

On June 24, 1537—the Feast of St. John the Baptist—the nine members of the Company were ordained priests in Rome. Scrupulous to a fault, Iñigo waited another eighteen months before he felt he was ready to say his first Mass. That was at Christmas 1538, and he chose the church of Santa Maria Maggiore, where the crib in which Jesus had been placed at his birth was believed to be preserved. If Ignatius could not go to Bethlehem, he would bring Bethlehem to him. But from now until his death, Rome would have to serve in place of Jerusalem. How long this process of discernment, of trying to determine God's will for you, can be, even for someone with a genius for discernment like Ignatius.

Down in the tiny poetry section of the library my eye caught an old familiar title: *The Selected Poems of Gerard Manley Hopkins* in the old Penguin paperback edition, a copy of which I bought as an undergraduate at Manhattan College forty years ago. I took it back to my room, where, after finishing for the time being with Ignatius, I decided to read through a poem I've loved since I first read Hopkins: *The Wreck of the Deutschland.* Really, I was surprised to see how much better I understood the poem—all 280 lines of it—now that I'd begun the *Exercises.* What a giant of a poet this Victorian Jesuit was, even though his greatness was hidden in his own lifetime. In spite of having written so often about him, I am amazed at the levels of meaning I keep finding in his work. For four decades he has been my wellspring and inspiration, and not just for his poetry but for his life. "Our one sane milkman" in the galaxy of poets, the poet John Berryman called him. Our one sane poet, who makes so many other poets seem lame, halting, and boringly narcissistic.

So for two hours tonight, I pored over the poem once again, stanza by stanza, probing it for some of the ways the *Exercises* inform it, until my heart lifted with some obscure joy. Hopkins in his room there at St. Bueno's in North Wales, meditating on the destruction of the German liner *Deutschland* in the mouth of the Thames River in the winter of 1875, going over and over the words of the German nun (one of five) who was drowned that night. No poet touches me like this man. Have I not like him thrown in my lot with this Company of men and their heady ideals? A poet of the heart *and* the head, a man who needed the orthodoxy of the

Catholic Church. A man who loved his country, a gentleman through and through, a saint, really.

And yet a man who single-handedly transformed the possibilities of English poetry. He spoke of a new rhythm haunting his ear, and you hear it in the oceanic swell in the opening lines of this poem:

> *Thou mastering me*
> *God! Giver of breath and bread;*
> *World's strand, sway of the sea;*
> *Lord of living and dead;*
> *Thou hast bound bones and veins in me, fastened me flesh,*
> *And after it almost unmade, what with dread,*
> *Thy doing: and dost thou touch me afresh?*
> *Over again I feel thy finger and find thee.*

Have I too not felt that finger and that dread? And the consolations which have followed as well? How powerful, how majestic and consoling, the nun's utterance, "Christ, come quickly!" even as the waves drowned her and her companions. *Who am I?* Christ keeps asking me here in my own cell, with another winter sea crashing against the shore just beyond this window. Now, at the end of the first day of this retreat, I too find myself, like those sisters, like Hopkins himself, whispering into the surrounding darkness: "Christ, O Christ, come quickly."

DAY 2: FRIDAY, JANUARY 7

1:00 P.M. Up at twenty past five this morning. The world lay in total darkness, and yet the old Christmas song "Joy to the World" kept playing over and over in my head. Above the song I became more and more aware of the words *Here I am, Lord,* as if my soul was waiting for some message. Then the passage from St. John that has been vexing me becoming more and more insistent: Jesus going up to Jerusalem only to be rejected. Isn't this my own childhood anxiety again of being abandoned?

Then the nagging thought of going to Boston College and meeting the English department. And what if it should be *Thanks, but no thanks?* O.K. So be it. All I can do is present myself. It will be theirs to say yes or no. But then what was the calling really all about? An illusion? Am I jerking myself around for some reason too deep to fathom? Maybe there's a joke in all of this, after all. But if so, what's the point? And is there a point?

And why should I be thinking now of something that happened forty years ago, that night I went to the assistance of one of my freshmen at Colgate because the kid was staggering up the frozen streets of Hamilton in mid-winter? Did I really follow him because I thought it was my duty? Then the kid disappearing between the man-high snow banks into one of the frat houses along Main Street, the music and the sexual shouts acting on me like a drug. Then my charge showing some mark on his hand to a small dapper fraternity boy at the door before he went round the corner and was swallowed up in the crowd, and me following after, showing my hand quickly, though there was nothing on it. And then the bruiser coming at me out of nowhere, slamming me up against a wall. *I'm a faculty member,* I managed, weakly. *A preceptor. I'm following one of my freshmen, who's drunk out of his head.* Though at that particular moment I couldn't have cared less about the kid. Finally, Bruno put me down, shaken and furious.

And the damn thing is this: I didn't belong there. Hadn't paid, wouldn't have. And yet, part of me really did want to be at that party, which I'd avoided because I was engaged. Of course I had an excuse. I was a preceptor, and since I was looking after one of my charges, I might have gone directly to campus security and played the offended junior faculty member. Me, at twenty-two, fresh out of college myself. Instead, I let it go. Except for the bruised ego that can still nurse a resentment forty years later, and the resolution never to get into that kind of situation again. Vivas for the brute fascism of American fraternities, smashed noses, date rapes, vomit-laden rugs. Vivas too for the illusion of entitlement. Professor so-and-so, huh? Oh yeah? Show us a sign. In the meantime kiss this, pal. Bruno, Bruno, the angel at the gates.

Clouds half-hiding the risen sun as I went down to breakfast, resolved to eat more sparingly, as Ignatius suggests. A banana and raisin bran with a mix of skim and two-percent milk, a mug of coffee. But the box of cereal being "almost" empty, I decided to empty it, for the thousandth time smashing my resolve as I sat there with a bowl of cereal that kept multiplying like the loaves and fishes. And how, at this rate, will I ever achieve my twenty-five-year-old svelte shape again?

After breakfast I returned to the two Psalms for a final time before I went to see JJ and saw them suddenly in a whole new light. "Your eyes could see my embryo," my translation reads, and suddenly I was recalling the nerve specialist telling me a dozen years ago that it wasn't just the genetic loss of hearing in my right ear, but that—looking at me—I seemed to have been damaged *in utero*. Was I nearly rejected even then by my too-young mother, then spared? Only when I was fifty did my father tell me he had consoled my teenage mother when she found herself pregnant by saying that at least she would have a son to take care of her in her old age. Then lung cancer snuffing her life out at sixty-five.

Another emotional meeting with JJ this morning. It is not how I thought things were going to proceed. I had it mapped out that the retreat would start with ground well covered: The First Week with the universe as God had laid it out, then mankind's fall, and the need to recover as we can that world of innocence and friendship with the Lord. I figured it would be like looking at a history play with myself as interested onlooker and no more, the important episodes having played themselves out generations before I ever came on the scene. What would be so hard about all that? It looked easy enough on the page. Later, in the Third Week, when it would mean spending days meditating over Christ's Passion: all right, then the tears might come. On the other hand, I have gone into this retreat expecting nothing, or everything, and have told myself I will try to do whatever it takes to meet Christ on this journey. It's just that I didn't think the trip would hit two emotional landmines—Wham! Wham!—in my first two meetings. This was supposed to be dry-eyed, mapping-out, abstract stuff, and instead I must have used half a box of Kleenex. Welcome to the *Spiritual Exercises.*

JJ was calm, sympathetic. We talked. Or rather I talked and he listened. I came back to the Gospel of John a second time, focusing on Jesus' rejection by the religious authorities. What was it about the passage from John that so troubled me? Finally I saw what it was: a sense not only of Jesus' being rejected but of my being rejected. I thought of my father's mantra: that he wished us kids would get married and move on. Then of my poor romantic failure of a mother drinking for solace, then abandoning the house altogether for weeks at a time.

Did I think God could heal all this? he asked. Heal it, I thought. Just like that? I deflected the question, afraid of what I might say, and talked instead of my passion for being treated fairly, a passion that had come out of being unjustly treated too often when there was nothing I could do about it. Part of it came from being lied to constantly by my mother, in small ways mostly, exaggerations, broken promises, until I couldn't tell what was real and what wasn't. I told him of my zero tolerance for all sorts of lying, for cheating, for passing off as your own what wasn't your own. Like the New York City detective in my prose composition course back in '68 who tried to palm off someone else's essay as his. Only by luck did I discover the offending essay he'd given me in a brand-new blue-backed textbook some publisher had just mailed me at Hunter, and which I had opened on the subway on my way downtown to teach at the Police Academy on East Twenty-third.

"I didn't do it," he kept saying, even with the goddamn essay right there under his nose. A tough Irishman with a pockmarked face: tall, wiry, his fists opening and closing as if squeezing something. Capable—I realized—of real violence. *Just do the goddamn thing over,* I told him, *and we'll forget this episode.* His lying had the smell of rotten cheese, and he was right in my face with it. If he persisted in lying to me, I told him, I was going to the dean with the evidence. And with that he turned and left.

It was after 10:00 P.M. when the class emptied out that I noticed another of my students—a young cop fresh out of the Academy—had also stayed behind. I glanced up in the midst of my argument to see him staring intently at the bulletin board, and suddenly the classroom felt very big and very impersonal. After the detective had left, the young cop came up to me and told me that that man had a very bad reputation on the street. It was late, he reminded me. How was I getting home? The Lexington Avenue, I told him, with a transfer out to Flushing. *Stay under the streetlights,* he warned me, *and make sure no one is following you.* His comment caught me by surprise, and I realized only then what might happen. All the way home I kept looking over my shoulder. The following week I received a bad essay from the detective. For three pages it focused on the broken toilet in a suspect's tenement room. At least this time I knew that his description of the intricacies of various cloacal patés had to be original work, and work closer to his heart. Injustices. Ten thousand everyday, run-of-the-mill injustices that darken our lives. Including my own, and those not so incidental, and for which I beg now for forgiveness.

JJ's question, so unlike what any psychotherapist might ask you: *Can God heal all this? Can He at least give me a right heart?* At the end of our session he gave me a map of Eastern Point and Gloucester and told me to get some exercise. I think he could see that I was getting overheated and needed to relax and let God work in God's own time. It's a control issue, still, I see: that *I'm* somehow going to cure all this rather than God. That's what JJ was saying to me, I see now, by his question. "Take Farrington Avenue," he said, pointing it out on the map. "Take it over to Atlantic Road and follow that up the Atlantic side of Eastern Point to Bass Avenue. There's a beach there called Good Harbor. Sandy, broad, a place where you can walk." After prayers in Chapel, I put on my light jacket and ski cap, got in my spiffy Sable, and went to check out the beach. Cars were parked along the left side of Nautilus Road, and people down on the beach were walking their dogs.

Forty degrees, blustery, clouds half-hiding the sun, low green waves rolling in and crashing against the sandy shore. I walked across the bridge that fords the creek, an estuary of bluegreen water that was now flowing backward out to the ocean. An old man was powerwalking, lifting his arms and shuffling a bit pathetically, like a character out of a Beckett play. Myself in fifteen years, I thought. Only fatter. Two women in their twenties took off at a brisk pace, one jacketed, one leotarded, their two golden Labradors circling them. One of the dogs dashed into the icy water like a crazy teenager for a dip: circling, running out again, then whirring itself dry before sprinting up the beach. I trudged on, following in their fast-receding tracks, lost in thought. I felt happy, already relieved of some great but undefined burden. How simple life could be if you let it. A walk on a beach in the wake of two happy dogs.

By then the two women and their dogs had made it to the stone wall three hundred yards ahead. Even the old man had outstripped me, turning once, I noticed, to see if I was following too closely (I wasn't). Then the women headed back, walking past me at a clip, intent on getting back to their cars, the dogs following in their wake in loops, sniffing. I reached the wall, then turned back toward my car, green and expectant in the distance. As I crossed over the bridge, a woman with a small black poodle darted me a quick smile. I thought of movie clips, of how we enter and exit each other's lives, before the film wears out or is erased. Hello. Good-bye. How was your life?

The car clock read 10:54. I drove into Gloucester, this time intent on finding the statue of Our Lady of Good Voyage that looks out to sea and beckons her mariner children safe passage, going and coming. Ten thousand fishermen from Gloucester lost to the sea in the past 350 years, and Our Lady of Good Voyage: mother of the sea, her eyes full of concern and caring. A woman holding in her large capable arm—her left arm—a schooner, while her right hand is raised in blessing.

"Look for the two blue-domed towers," JJ had said. "Up Prospect. You'll see her up there." I parked in the lot off to the side of the church. The building is Portuguese in design, modest, five-windowed, with a school off to one side and a statue of the Sacred Heart off to the other. This is working-class Gloucester, the kind of place I've always favored. And there, above the school and a package store: Our Lady between two towers, the left one empty, the right filled with four bells. The church itself—like most churches now—was locked against vandalism, theft, or outright desecration. But there she was, standing above me, cradling her schooner, double masted, nestled there like her child. "Captains coming into the harbor use the towers to bring their boats in safely," JJ had said. Looking up at her, I could believe it.

I drove about the streets, thinking of the poet Charles Olson, a.k.a. Maximus, that six-foot-six poet who loved Gloucester as William Carlos Williams loved that other working-class town, Paterson, New Jersey. The filthiest swillhole in all Christendom, Williams had once called his beloved city, the place where my mother's mother grew up, working in the mills along that river. One comes to love such places, no matter how plain or ugly to an outsider. Besides, there's something in the blood that keeps coming back to the mother, isn't there? I thought of my friend Phil Levine, of his love for Detroit, of all poets from Whitman on who have sung our debased, beautiful, democratic cities, our people, our unsung masses. Blessings on them all. And on all unknown poets and on all those who sing, or even croak, a song of joy.

It was nearing lunchtime as I headed back to Eastern Point, driving as slowly as I could to absorb the actuality of the shorescape I was passing. Inside the compound marked by the twin brick columns and the No Trespassing sign a mile from the retreat house a backhoe was opening a trench from the front porch down to the stone gate entrance of one of the grand houses that front the eastern edge of the harbor. *Laborare est orare. To work is to pray.* Everything seemed to glow just then with a whole new life. This, I thought, is how Emerson and Thoreau must have seen things on good days. Rinsed and whole.

4:00 P.M. Ignatius asks us to consider God's kingdom, as it was in the beginning. And here it is all around me, as in the opening pages of Genesis, when God saw that all He'd made was good. A New World Naked. Taking my cue from the field guide to North American birds on the small stand by the dining room windows that look out over the ocean, I write out now a litany in celebration of the birds that flock along these Eastern coastal waters: the Snowy Egret and Great Blue Heron, the Bittern and the Sandhill. The Kittiwake and the Black-backed Gull. The Terns, the Skimmer and the Noddys, brown and black. The Gannet, Cory's Shearwater, the Frigate and the Tropicbird, the Jaegers, among them the Long-tail, Pomarine, and the Mick. The Teal, the Widgeon and the Canvasback, the Hooded Merganser, the Bufflehead and Goldeneye, the Coot and Brant. The Canada Goose, the Mute Swan, the Whistler, the Grebe and Loon. The Sandpiper, Plover, and the Dunlin. The Willets and Phalaropes. The Oystercatcher, Stilt, Whimbrel and Curlew. God made them all and saw how very good it was.

And now for the two passages for today: Hosea 11:1–9 and Micah 6:6–8. The passage from Hosea is stunning. It's about God's covenant with Israel and us, and turns on the metaphor of fidelity. Israel has abandoned her Lord to follow the ways of the Canaanites, those practitioners of sacred prostitution. *No need now to go back to Egypt,* God tells his people. *Assyria will serve well enough as your new master. How could you break my heart like this?* He pleads with his people. And yet He will not destroy His people again, as He did at the time of the Flood. *For I am God,* He says, *and not man.* He shows Himself in compassion and forgiveness, rather than wiping us out again. Given my own track record, that's comforting to know.

What is it that God demands of you? the prophet Micah pleads. The burnt offering of bullocks? The sacrifice of oil? Not these, but *to do what is right: to love loyalty and to walk humbly with your God.*

Be faithful and walk humbly. Walk humbly.

I went down to Chapel as the afternoon shadows grew longer, praying over these passages again, the room illuminated only by the candle signaling Christ's presence in the consecrated bread in the Tabernacle. The Ark, the Tent. It was very peaceful there, and when I came out shortly before four and walked past the sideboard in the Main Hall, I spotted Eileen's handwriting on an envelope. My first letter from her. I picked it up and tucked it inside my journal until I could get back to my room. Paul is well, she says, and enjoying his theology classes at Berkeley. Our firstborn. Doing what his father—who spent ten months in a seminary prep school forty-five years ago—could not.

7:45 P.M. Tonight it was Fr. Tim Shepherd, the tall, tousled-haired Jesuit Novice Master from Detroit, who said Mass. A stand-up comedian. He began his homily by telling his Chicago/Detroit novices that Rita Jensen, the teacher who had spoken of a "Gawd" in this evening's readings for the Mass, was in fact speaking of the same God the novices themselves worship. "Gawd," he explained, was merely the eastern Massachusetts name for this Deity.

His homily was based on the First Letter of John: *Whoever pos-*

sesses the Son possesses life; whoever does not possess the Son of God does not possess life. So, he concluded, if we want to know what God wants of us, watch how His Son acts. For Jesus did nothing apart from the Father, the two working as with one will. And in truth, my heart lifted to be there in that room with that community of retreatants and directors, to eat God's body and drink His blood, there for the asking. *Lord, if you want to, you can cure me,* the man with the withered arm had begged. And Jesus, stretching out his hand to touch him, saying, *Yes, I do want it. Be cured.* And that was it: The man was cured. Lord, I, too, want to be cured. Cured in mind and heart. Help me.

After dinner, I slipped into the small room adjoining the main chapel they call the Mary Chapel to talk with Mary. A single candle flickered before a statue of her holding her child. It was so quiet I could hear the waves pounding against the rocks a hundred yards away. Then I went down the hall to the Fireplace Room again and sat there before a crackling, welcoming fire, warmed by it as well as by the presence of the others. By the light of a night lamp I read my evening prayers from *The Magnificat.*

As I was leaving to go back to my room, I saw a copy of the Jesuit magazine, *Company,* which I took back to my room. In it is an article listing some of the 342 Jesuits martyred in the late, great twentieth century just completed: witnesses to their faith, for which they paid with their lives. How can I not think of my own son, and the many Jesuits who have helped me along the way? Among the most recent casualties, in fact, was a young Jesuit killed just last fall in the violence in East Timor. He was thirty-four, Paul's age exactly. His name was Fr. Tarcisius Dewante. He had just been ordained and had been murdered along with four nuns and three other priests and one hundred refugees, all of whom had fled to the Jesuit schools in the towns of Suai and Dili for refuge. All died on September 7, 1999, during the reign of terror that swept over the island in the wake of the elections for independence there. Four days later a seventy-year-old Jesuit priest, director of the Jesuit Refugee Service in Dili, was killed by intruders. I cannot get out of my mind the video pictures taken by cameramen from the besieged hotel lobby in Dili and broadcast on the evening news as I ate my dinner that night. They show men pouncing on unsuspecting victims, then yelps of pure fear, then machetes hacking them to death.

Here I am plotting a comfortable retirement, when throughout the century—as in all the previous centuries of their five-hundred-year existence—these Jesuits, like so many other men and women, have given up their lives in pursuit of an ideal. French Jesuits in China during the Boxer Uprising of 1900. Jesuits in Armenia during the genocide there. Fr. Miguel Pro in Mexico under the anticlerical government of Plutarco Calles. Another eight Jesuits murdered in China in the '30s and '40s. In Loyalist Spain, in the course of a few months: 122 Jesuits executed. Sixty Jesuits in Europe under the Nazis: Polish, Czech, Slovak, Slovenian, French, Dutch, Austrian, and German. They died in prisons, concentration camps, or were shot where found. Dutch Jesuits in Japanese concentration camps in Indonesia, Spanish Jesuits in Micronesia, Canadian Jesuits in China. A Jesuit killed by the Gestapo in Minsk, where he had gone at the local bishop's request, marked missing for nearly half a century, until police documents were released after the Communist regime collapsed.

The deaths, too, of other Jesuits at the hands of the Communists in Albania, Bohemia, Croatia, Hungary, Lithuania, Romania, Poland, Slovenia, China, and the frozen Siberian gulags. A Jesuit demanding to know what the Brazilian police had done with several of the *desaparecidos,* shot dead by an irritated junior police officer. Three Jesuits—two English, one Irish—along with four Dominican sisters, killed in Zimbabwe when their mission was overrun. Fr. Rutilio Grande, Archbishop Oscar Romero's friend, and two lay companions: ambushed and shot in El Salvador as they drove to evening Mass. Those six Jesuits killed in 1989 in San Salvador, along with their housekeeper and her fifteen-year-old daughter. All awakened in the middle of the night by soldiers, several trained at our School of the Americas. Isn't that what's so attractive about these Jesuits, these martyrs to the truth? Consider Pilate, facing the Jew from Galilee, whom he would kill that same day. *Truth?* he mutters. *What's that?*

10:00 P.M. Have been meditating on Ignatius's *Principle and Foundation* again, the keystone of which is the following: "That we are created to praise, reverence, and serve God our Lord, and in doing so to enter into union with God." And so we are to use the things of this world to help us achieve spiritual union with God. Which means balancing things and discerning what is the best path for us, insofar as we have a choice in the matter.

When, therefore, Ignatius speaks of remaining "indifferent" to all material things—money, clothes, a house, wine, food, cars—he means things that are in themselves morally neutral. I am not *compelled,* therefore, to give away my life savings for some greater good, nor am I *compelled,* say, to protest the atrocities committed by soldiers trained by the U.S.'s School of the Americas. But to become more perfect—*be perfect as your Father is perfect,* is Jesus' injunction in the Gospels—I must be willing out of love to go the extra mile to make all progress possible, wherever the possibility of such progress shows itself. This certainly follows. It doesn't make it easier to follow, but the logic points in that direction. And there you have it.

11:00 P.M. Still too wide awake to sleep, so let's look at Ignatius again. In the winter of 1537–1538, by which time Ignatius was forty-seven, the year of waiting for safe passage to the Holy Land finally came to an end with the sea routes still closed. And so, Ignatius resigned himself to the fact that they would not be going there after all. At once he set off for Rome to offer the Company's labors to Pope Paul III. Ignatius sent the others out in pairs to the neighboring university towns in Italy to preach, while he set off with Frs. Faber and Laínez. A few miles north of Rome, at the village of La Storta, he had a vision in which it seemed to him that God the Father was linking Ignatius to His Son, who spoke these words to him: *Ego vobis Romae propitius ero.* "I will be propitious to you in Rome."

What did the vision mean? That the work Ignatius had undertaken would flourish? That God would treat him benevolently? Was God telling him in effect not to be anxious—*do not be afraid*—that he would be there for him, just as the angel had told Mary when she found herself pregnant with Jesus? Isn't it the same message the angels brought to the shepherds in the fields that first Christmas, or to the women that first Easter morning? *Do not be afraid.* Later, when others of his Company asked Ignatius what he thought the message might have meant, he merely shrugged. "I do not know whether we shall be crucified in Rome," he told them, "but Jesus will be propitious."

It was now that Ignatius suggested that the little brotherhood that had formed around him call themselves the Company of Jesus. Company: a military term no doubt, and also a term meaning "friends of the Lord" or members of a confraternity. Not the Company of Ignatius, I see, but the Company of Jesus. After all, it was Christ who had gone before, showing the way with his own life. *He* was the one leader truly worth following. As it turned out, Paul III did smile on the Company, summoning them to Rome to work with him. Faced with the burgeoning of new souls to care for in the Americas and the Far East, as well as by the threat of the Protestant Reformation in northern Europe, he asked Ignatius's men to act as missionaries. At the same time, a rule would have to be formulated if the Company was going to attract and hold new members. But if the men agreed to take a vow of obedience and become an Order in the traditional sense, would they then have to adopt the older rule of stability that defines all cloistered orders, and thus remain attached to a particular monastery? And if they did, what would become of their ability to go where they were needed most? Paul was a far-ranging and liberal pope, but what if a more conservative pope replaced him? Would he quash the new order, insisting that its members stay put?

After much prayer, and in a world where entire nations were breaking away from the pope's allegiance, the Company came to the unanimous decision that, yes, they would, after all, have to take the vow of obedience as other orders had. In spite of the fact that there were tremendous obstacles within the Church hierarchy that threatened to sink the Company, the Company was officially recognized and sanctioned in September 1540. The following April, Ignatius reluctantly consented to become the first Superior General of the Order. Once he had, he and his companions professed their vows at the Church of St. Paul Outside the Walls, on the site where the Apostle had been martyred fifteen hundred years before.

A modern Order then, the pope's special forces, ready at a moment's notice to pick up and go where they were needed, whether to the courts of Japan, China, and India or the jungles of Paraguay and Brazil, or among the Hurons and Iroquois in North America. What a group! How many martyrs there were among them, how many witnesses to the faith. How many deaths by drowning, by malaria, by torture, by exhaustion these men underwent. And so the Jesuits enter history, for better or worse: Xavier, Faber, Gonzaga, Peter Claver, Alphonsus Rodriguez, Hopkins, de Chardin, Rahner, Arrupe, Dulles, and untold thousands of other extraordinary and selfless men who gave everything they had to the Company and its Captain. Like Fr. Duffy, counseling me, here at Eastern Point, in the autumn of 1984, and giving me hope. Unsung in the world beyond these walls perhaps, but sung now by me. Multiply *that* example by a hundred hundred thousand.

DAY 3: SATURDAY, JANUARY 8

7:30 A.M. A rough night, filled with dark dreams that evaporated on waking. The first time I awoke it was one in the morning, when

I swam into consciousness to find myself with a leg cramp and surrounded by an eerie silence, my chest feeling as if a succubus were squatting on it. I got up trying to breathe, then lay down again, prayed for calm, and somehow fell back to sleep.

Then at four—the hour of the wolf—I woke again with a start, unable to breathe. A shadow of death seemed to lie over everything. The passage from Hosea about our infidelity to God filled my mind and erotic images began crawling over me and the bed. They were everywhere, though I could see them for the empty illusions they were, there to steal my peace and leave nothing but ash in their place. The Evil One, Lucifer, hiding behind his puppet theater, manipulating his glitzy, tinsel-strewn sex puppets. Once again I turned to the Father, begging Him to banish these images. Then to Christ, pleading with Him to hide me in His wounds, the image itself picked up from the *Anima Christi.* The images, I told Him, were robbing me of my peace.

And then, like that, the Enemy, that charred, ruined aristocrat, that great fallen angel, like something out of Kubrick's *Eyes Wide Shut,* hovered off, black wings flapping. Slowly, the darkness lifted and calm returned. I kept saying to myself, in words that surprise me now, for they seemed to arise spontaneously: "I am His Son. I too am a prince and no slave, made His son by His Son's sacrifice. He will watch over and protect me." Then, quietly, I fell back to sleep, waking strangely refreshed a few minutes ago. Light, sweet light, was just breaking through the low-lying clouds, revealing a plum sea, shading to slate blue. Orange-mackerel clouds, then the royal sun stepping over the sea as if to greet me.

11:15 A.M. Spoke with JJ this morning of what had happened to me in the predawn hours. I told him that I sometimes feared I was still a two-percent Manichaean. Yes, God's light shone on most of my life, but there was some secret two percent that the Ruined Aristocrat seemed to have control over, and that I hated myself for it. "If the Devil can get hold of a single hair of a person," St. Francis once wrote, "he soon has it enlarged to a cable. And if for years on end he is not able to down the person he has been tempting, he does not haggle over the delay so long as the person gives in to him in the end. That is his business. He thinks of nothing else day and night." That, and the poet John Berryman's Evil One saying, "I smell you for my own, by smug," with sulfur suffusing the room. But as I thought about this, there in JJ's office on a Saturday morning in January, it struck me that it was *I* who had allowed myself to become a slave. I think that is what this night has taught me.

JJ opened his copy of the *Exercises,* looking for something. He seemed in no hurry as he patiently, steadily searched until he had found what he was looking for. It turned out to be the Thirteenth Rule for the *Discernment of Spirits,* folded in under the *Supplementary Matter* at the end of the *Exercises.* "Sometimes the Enemy acts like a false lover," he read deliberately,

> insofar as he tries to remain secret and undetected. For such a scoundrel, speaking with evil intent and trying to seduce the daughter of a good father or the wife of a good husband, wants his words and solicitations to remain secret. But he is deeply displeased when the daughter reveals his deceitful words and evil design to her father, or the wife to her husband. For then he knows he cannot succeed in the design he began. Just so, when the Enemy turns his wiles and persuasions on an upright person, he intends and desires them to be kept secret. But when the person reveals them to his or her good confessor who understands the Enemy's deceits and malice, he is deeply disappointed. For now he sees that he cannot succeed in the malicious project he began, because his deceptions have been found out.

I was stunned by the brilliance of this insight. And so I have been thinking about Satan's strategies all morning, of the devious ways in which he stalks us. I know this Enemy all too well. We became intimates years ago, in the way an older man, oiled and perfumed, aristocratic, self-assured, self-loathing, will keep a boy in bondage, sometimes with blandishments, sometimes—as necessary—with threats. Ignatius understood clandestine love trysts—the thrill, the shame—having witnessed these trysts at court. He knew the damage they did to men and women both. So, too, with soft porn on television, or the stuff on the Internet: the exhausted faces of the women, drug-fed, threatened with violence, beaten, often killed by pimps and smalltime hoods, anonymous, dull, murderous. The cold end of a gun held to the head. Or taken to the edge of a roof to stare five stories down.

Have I not prayed all these years to have my passions brought under check? Angry flare-ups against my wife and sons, damaging to their self-esteem. The refusal to enter bars, my insistence on keeping the door open to my office when students are there, getting up each morning at six to get down to daily Mass, kneeling on the cold floor, asking for His grace that the Enemy, in whatever form he might take, might not insinuate himself, knowing that on my own I could fold like a house of cards, for it is only God who can see me through this. I have not asked that passion be taken away—for passion is what keeps life fresh, what gives me the spring to place my two feet over the edge of the bed each morning and get up—but rather that my passions might be channeled. God's beauty is everywhere, including the beauty of women, to be admired, then let go. "Sometimes, Paul," a priest told me years ago, "the hamburger stays on the table." He meant that not everything had to be taken and later discarded. Besides, he reminded me, it wasn't mine for the taking, even when—as sometimes happened—it was offered.

Somehow, in getting this out into the open I felt deeply at peace again, as if a boil had been lanced. As I was getting up to leave, JJ gave me John 15:12–17 to read and asked me to reflect on Ignatius's description of the Three Sins: the rebellion of the angels, the rebellion of our first parents, and—finally—my own sorry rebellion. Then he asked me to look over the first nineteen verses of Genesis 3, as well as Psalm 106. I had my homework for the day.

I walked out into the Main Hall where Marcie was looking out the window and meditating, so as not to intrude on my solitude, and went into the main Chapel to pray. There, against the window, with the waves crashing against Brace Rock in the background, I sat down before the Blessed Sacrament. The morning sun was streaming in through the large bay windows. I sat on three blue pillows with my head against the wall, light washing over my hands and legs, and shut my eyes, sitting like that for an hour in deep peace, relishing my new sense of sonship. *I am convinced,* St. Paul says in this morning's meditation from the *Magnificat, that neither death, nor life, nor angels, nor principalities, nor present problems, nor future difficulties, nor powers, nor height, nor depth, nor any other creature will be able to separate us from the love of God in Christ Jesus our Lord.* So be it. So be it.

I've been thinking how anticlimactic the last chapter of Ignatius's life turns out to have been. Like my own life, it seems: one more teacher and writer alone in his office cell ninety percent of the time. No crowds, no instaurations, no tinsel *gloire.* Why is it that a life as stirring as Ignatius's had been up through his fiftieth year should—from the outside at least—end up with all the appearances of some bureaucrat shuffling papers in his office in Rome? A cardinal, who knew him only in these last fifteen years, found nothing extraordinary in him, other than what one might have found in any conscientious priest carrying out his quotidian duties. The man who had once fervently hoped to spend his life in the Holy Land did not now go off to China or Brazil or even Germany or Portugal. Instead, he read it as God's will that he stay at the helm in Rome, running the affairs of the entire Society while living with forty other Jesuits on the Via Aracoeli, in a house attached to the Jesuit church.

He was a brilliant administrator and C.E.O., who in these last years wrote over seven thousand letters to members of his Company, already scattered as far as Japan in the one direction and Brazil in the other, asking for news and offering pastoral advice, whether gentle or—where necessary—admonitive. In 1551, when he was sixty, he gathered the elder fathers of the Society to once again revise the constitutions, and tendered his resignation as General. He was in poor health, he explained. Perhaps it was time to pass on the reins to a younger man. But his letter of resignation was refused. Three years later, in failing health, he tried again to resign, and again his resignation was rejected, though he did succeed in turning the practical aspects of his office over to Fr. Nadal. Ironically, as it turned out, Ignatius himself soon after had to send Nadal abroad on urgent business, and so once more he found himself at the helm. So much work, so few hands to do it.

As soon as the pope had sanctioned the Society in 1540, Ignatius's tiny Company was scattered to the four winds. One of the Company was sent to Lisbon to found the Portuguese province of the Society. Xavier sailed for the Far East, eventually becoming Provincial of India. Two others were sent to Ireland on a clandestine mission to aid the Irish in the wake of England's suppression of the Catholic Faith, and barely got out of the country with their lives. In 1542, four Jesuits were dispatched to Germany to found a province there. Four years later, five Jesuits found places at the Council of Trent, two as influential papal theologians. Five years after that, Ignatius founded the Roman College for the formation of his Scholastics, thanks in large part to the munificence of another Jesuit novice, (St.) Francis Borgia, father of eight and a widower, who turned his vast wealth over to the Society when he joined the Order. Rome became the center of a great wheel, from which Ignatius tirelessly exhorted his brothers to do everything *ad majorem Dei gloriam:* for the greater glory of God.

Then, in the summer of 1556, Ignatius, now sixty-five, was hit by the dreaded malarial Roman fever. Because he did not complain, no one realized how ill he was. On the evening of July 30, he asked for the last sacraments and a blessing from the pope, but was told by his physician that there was no immediate danger. The following morning the infirmarian in the next apartment found him at his prayers, and so did not suspect that he was dying. Then, quietly, imperceptibly, two hours later, Ignatius was dead.

It took fifty-three years to beatify him, and another thirteen before he was canonized. "He looked at his life as an offering to the God he called *liberalidad,* freedom," Ron Hansen ends his essay on Ignatius with his characteristically grounded eloquence, "and God blessed that gift a hundredfold in the Society of Jesus. The house of Loyola ended when Doña Magdalena de Loyola y Borgia died childless in 1626, but in that same year there were 15,535 Jesuits in 36 provinces, with 56 seminaries, 44 novitiates, 254 houses, and 443 colleges in Europe and the Baltic States, Japan, India, Macao, the Philippines, and the Americas." It is this man—this Ignatius, this bantam Basque—whose directives I am trying, like a good soldier with a hearing problem, 450 years down the line, to follow.

12:45 P.M. I notice that, imperceptibly, the other Thirty-Day retreatants seem to have settled in for the duration. Most seem relaxed and stare out on the ocean for long moments. A few A-type personalities (my kinsmen, if the truth be told) seem intent on reading every book they can lay their hands on and listening via headsets to every CD they can find. Others jog or run or go for long walks into town, or along the rocks here, lost in thought. The novices seem to have mastered a sort of shorthand sign language, by which they communicate at meals and in the evenings. I've begun reading a fascinating book, *Jesuits Go East: A Record of Missionary Activity in the East, 1541–1786,* the two dates bracketing the 245 years from St. Francis Xavier's setting out for Japan to the suppression of the Jesuits by Pope Clement XIV in 1763 and the aftermath of the suppression. It's an old book—fifty years old—but it tells the story sure enough.

4:30 P.M. A sweet deep sleep after lunch today. Delicious, really, and it made up a little for the terrors of last night. Afterward, I donned a sweatshirt and ski cap and took off on foot down to the lighthouse, walking the half mile out to the end of the granite breakwater. To the north, at the far end of Gloucester Harbor, I could make out the twin towers of Our Lady of Good Voyage, with the statue of Mary between them. The last time I walked out to this point was back in '84, a time that stands now as a nadir and as a beginning, when I was tortured with the thought of how I was ever going to put my marriage back together again. Standing here now, facing the sea, it all came back with a terrifying rush. I could feel the desolation all over again, my body floating off in the waves there, returning now to its first elements. Unless, that is, the time were somehow redeemed, unless God really did care about us, and the mess we too often make of our lives.

I've been meditating here in my room on the passages JJ gave me this morning, with the focus first of all on Genesis 3:1–19. The Fall of God's First Kingdom. God's Adversary, the Enemy, in the garden in the form of a serpent, urging the woman on, who will in turn urge the man on:

> *Now the snake was the subtlest of all the wild animals that Yahweh God had made. It asked the woman, "Did God really say you were not to eat from any of the trees in the garden?" The woman answered the snake, "We may eat the fruit of the trees in the garden. But of the fruit of the tree in the middle of the garden God said, 'You must not eat it, or even touch it, under pain of death.'" Then the snake said to the woman, "No! You will not die! God knows in fact that the day you eat it your eyes will be opened and you will be like gods, knowing good from evil."*

You will be like gods, for you too will know what evil is. And you will, you poor slobs, learn what death is. I know. I have been there myself, thank you. And so: a man and a woman, at odds with each other, and their God, and everything askew. The man looks at the woman and sees her now not as his lover and partner but as someone out to hurt him. Suddenly, she has become the seductress, who can only be tamed by domination. For her part, she will take counsel with herself and not with him and will suffer the pains of childbirth, which she alone will feel. The man will labor, often for small enough or even illusory rewards. God's balance has indeed been thrown off kilter. From now on the wheel that should have run smoothly will wobble eccentrically, like a bike wheel after hitting a stone wall. The intimacy and free play each felt with each will be gone. Worse, the intimacy both shared with God, who walked with them in the cool of the evening, has been lost. And if it is gone, how can we ever recover it?

8:00 P.M. Mass and dinner, after which I went over to the library room to catch up on the news, in that way hoping to keep at least one foot in the world I have inhabited these past fifty-nine years. Strangely, the need to know what's going on seems more urgent now than ever. It's as if I had new antennae and were listening for the pulse of the human race. I, who daily confine myself to half a dozen comic strips and the stock market reports.

And so: a report in the *Boston Globe* on Ehud Barak of Israel and Farouk Sharaa of Syria, negotiating the return of the Golan Heights, sitting opposite each other in West Virginia, with Clinton between them. Clinton, at least, seems optimistic about arranging a peace settlement, but I notice that Sharaa is not even willing to shake hands with Barak. Besides which, there is still Sharaa's unshakable ultimatum: return the Golan Heights as those borders existed on June 4, 1967, just before the Israelis took the high ground in the Six Days' War, or there will be no talk of peace. How long, O Lord? These neighbors—cousins, really—who distrust each other as much now as they have any time these past four thousand years.

On the opposite page: a photograph of a Russian officer uncovering the face of a Chechen soldier, the man's mouth still tightly wrapped with duct tape, a ski mask roughly removed. There's a dazed look in the man's eyes, like a toad caught in a snake's grip, conscious that its life is over. The Russian officer clearly means business. How many of the twenty thousand civilians inside Grozny will be dead when I leave this place? How many young Russian conscripts?

Back in my room, I began going over Psalm 106: *Give thanks to Yahweh, for he is good, / his faithful love is everlasting!* It's a hymn recalling the collective guilt of a people. Yes, but my guilt as well. Our ancestors defied you, the Psalm laments, defied you even with their backs against the sea. And though you saved them, they chose to forget you yet again, trading away your glory for the image of a grass-eating bull. They chose the child-slaying god, Moloch, and they did not root out his followers as you insisted but slept with them, and wound up seduced, until they, too, were sacrificing their children to him. And still, when they cried out in their agony, you took pity on them again. Why? Why do we keep returning to our sins like a dog to its vomit?

And, finally, the passage JJ gave me from John 15:12–17, after I'd mentioned my keen sense of sonship with God. If I have chosen God, the passage reads, it is because God first chose me. *I shall no longer call you servants,* Jesus tells his disciples in the hours leading up to his death. Instead, he says, *I call you my friends, / because I have made known to you / everything I have learnt from my Father.* Then he tells them to *go out and . . . bear fruit, / fruit that will last.* Finally, he gives them the command to *love one another.* So: it is God calling out to me, isn't it, as much as my calling out to Him. Amazing to realize this again.

9:15 P.M. Down to the Fireplace Room for a short break. I sat and stared at the fire for a few minutes, then went into Chapel to pray. Only now, one hundred hours into the retreat, does it really seem to be getting underway. It's like the first plunge into the depths after footing it around the beach. Now land's end at last begins to fall behind.

Then back to my room to meditate on the First, Second, and

Third Sins, in order to understand better what sin really is. What is it but the attempt to frustrate God's plan of creation? And so, a meditation first on the sins of the angels; then on the sins of our first parents; and—finally—a meditation on my own sins. If evil balks at God's plan, how shall we get rid of it? Begin by praying, Ignatius exhorts us, begging God for the grace to turn ourselves over to His service and praise.

And so, to first meditate on the nature of Evil and the heart's proclivity to gravitate toward it. This, Ignatius explains in the Prelude, will be "a composition by imagining the place." When, he explains, "a contemplation or meditation is about something abstract and invisible, as in the present case about the sins, the composition will be to see in imagination and to consider my soul as imprisoned in this corruptible body, and my whole compound self as an exile in this valley [of tears] among brute animals."

A hard thing to do, meditating on the abstract, but I gave it my best shot. I thought of the body's weight and gravity trapping the soul, the essential Self steeped in the self, and asked the Lord for a sense of shame and confusion about myself when I thought of how many have been damned for one willful defiant act against God, and of how many times I have escaped with my own life. Then I began to meditate on my own unworthiness and of God's mercy toward me. I thought of Poe's narcoleptic dead, locked in their coffins and pounding to be let out as the dirt fell on the lid: an image of death-in-life. It is certainly an image with the power to unsettle.

And so to the *First Point:* the sin of the angels, with their non-corporeal intelligences. Hopkins is very good on this. In his own notes on the *Exercises,* for instance, he speaks of a choir of voices singing the praises of the Eternal One, and then of Lucifer and the other angels falling in love instead with the sound of their own voices. For Lucifer, the original sin must have been one of pride: the setting himself up as a god in place of his Creator. And so a fractious cacophony intruded where there had been cosmic harmony, a palace rebellion doomed to failure from the start but which did not stop the Promethean Lucifer from acting anyway. He had free will, he had grace and intelligence, he was a great prince, an aristocrat, a world wielder in his own right. And with his *non serviam—I will NOT serve anyone but myself*—there followed a battle of titanic proportions. Of course Satan was toppled, but not without a fight that shattered the heavens, his fall likened in Revelations to some gigantic comet plunging through the heavens to crash into the earth's crust.

Grand Guignol? O.K. Then how treat of the problem of real evil? Who, after all, is the most evil figure in history or literature you have ever encountered? And what is it that makes that figure so evil? Consider Faulkner's Popeye in *Sanctuary,* raging like Satan, and as impotent, in his malevolence raping a woman with a corncob. Or Shakespeare's Iago, spreading murderous dissension and suspicion in *Othello,* until the general destroyed both his wife and himself.

Hitler in a rage, killing first his niece, then how many millions of Jews and Germans and Poles and Hungarians and others. The prison guards at Auschwitz. The Kommandants. The Nigerian Muslim officer who cold-bloodedly shot my former teacher, Brother Roman Wyzcinski, through the head. Those machete-wielding jackals in East Timor. The three Texans who chained a black man to the back of their pickup and dragged him to his death. Any one of ten thousand torturers, trained in their techniques, showing no mercy, deaf to the screams of their victims. Thank God that in my own life I have met no one this evil.

The Second Point: Adam and Eve's sin, the original fall, and the catastrophic ripple effect from that fall. Like passing AIDS from parent to child, and on down the line. The DNA genetic model permanently warped by fallout from a nuclear catastrophe. The story itself is so pitiable. Satan undermining, then refuting God's word. *You will not die,* he assures Eve, though of course she will. Then the angel with the flaming sword and the expulsion from the garden. If this is myth, it reveals a profound truth: that somehow things have gone horribly wrong with us. Studying the history of our species, we find enormous suffering and loss running through everything. Yeats—good Nietzschean that he was—speaks of a kind of fatalistic tragic gaiety in all of this. Laughter in the teeth of the inevitable. But on closer inspection, I think my old Bread Loaf colleague, Tim O'Brien—arguably the best novelist to come out of Vietnam—was closer to the truth when he spoke of the real losers in any large-scale conflict as the parents, children, and wives of the maimed, the missing, and the dead. As long as these breathe, they will suffer the loss of those who fought. And where is the tragic gaiety in so much sorrow?

The Third Point: my own sins. What, Ignatius asks us, of those who died and were lost because they committed only one serious sin? Or two? Or five? Or any number fewer than mine? But this kind of reasoning I find too abstract. Consider instead if I had died in a car crash, say, in October 1984, after leaving Eileen. Or at any time when I was deep in transgression. Or been found out, say, the way Bill Clinton was found out by a Starr Chamber sniffing for blood. A man ruined by his sexual misconduct, the affair all over the newspapers, the girl's transcripts on the Internet. A charismatic president ruined, his power to do good severely compromised, the nation hurt in a thousand ways, treaties left unsigned or rejected by a vindictive Congress, his moral stature shrinking in the aftermath. Is not scandal of this order itself a kind of death?

10:30 P.M. Overwhelmed by it all, I went down to Chapel to collect my thoughts. For the most part I have been spared the experience of raw evil. Perhaps not. Perhaps I am only fooling myself. I do not know what sin our first parents committed, or who they were, or even if there were two original parents. But when I look back, I see an appetite for evil in us humans, a self-aggrandizement, greed, lust, a death urge, a willingness to do harm to others and to oneself. How often we screw things up, or cover over the truth, or lie, hurting others to get what we want.

One learns good from one's parents and the larger world beyond. But one also—alas—learns evil. Cities put to the torch, the inhabitants executed. Babi Yar, Nigeria, Somalia, Chechnya, Shanghai under the Japanese occupation, Antietam, the Wilderness, Little Big Horn, Wounded Knee, my own Turners Falls, Dresden, Nagasaki, Hiroshima, Columbine, Jericho, Mosada, Megiddo, Waterloo, Normandy, Acre, Stalingrad, London during the Blitz, Verdun, the Somme, Dublin, 1916. Prison riots, lynchings, dismemberments, drawing and quarterings, the Inquisition, the McCarthy hearings, cross burnings, Nazi interrogations, the Salem Witch Trials, beheadings, the bullet to the nape of the neck, the rough Roman justice that crucified God's Son.

I kept thinking of my old friend Barry Moser's images of the mockers at the crucifixion, the ones he showed me just after he'd etched them in blocks for his Bible: the upright poles just outside the walls of Jerusalem, and three men crucified. I thought of crows jellying the eyes of the condemned, the mob-style executions, sex murders, untold millions of abortions, viable fetuses churned to mush with razorlike rotary instruments.

Then I thought of God's Son entering the world, the Word made flesh, coming to proclaim a year of jubilee, of mercy, for the people. Jesus, Yeshua, who would die in the maelstrom of human history, like the Jewish prophets, like Gandhi and Martin Luther King and Robert Kennedy and so many others who made too-easy targets by preaching peace and love in a world bent on murder. I thought of Herod, that old fox, near death, trying to snuff out this tiny interloper. Business as usual at any time since the fall.

It's after eleven. *Basta!* Enough! Lights out. Try to get some rest.

DAY 4: SUNDAY, JANUARY 9

12:30 A.M. Awoke with a start at midnight from a suffocating nightmare. Once more, as I have for years now, I felt as if I was drowning. I looked around for Eileen and then remembered where I was. I got up and rushed to the window, prying open the outer aluminum storm window, and greedily sucked in all the air I could. It took ten or fifteen minutes to steady myself, and when the panic began to subside, I went down to Chapel to pray and re cover some vestige of peace. The candle before the Blessed Sacrament flickered and comforted. No one else was about.

As much as I admire this tough, little Basque, there's something about Ignatius's intensity that threatens to overwhelm me. His face is turned toward the work that must be done, and he will not flinch, even when his beloved Jesuits begin dying in the field. Over and over, he and his followers keep playing for the highest stakes, so much so that I want to turn aside and rest, or go back to terrain I recognize. From where I stand I can see the French cannon in the surrounding hills, the fear on the faces of those I meet in the streets here. Let's negotiate, I want to tell him. Let's go home. But no, he says, face forward, in the teeth of the enemy, waving his little sword. If God is with you, he seems to say, quoting the Psalmist, who can be against you? Still, those are pretty big guns out there ranged against us.

He keeps asking the most fundamental questions—metaphysical questions, theological questions, questions about the nature of existence. Deeply disturbing questions about what is and is not important in the long run. Which doesn't seem all that long anymore. Like so many saints, he runs counter to the warp and woof that make up the texture of our small, comfortable lives. I keep thinking, for instance, of those thirty-odd Jesuits off the Azores in the seventeenth century, bound for the New World missions—Fr. Diaz and his companions—their ship captured by French Huguenot Corsairs off the Canaries. The arduous making of the *Exercises,* the years of training in the classics, philosophy, theology, pastoral care, works of charity done, the work left undone, all that promise snuffed out in a matter of a few hours when they were forced overboard. Multiply such self-sacrifice a hundredfold, a thousand, ten thousand. Then the Order itself suppressed in 1773 by a weak pope caving in before political expediency.

The truth is I am afraid, afraid that I will not be able to say yes when the time comes, yes to the necessary sacrifice of my own will for something larger and greater, a yes that might allow me to break out of my own self-imposed limitations and reach for something greater. And yet, something seems to be steadying me, as I was steadied back in October 1975, when I was the too-young Rector of a Cursillo weekend in North Adams, JJ's brother-in-law—Big Abe—there to steady me then with his humor. That first night I left the community room because of the noise and banter so I could get some rest and fell asleep in a classroom where the Blessed Sacrament was kept. A candle flickered before the makeshift tabernacle, and when I fell asleep I dreamed I was being lifted and enveloped by God's soft comforting light. Next morning I woke, deeply refreshed, ready to do His work. May it be so again.

9:45 A.M. Fell asleep again and woke just as the sun was breaking above the ocean through low-lying clouds. My head was pounding with the stress of the night just finished, and I wanted to stay where I was, hidden under the covers. But it was time to get up. I dressed and went down to breakfast, lingering over my coffee, unwilling to leave the human contact there. No sooner was I with JJ than I was laughing about the crazy night I'd had.

He seemed more concerned for my health than I was. I *must* begin the reflections earlier in the day, he told me. I could not wait until 9:00 P.M. to begin a new set of meditations, as I had with the Three Sins. The point, he explained, was to meditate on each of the passages at least three times during the day, starting when I am still fresh. I think the intensity of these daily discussions has got to be wearing on JJ as well, though he never says so, but simply listens, following, checking internally against what Ignatius has to say on a particular point, and stroking his beard. Nothing I say seems to escape him. Both of us, I am beginning to understand, are being fed by the same spiritual conduit, as director and retreatant respond to each other, as well as to the promptings of the Spirit. Call and countercall. And look at this. The sun is shining on my hand, warming it, caressing it, as I write these words here in Chapel. How warm and life-sustaining the river of God's light can be. Praise Him.

11:45 A.M. Donned my light windbreaker, black gloves, and ski hat and strode down toward Niles Pond at a brisk pace, breathing in the sea air. Then out through the gates and north to Bemo Road, then east. Off St. Louis Avenue a mother was playing hide-and-seek with her two small boys. They were hiding, the little one behind the older, in among a row of tall evergreen bushes—eight or ten feet high, thick to the very base. Still, you could pick the two brothers out even at a distance, because the older boy had an orange strip on his black ski cap so bright you could have navigated by it, and his little brother was making sure he stayed within two feet of him. A tough little sport but not yet willing to go it alone.

"Oh my, where are my little boys," the mother was saying, playing along. And then the older boy, unable to contain his happiness any longer, popped out from the bushes, giggling, "Here I am! Here I am!" Then the little guy, waiting just a bit longer, also making his triumphant appearance, beaming like his brother. And isn't that what God has been saying to me all along, if I would only listen? "Here I am," He keeps saying. "Here I am!" If you are looking for the Garden of Eden, friend, you will find it just off St. Louis Avenue on Eastern Point, and its face will be a young mother with her two little ones. I laughed with joy at the delicious spectacle.

Farther down the road, where it opens into the ocean again, I caught sight of the Retreat House across the cove. It looked peaceful, solid, beckoning. A woman jogger ran by me, smiling a hello. I smiled back. After a bit, I headed back. A hundred yards ahead as I came out onto the main road a young woman with abundant hair and a black and purple ski jacket was walking in the same direction I was. I saw her turn once and wondered if my presence had interrupted her thoughts. How easily we intrude upon one another's solitude. I wish somehow we men might wear some sign to say Harmless. Completely Harmless. Have a Nice Day. But are we? And isn't that what the meditation on my own sinfulness and the disorder it brings with it are all about?

1:15 P.M. Chicken soup and a sandwich of imitation lobster, shrimp, and bottom feeder, the silence in the dining room broken only by the sound of eighteenth-century flute music trilling up and down the scales, the strings waiting to respond. Then the violins and viols, a flight of them. Some could say from their vast reservoir of knowledge just whose music this is. But for now—though nameless, like the Great Spirit—the music belongs to me, and equally to the others sitting about me. It's there for all of us, the way one owns a landscape—this landscape—without needing to put up a single fence or pay a single penny.

2:00 P.M. Sitting here in Mary Chapel, I was meditating on my own sinfulness, as Ignatius instructs us to do, asking "for a growing and intense sorrow, and tears, for my sins," and calling "to memory all the sins of my life, looking at them year by year and period by period. Where I lived. My associations. The occupation I was pursuing at the time." I was doing this, when, suddenly, I seemed to see myself looking down from the cross as if through Jesus' eyes. How strange it was to be looking through *His* eyes!

And there they were: Mary, my mother, distraught, her own heart broken, mute, looking up at me, trying even now to comfort me, with the nails through my wrists, one foot forced over the other, sole to heel and splayed together. And Mary Magdalene, a tough woman who would not scare, faithful from the start. Faithful even now. John, too, trying to comfort my mother, his own heart broken. Four soldiers squatted in a circle, while one of them threw dice for the cloak my mother had sewn for me. The mockers were still mocking, though their shouts were lessening now. Or was it that I could no longer hear them? Worse even than the pain, though, was the sensation of drowning as I tried to lift myself high enough to suck air into my lungs.

So this is how it ends. It's dark. *My God, my God,* I cry out, *why have you abandoned me?* David's words, Psalm 22, a son of David uttering them now, a thousand years later. A Jewish king hung out to dry.

I've come down to the dining hall to write. It's going to be a long afternoon, for sure, as I go step by step through this self-scrutiny. A review of my sins "year by year and period by period. Where I lived." Begin at the beginning, then. What did I know of sin, growing up in our corner of New York City? I remember my mother visiting a girlfriend whose husband had been killed in the Battle of the Bulge. The year is 1946, and we're up on East Sixty-fifth. I've walked down the mean street with a little girl—the five-year-old daughter of my mother's friend, and I spot a grocer throwing a box of sugar-dusted donuts into a large garbage can. I pluck the box out and hand one to the girl, meaning to impress her with my largesse. My four-year-old brother, Walter, is standing there, demanding a donut. Instead, I pick up an empty brown whiskey bottle from another garbage pail and bring it down on his face, opening a huge gash on his mouth. He stands there, stunned, and then he is bawling, his face suddenly spurting blood. And now my mother is running down the street, frightened, trying to stop a Yellow Checker cab to get her baby to the hospital. Young Cain. Younger Abel.

My parents have just had cheap new linoleum installed in the kitchen of our railroad flat on Fifty-first Street, and Walter and I have been watching the man install it. When the man leaves, I find the sharpest knife I can and begin cutting small pieces of the new linoleum out from under the sink, the way I've seen the man doing. My father's belt comes off and, as his father had no doubt done to him, he beats me—it doesn't take long—until there are huge welts and blood across my bottom and the backs of my thighs, and finally, appalled at what he has just done to his small son, he stops.

"If *you* won't beat him," the woman across the hall tells my mother, "then let me have at him. I'll teach him how to be good." No doubt I have been misbehaving in some way, but mercifully my mother does not offer me up.

My mother cuts a piece of my birthday cake for my godmother to take home. "No," I scream, "that's my cake. My cake. She can't have it." My mother stares at me. What, she wonders, has gotten into her oldest?

A fight up the street, in front of the synagogue. Harry Caufield, eight years older than me, and the leader of the pack who live here in the shadow of the Third Avenue El, forces me and Bobby to punch each other. Bobby's the only kid on the block actually smaller than I am. The older boys surround us and egg us on. Neither Bobby nor I want this fight, so Harry tells Bobby to push me. I push Bobby back. Now Bobby begins to cry. His older brother, Skip, steps in and pushes me hard. How do you win these things?

Here, Harry says on another occasion. Jiggle up and down with Bobby. We are both standing on the corner with our arms around each other and we jiggle up and down in our coats. "That's called *fucking,*" Harry says, explaining the Eleusinian mysteries to us. "Say 'fuck,'" he says, and I say it, then bring the word home, having just eaten of the fruit of the Tree of the Knowledge of Good and Evil. And with that my mother proceeds to wash out my mouth with soap.

A kind old Jewish man passes out a dark fruitcake from the portal entry to the synagogue on Fifty-first to the boys gathered there, myself among them. I take a piece and eat it. It tastes sweet and good. When the old man goes back inside, Harry starts. "That's Jew food," he says. "Throw it away." Harry hurls his at the door, and the others follow, though I continue to eat mine. Then Harry's face is up against mine. "Throw it," he rages, and I throw what is left. Half a century and more, and I can still imagine the old man's face. It is an image I will carry to my grave. Twice as an adult I have gone back to stand in supplication before that holy ground. The synagogue itself was long ago refurbished, and the old man must have gone to his eternal rest, having seen enough hatred and stupidity in his time. And still the image burns, because these, I have come to believe, are *my* people. Flesh of my flesh, bone of my bone, breath of my breath.

Mr. Coyne, the Irish janitor who lives on the first floor, has built me a racing car with a few two-by-fours, some rope, and the wheels from an old baby carriage. I take the cart out onto the sidewalk with my friend for a ride, first him pushing, then me. Then, like an animal scenting carrion, Harry is standing there. He jumps up and down on the wheels, laughing, as he breaks each in turn.

Coming home from the movies one evening after Christmas, I spot Harry and his gang burning discarded Christmas trees on the cobblestoned street between parked cars. I have just been to see Walt Disney's Uncle Remus and Br'er Rabbit and I'm singing "Zippety doo-dah" to myself, when Harry spots me. He has just spotted bigger game than Christmas trees to burn. I try to run, but they have me. He douses the sidewalk with lighter fluid, and then he douses me. He lights a match and holds it up to my face. I scream for help, but nothing happens. A man walks by, his face averted, minding his own business. Another crosses the street. No one has a telephone on our street—at least no one I know. But there is my mother, running up the street in the early dark, dragging my brother and pushing my sister in the stroller ahead of her, screaming so loudly that Harry and the others finally break and run.

Later that night, when my father gets home from working on the Calavo Dried Fruit trucks over in New Jersey, he tells my mother he will handle this himself. Early next morning he wakes me to show him where Harry lives. He rings the buzzer to gain entrance through the front door, walks down the long dark hall of the railroad flat, and bangs on the door to Harry's apartment. Harry's father answers: a gray-haired, ancient man. Then Harry's older brother is standing there in a white sleeveless undershirt. He is just out of jail, I will later find out, and my father knocks him across the room with one punch and tells him and the old man that if Harry touches his kid again he will kill him. *Capisce?* And for a while there's a truce. At least, I don't see Harry. And then one morning my father goes out to find that all four tires on his Calavo truck have been slashed and *Dago* painted in red on the sides. Time to move on, my father says.

Then the move to Levittown, and the Cape Cod, one of thousands of look-alikes, all sprouting from what two years before had been potato farmland. The incessant bullying endemic among kids. The sexual abuse and the rest of it, memories that I repressed for years. And then, in my forties, fantasizing that if I could find the kid who had hurt me I would pistol-whip him until he begged for mercy. Last year I even went back to find his house. But of course the kid—who would now be retired—had long since moved away. Maybe he's dead, for all I know. I have had to pray very hard to let my hatred for him and the others go, for it was they who stole my innocence. I have prayed for the rage I feel to abate and often it does, though from time to time there have been flare-ups and brushfires, and I find myself praying again to let the thing go.

When I was eleven, we moved to a brand-new Levitt ranch house a mile away. I remember the pretty Jewish girl who lived across the street and my awkward sexual feelings for her. A strange, new experience for me. Years later, when the sexual urge finally did awaken in me, belatedly, it came with a power that surprised and confused me. But why is it that for Catholic men especially all our early transgressions seem sexual in nature? Surely there are more important issues we should be looking to root out: rage, cruelty, pride, greed, indifference to the pain of others. So what is it in our education that seems always to bring the issue back to sex, as if we didn't have to grow up and fumble through our adolescence? Is it that we *are* our bodies? Masturbation. The awkward fumbling with girls. Comic, crude stuff. "I know what *you're* trying to do," one heavyset pubescent blonde told me, which ended *that* short-lived relationship.

Fist fights, sometimes winning, sometimes losing, but somehow never really getting hurt. No ribs stomped. No head broken. And—mercifully—no knives or guns, unlike the stories my kid brothers told me of shotgun explosions taking out windshields and heads. At thirteen, I entered the ninth grade at Chaminade High, a prep school run by the Marianists in Mineola. A year later we moved there so my father could be closer to his Esso gas station.

At the start of my senior year I entered the Marianists' preseminary school in Beacon, New York, fifty miles from New York City on the Hudson. I stayed there from September 1956 until the following July, when I came home for vacation and never went back. And why *did* I enter the seminary? I ask myself now. In part, because a priest had told me I might have a vocation. In part, because I liked the idea of doing something large and important. But also because Beacon offered me a way out of our small crowded Cape Cod in Mineola, already bulging with six kids and a seventh who would soon be on her way.

I remember the black-and-white *Life* magazine photographs of the Hungarian Revolution that fall. Kids my own age with automatic weapons, the lime-eaten faces of the dreaded Russian NKVD shot in the streets of Budapest. A black-and-white TV commentary on Castro and Che in the mountains of eastern Cuba. Was Castro a hero? I asked Brother Luke afterward. "I don't know," he said, shrugging. "It all depends on what he does when he comes to power."

When I returned home in July, the headiness of seeing girls again was too much for me. I wanted all of it. And, since it was too late to apply to college, I did a fifth year of high school instead, public school this time, with real girls in the class. And so the dense emotional jungle of sexuality all over again. By then I understood that I was entering a world of feelings and emotions bigger, surely, than anything *I* was ready to handle. The last thing I needed was to become a nineteen-year-old father, like some of my friends. Somehow, all through my college years and my courtship with Eileen, until we married, I remained celibate. I met her my sophomore year at a fraternity party in Mineola and fell in love with her at once. We married in August 1963, a year after I graduated college. I was twenty-three, going on fifty in terms of my sense of responsibility, sixteen in terms of emotional development. The boys came in '65, '66, and '68.

Years then of teaching, writing, flirtations. Then, beginning in 1980, the Bread Loaf Writers' Conference, a summer workshop where, for twelve days each August, I talked and bantered with novelists and poets I liked and admired. At forty I had my first heady taste of being accepted into the world of writers. In the summer of '84 began the affair that nearly ended my marriage. Where was this going? she wanted to know a month into the relationship. Going? I asked. I'd thought we were there already. Why, she insisted, didn't I just follow my natural instincts and break with my wife? Dazed to the point of stupidity, I watched myself one late September day suddenly walk out on my family.

It took me a little over a month to wake up to the enormity of what I had done. I was drowning. I wanted to stay with the woman. Why not? No responsibilities, just a little pasta cooked up, a glass of wine, a few laughs. But I also knew I was never really going to leave Eileen. So what the hell was going on? I was terrified by what I had done, yet unable to extricate myself.

The one thing I had left—besides my teaching job—was Mass, and that I refused to give up. *That* would be like letting my last lifeline go. So each Sunday I sat in the back of a church where I hoped nobody knew me. After a month I came home again, telling Eileen it was over. But it wasn't, and soon I was seeing the other woman again. It didn't take Eileen long to figure out what I was doing, and now it was she who told me to leave. Leave, and find out who I really was. Put an end to this double life, to the deceptions and rage.

Somehow, I found the strength to pull myself away and make a retreat. Part of me pined to be here, while another part sniggered. In early November 1984, at the suggestion of my former parish priest and spiritual director, Fr. Rich Meehan, I canceled classes for a week and drove up here. Fr. Brian Duffy was my director then, and I actually told him that I'd come here to find a way to accommodate myself to two women, as other men I knew and admired—sophisticated, worldly men—had managed to do.

He listened to me go on, then wrote out on a tiny slip of paper the following: Isaiah 30:15–18. "Go back to your room," he said finally, "and pray over these verses." *For Lord Yahweh, the Holy One of Israel, says this,* the passage from Isaiah began:

Your salvation lay in conversion and tranquility,
your strength in serenity and trust
and you would have none of it.

The footnote explained that the passage referred to Israel's refusal to trust in the Lord, instead trusting in a foreign alliance for her safety. And where had it gotten her? Nowhere. I had allied myself with another woman instead of remaining faithful to my wife and my God. *"No," you said,* the passage went on,

"We shall flee on horses."
And so flee you will!
And again, "We shall ride on swift ones."
And so your pursuers will be swift!

Then the passage changed, as God welcomed his errant people back:

But Yahweh is waiting to be gracious to you,
the Exalted One, to take pity on you,
for Yahweh is a God of fair judgment.

It was here at Eastern Point that the fever finally broke. I made my confession. I promised to go back home. I promised to change. And slowly I did. Eileen's friends had advised her to get rid of me, as they would have gotten rid of their husbands in a similar situation and—in several instances—already had. But she didn't. She knew something had broken open in me and that I wanted to change. She knew I was trying to figure out what a marriage could be. She wanted that too.

"My eyes have seen what my hand did," the poet Robert Lowell wrote at the end of his brilliant, flawed life. My own sentiments exactly. Regardless of how I was sinned against, I see now more clearly than ever just how deeply I have sinned against those I love. And what of my anger, the way, like my father, I have chilled the temperature in a room simply by walking in with some grievance? Why has it taken me so long to see what my family and friends could see coming, like bad weather, miles away?

And where did Eileen get the strength to forgive me? I would work at opening myself to the love that was offered me by Eileen and my sons. Every day I would work at it. I would work at controlling my anger, my impatience, my need to be always in control. Only when I abandoned myself to God, the way an alcoholic gives himself over to a higher power, did I have a chance of getting better. I had to learn that I too was powerless without His help.

I cannot fight the disorder of sin alone. Each succeeding year has told me this, until five years ago, teaching my Confirmation class about the reality of evil, and how easily one can slip back into the old ways, even in one's heart, I began attending the 7:00 Mass each morning. You learn, finally, to take nothing for granted. If you're not on an upward spiral, you begin to spiral downward. The Enemy's out there, an Enemy who knows every unguarded culvert and abandoned conduit into your fortress. He hates you, hates your joy, and he will stop at nothing, except the Cross. Isn't that what Satan—that counterintelligence officer, that spy, that carnival circus barker—most enjoys doing to us: pulling us in with all sorts of enticements, then springing the trapdoor shut and handing us a knife, asking if we wouldn't be better off now cutting our own throats quietly?

I remember praying afterward that erotic desire might be taken away, and for a short time that strange life-denying prayer was answered. What I was left with was a kind of zombie existence, a strange sort of death-in-life. After all, a zest for life is good. It's all in what we do with it. A matter of balance. My hardest struggle, let's face it, has been to develop a real intimacy with anyone. Over time, I have come to learn that my best chance at intimacy is with my family and in my marriage. After all, it's what marriage and family are really all about. Somewhere I have the large blue letters Eileen wrote me when I left back then. In them she told me she was still there, still waiting, when—and if—I ever woke up. Most of those letters I never answered. But I cherish them and the memory of them, every cursive jot and tittle.

The night I left, she told me years later, she gathered our two younger sons and prayed for me. *Prayed for me!* Then she drove to Harvard to tell Paul what I'd done, and asked him to pray for me. Somehow, I will have to live with these memories. But how proud I am of her, of all of them. What soldiers they were. What real soldiers. I have seen the face of Christ in each of them. Have seen how they answered my betrayal. By praying for me. Quid pro quo.

7:20 P.M. At a quarter past four, my right hand cramped with fatigue from writing all afternoon, I finally got up and walked down to the entrance gate at a brisk pace, breathing in the fresh air, then turned around and walked back to my room. I showered, shaved, then hurried down to Mass. There was still a wisp of blue afterglow out the western window: the faint, steady promise of the year's light returning. Young Fr. Joe celebrated Mass tonight, sprinkling us all with water for this, the Feast of Christ's Baptism. How lovely and simple the ceremony was: a clear bowl of water, a sprig of hemlock, a vase of white roses, harp music in the background. In a voice cracked with laryngitis, he managed to speak of the Father's love for the Son, and for all who follow Him and do His work. Then Eucharist and the deep peace that comes with that.

For supper tonight: mashed potatoes, succotash, roast beef, and peach pie. Then back to my room to go over my sins again. "I will reflect upon myself, by using examples that humble me," Ignatius advises, which is certainly what I have done all afternoon until now. I am exhausted. Still, I feel I have only scratched the surface, that there is much else swarming down there.

"First," Ignatius asks, "what am I, really, compared with all other human beings?" A man of modest achievements, a man who has hurt others. One more academic, no doubt overpaid, compared to others in the world. A self-important figure of no importance, someone with little courage or common sense, one who has often "seemed busier than he was." A poet-dabbler, a scribbler, most of whose work will no doubt shortly be forgotten. One who pales when measured against any number of other men and women: administrators, generals, presidents, C.E.O.s, mathematicians, philosophers, police officers, firemen, pilots, news commentators, editors, artists, musicians, gymnasts, professional ball players, actors, software programmers, priests, bishops. Measuring my true worth is not one of my favorite activities. I'd rather watch television.

"Second, what are these people when compared with all the angels and saints in paradise?" And, in fact, what is all creation—even in an expanding universe Ignatius himself only vaguely guessed at—compared to the Creator of all of this? Really, what does it all amount to, the prizes and awards and public recognition, as against the real work that goes on in hospitals, food centers, schools, prisons, monasteries, mosques, and Buddhist temples? And how many saints have I ever seen anyway? Mother Teresa at a distance in the UMass football stadium? On the other hand, I may have actually seen hundreds, none of them officially recognized, of course, but saints for all that. Priests, nuns, rabbis, doctors, nurses, mothers, several of my best teachers, people who gave without counting the cost.

"Third, I will look upon myself as a sore and abscess from which has issued such great sins and iniquities and such foul poison." How many have I hurt? Rejected? Snubbed? Used over a lifetime? Please God, don't ask me to go over this again. Too many. Some remembered vividly, others almost forgotten, at least their names. Mistakes made, cruelties enacted, letters unanswered, the finger given to how many motorists? Thank God the military rejected me and that I have never had to kill another human being, as some I have known could not avoid doing.

I don't think I can go much further in this direction without nausea overtaking me again. I ask then for mercy, and thank the good Lord for granting me life and for having preserved me so many times. I promise too, with His grace, to do better in every way.

And what is it that sin does? I've been meditating on the passage JJ gave me from 2 Samuel 12:1–14 at odd times since this morning. It's the story of the prophet Nathan confronting David and telling him the parable of the poor man who had only a single lamb, which the rich man insisted be sacrificed in place of one of his own lambs. David listens to Nathan's parable and becomes enraged at the rich man's injustice toward the poor man. *As Yahweh lives,* he tells Nathan, *the man who did this deserves to die.*

You are the man, he tells David, and then adds:

> *Yahweh, God of Israel, says this, "I anointed you king of Israel, I saved you from Saul's clutches, I gave you your master's household and your master's wives into your arms, I gave you the House of*

Israel and the House of Judah; and, if this is too little, I shall give you other things as well."

This being so, God demands to know how David could show such contempt for Him as to have Bathsheba's husband, Uriah, murdered so that he—David—could enjoy Bathsheba. From now on, God promises, David's house will never be free of trouble. His own sons will turn on him. *You have worked in secret,* God tells David, *but I shall work this for all Israel to see, in broad daylight.*

David breaks down. *I have sinned against Yahweh,* he says. Nathan listens, then tells him that *Yahweh, for his part, forgives your sin; you are not to die. But, since you have outraged Yahweh by doing this, the child born to you will die.* The story is instructive. How often, in our greed, have we snatched after what did not belong to us? "Sometimes, Paul, the hamburger stays on the table." By deliberately sinning, have I not set myself up as a two-bit god, snatching at what was not mine? And how shall I repay the enormous debt, now in the billions? Consider St. Paul's profound insight into the divided will. *In my deepest self I dearly love God's law,* he says. *But I see that acting on my body is a different law which fights against the law I know in my mind. And so again and again I find myself becoming a prisoner of that law of sin which breeds inside me.*

9:15 P.M. When I could take no more of this, I walked out under the stars, circling the small rotary three times, gulping in the cold, bracing air. Finally, I came back in and sat before the fire, like an outcast seeking comfort and companionship. Several women and men were sewing images with thread or yarn. Afterward, I went into the dining hall for a cup of hot chocolate. Here and there splinters of light glanced off the glass surface of the ocean. I saw Devon off to one side, nodding his head to the beat coming from his headset. I sat next to him for human comfort and stared out into the vast ocean of darkness before me.

DAY 5: MONDAY, JANUARY 10

5:30 A.M. Clear, warm, peaceful, dark. Finally, a good night's sleep, breaking the previous nights' string of choking nightmares. But now, here at my desk, by the light of a single bulb, I find myself going over what I wrote yesterday, discouraged most by my failures as a husband and as a father. Anger issues, especially. In this I have acted no differently, I suppose, from my own father. A little more cultured and cultivated, perhaps, but both the same animal underneath. Yes, he's slowed down a good bit, incapacitated by two operations in the last year, the first of which nearly killed him. How small and bent the old king seemed in his wheelchair when I flew down to be with him last November. And yet, how his eyes glinted when the young nurse walked into the room. The old fox watching the songbird. Eighty-two and still on the lookout, this man I love like my own life.

9:20 A.M. Went back to sleep at six, and woke at eight, into a world of gray, displaced light. I raced down to a breakfast of toasted English muffin, jelly, and a cup of coffee. I'd been told that two harbor seals come to bask sometimes on the rocks when the sun is shining and stay there until the tide comes in and lifts them off. I have yet to see them myself, though. When I saw JJ, he said he'd seen one out there just this morning.

The sessions have become more informal as I have come to trust myself more to JJ. Mostly he listens. He doesn't say much about himself, for the *Exercises* are about where the retreatant is headed. I think he would like to share more, but mostly he refrains so that we can get on to the next step, whatever that may be. I'm never really sure, for the map I have—the text of the *Exercises*—and what actually happens in any given day seem to have only the vaguest connection. The fact is that I'm constantly surprised by the dryness and distance of the words on the page of the *Exercises* and the drama of my own confrontation with the immense spiritual realities the words conjure. There's no use planning any of this, except in the broadest way. It's the difference between having a map of Marrakech and being in Marrakech.

I began the session this morning by telling JJ all I'd written yesterday, as I remembered my past in detail. Even as I reeled off the incidents, he seemed to wave away the particulars, looking for something deeper. Finally, he asked me if Christ had entered into these recollections, and if so, how? So all the meditations on the nature of sin and rebellion yesterday come down to this: a search for the deeper spiritual patterns that have shaped me. The first step, then, is to learn from the mistakes I've made, evaluating what sin actually does to one: the illusory sense of getting somewhere and the sorry outcome and self-loathing that follow after each fall. Add to that the inestimable loss of centering, of peace, of walking in the cool of the evening with God.

Like a strategist studying the history of military campaigns, I told JJ, I must learn how to make my fortress more secure against this Enemy who never sleeps. After each failure I've always tried to rebuild: constructing redoubts facing north, south, east, and west and setting up guard posts in between. How often I've promised myself to avoid this situation and that temptation. I promised to talk straight, care for others as if they were my brothers and sisters, work at being more patient, and give alms generously. But how many times in the end has Satan managed to outfox me, finding the weak point, like David's soldiers entering the enemy's fortifications through underground conduits, then taking the city from within.

I could see JJ looking for something in his copy of the *Exercises*. He took a full minute or so, patiently searching. It turned out to be Paragraph 327, Rule 14, from the section on the *Discernment of Spirits for the First Week*. "To use still another comparison," the passage begins,

> the enemy acts like a military commander who is attempting to conquer and plunder his objective. The captain and leader of an army on campaign sets up his camp, studies the strengths and structure of

> a fortress, and then attacks at its weakest point. In the same way, the enemy of human nature prowls around and from every side probes all our theological, cardinal, and moral virtues. Then at the point where he finds us weakest and most in need in regard to our eternal salvation, there he attacks and tries to take us.

I know I must have read this paragraph at some point, but if so its full import had escaped me until now. Being the soldier he was, Ignatius studied military strategy and must have watched tensely as the French army deployed and trained its heavy artillery on Pamplona, where he was nearly killed in the attack. I thought of Russian field officers surrounding Grozny, scrutinizing the terrain, looking for weak spots, even as they pull the noose tighter on the Chechens.

"When he finds the weak point, where we most need God's help"—and Ignatius underscores the point—just there Satan "attacks and tries to overcome us." How utterly right this observation is, and how terrifying to know how often the Enemy has breached my defenses in the past. For there will always be some weak point through which he might surprise us when we least expect it. Which is why, years ago, I learned that I cannot win this war unless I first surrender to the Enemy's Enemy—God—and then only through that sign of contradictions, the Cross. It's like what they teach alcoholics in AA, that THERE'S NO WAY AROUND IT but to throw yourself on the mercy of a Power greater than yourself.

We're all obsessed in one way or another, aren't we, whether it's about money or the good life or power over others? Whatever the obsession—and there are obsessions a hell of a lot more subtle than what seems to be troubling me—they're all delusional and destructive. It's not a matter, then, of adhering to a script—the law, the commandments—but of attitude, of being willing to fundamentally change so that you come to align yourself more perfectly with your Creator. Having tried every other way but Him, all I can do each blessed day is ask for His help.

10:00 A.M. Here in Chapel I've been thinking again of Hopkins's portrait of Lucifer, and how I too have too often been more in love with my own voice than in getting at the deeper truth beneath the words. Ever since I began this journal, I've been aware that the writing itself may be keeping me from making real progress while I'm here. If that's the case, it's the writing that will have to go, and the thirty days will have to be made wordlessly as well as in silence. What is it, after all, that I am really doing here?

Does it come down, then, to a question of voice—of self-glittering, self-delighting song, artistic expression, the trenchant phrase—as opposed to becoming a clearer conduit for what God is trying to tell me? Am I listening? Am I listening even now? Is what I'm writing true? Remember that you're only a pilgrim here, trying to hear what God is saying to you. Everything else is extraneous.

Mary Chapel, with the waves pounding against Brace Rock. I've been trying to collect my thoughts, preparing to make what Ignatius, genius that he was, calls the *Triple Colloquy,* even as I consider for a fourth time—according to his instructions—the larger meaning of the Three Sins (those of the angels, the human species, my own). The focus, of course, must be on my own failures. Against others. Against God. I feel terribly weighed down by all of this. It's as if a doctor, performing a biopsy, should suddenly discover a more malignant cell disorder beneath a layer of benign growth. What the hell else is down here?

But this time I am asked to pray the *Triple Colloquy* as I approach my sinfulness, asking God to let me see my sins as He must see them. The *Triple Colloquy* calls for the retreatant to speak first with Our Lady, which is the reason I'm here in Mary Chapel now, to ask her and her Son for three things:

1. A knowledge and abhorrence of my sins.
2. An understanding of the radical disorder in sin and in my sins,

in order that I might hate them. And then to ask for the grace to change my life and put my house in order.

3. An understanding of how the Prince of this World works, and to hate those works, and then rid myself of all that is part of that disordered world, with its empty promises.

Then I am to say a Hail Mary.

After this I am to imagine myself going with Mary to ask the same favors of her Son, and then beg for the grace to avoid all such pitfalls. Then I will say the *Anima Christi,* a prayer formulated in the Middle Ages and the one that opens the *Spiritual Exercises.* It was a great favorite of Ignatius's. We say it far less often now, which is too bad, for studying it, I find it both profound and moving. Thirteen lines made up of ten petitions. In fact, it's a mantra, a psalm, and I have come in the past few days to love it:

Soul of Christ, sanctify me.
Body of Christ, save me.
Blood of Christ, inebriate me.
Water from the side of Christ, wash me.
Passion of Christ, strengthen me.
O good Jesus, hear me.
Within your wounds hide me.
Do not allow me to be separated from you.
From the malevolent enemy defend me.
In the hour of my death call me,
And bid me to come to you,
That with your saints I may praise you
Forever and ever. Amen.

After this I am to imagine myself as going with Mary and Jesus to kneel before the Father, the King of Creation, and once again to ask for the grace I need to change my life. Then I will say the prayer Jesus himself gave us, the Our Father:

Our Father, Who art in heaven,
Hallowed be Thy name.
Thy Kingdom come, Thy will be done,
On earth, as it is in heaven.
Give us this day our daily bread,
And forgive us our trespasses
As we forgive those who trespassed against us.
And lead us not into temptation,
But deliver us from evil. Amen.

Last March, when I made the *Triple Colloquy* in the dark halls of Campion Center, it seemed to unfold in a stately procession: an audition before a gracious Queen, her princely Son, and then the King our Father, and peace had come. But making it this morning, I found myself looking up at the statue of Our Lady, the child in her arms squirming as He turned to look at His mother, and I remembered Our Lady of Good Voyage. The two statues seemed to merge in my mind's eye now with that young mother with her two little boys, bundled against the cold. I stared at the statue before me, then closed my eyes. The face of a beautiful woman slowly began taking shape before me. There was a flicker of blue about her mantle. Then suddenly her eyes opened, and an intense light shone from them and flooded me so that I could not keep my gaze from her. Then her small son turned to look directly at me, His eyes shining with the same intense light as His mother's.

Just then one of the Thirty-Day retreatants walked into the room. I opened my eyes for a brief moment, then shut them again, for I did not want to be interrupted just now. I heard him sit down hard on the floor across from me and his breathing seemed labored. "I will not open my eyes again," I told myself, "for I want to stay here with Mary and her Son." I wanted to stay like that for minutes, hours, days, just gazing into their eyes. The only sound was the sound of troubled sighs entering this other dimension. It was like the cry of the whole human race, part of a medley subsumed by the gracious blue transparency of those eyes.

And then the Son, grown to manhood now, was standing there beside His mother and the infant who had been His younger self. His eyes, too, were open and smiling. So here they were: the infant at Christmas, and the young Christ just starting out after His baptism, His promise still ahead of Him, and all the eyes were blue, with the blue of the heavens, identical. And then I could feel the Father's presence there, and interlaced with it all the troubled breathing, and—as I looked on—the eyes seemed to become brilliant stars reflecting the heavens, the moon, the moons of Jupiter, the galaxies beyond. "It is good for us to be here," I said, and would not have moved for anything, not asking this to last forever, not asking for anything, just delighted to be there. Then slowly the scene subsided into a purple Rorschach, the other retreatant got up and left, and after a time I opened my eyes, deeply rested, and thanked Our Lady and her Son, and left the Chapel.

11:45 A.M. Down to the dining room, where I read the two passages JJ has given me for today. The first is Matthew 13:4–23, the parable of the sower who sowed good seed. The other is Psalm 51, in which David laments his sins:

Have mercy on me, O God, in your faithful love,
in your great tenderness wipe away my offenses;
wash me thoroughly from my guilt,
purify me from my sin.

What David lamented for himself, Lord, let me lament for myself, here, now, asking, as that complex, good man did, that You might "create in me a new heart":

Renew within me a resolute spirit,
do not thrust me away from your presence,
do not take away from me your spirit of holiness.

Then there's Jesus' parable: *A sower went out to sow,* the passage begins:

> *As he sowed, some seeds fell on the edge of the path, and the birds came and ate them up. Others fell on patches of rock where they found little soil and sprang up at once, because there was no depth of earth; but as soon as the sun came up they were scorched and, not having any roots, they withered away. Others fell among thorns, and the thorns grew up and choked them. Others fell on rich soil and produced their crop, some a hundredfold, some sixty, some thirty. Anyone who has ears should listen!*

It's a parable Jesus actually has to explain to his disciples. Pay attention, he tells them:

> *When anyone hears the word of the kingdom without understanding, the Evil One comes and carries off what was sown in his heart: this is the seed sown on the edge of the path.*
>
> *The seed sown on patches of rock is the one who hears the word and welcomes it at once with joy. But such a person has no root deep down and does not last; should some trial come, or some persecution on account of the word, at once he falls away.*
>
> *The seed sown in thorns is someone who hears the word, but the worry of the world and the lure of riches choke the word and so it produces nothing.*
>
> *And the seed sown in rich soil is someone who hears the word and understands it; this is the one who yields a harvest and produces now a hundredfold, now sixty, now thirty.*

May the seed sown scattershot here on this retreat fall on rich soil. And may it, please Lord, produce a hundredfold.

Walked up the main road before lunch. Four swans bobbed in the waves of Niles Pond, like Portuguese galleons, submerging their long necks beneath the water as they searched for food. I caught a glimpse of a swirl of starlings—hundreds of them—in the stark, majestic trees above me. The tide was coming in now, the white-caps crashing against the rocks, the horizon one great wash of pale gray blue. Nature played on, as she has these last billion years.

I tried imagining what a world devoid of God would be like, and thought of Dante's *Inferno.* The ultimate sadness of the philosophers in Dante's circle is of the human imagination constructing all sorts of orders, all of them missing the one thing necessary: God's Word, the foundation of all words, all language. Even in Hell, it struck me, we would have to make a bed of sorts for ourselves. In whatever hell we make for ourselves, we still need order. The truth is the mind needs order, craves it, simply because that is how it is made. But to be forever separated from God, the author of all order: that would be frustration indeed. True, the Good can be rejected, but there is still the mind's deep need for the very thing it has rejected, something that nothing else can ever satisfy. Thoughts against thoughts in groans grinding. Narcissism. Claustrophobic suffocating narcissism. That is what Hell is.

9:30 P.M. A whole afternoon away from my pen—in both senses of the word—and more in the moment itself. Lunch at noon, followed by a nap, and then—in mid-afternoon—another walk along the sea's edge, as the wind came on stronger and stronger. No one else was about as I clambered up onto the high rocks to the right of Brace Cove and stood there, watching the wave's spray rise thirty feet into the air as my windbreaker ballooned. A trawler far off to the right was making its slow way along the coast. I was praying the rosary to myself, when suddenly I began saying Hail Marys aloud, shouting them into the oncoming waves, my body rocking with the force of the wind. It was both exhilarating and terrifying at once, the feeling, for I knew very well what the water and rocks could do if I slipped or was lifted by the wind. Then, suddenly, rain, cold and lovely, began falling.

Fr. Frank Belcher celebrated Mass at five this evening. Advent and Christmas are now behind us, though the theme of God's love abides, as indeed it abides forever. I spotted another letter from Eileen—her second—on the sideboard as I passed on my way to receive the Eucharist and stuffed the letter in my pocket to read later. For dinner a salad with blue cheese dressing, noodles and creamed tuna, peas and onions, coffee, apple cinnamon flat cake. Blessings on the kitchen staff and on all who make our lives comfortable here. Then back to my room, where I read through Eileen's letter several times—how she missed me, and how long this time away from each other has hung on her. I held the letter to my lips and kissed it, then wrote her by way of return.

At half past eight I walked down to the Fireplace Room, then into Chapel to pray, then down to the Reading Room, where I browsed through a book on biblical archaeology and read some of John of the Cross's poetry. Then back here to my room. The rain has finally stopped, though the wind is still blowing fiercely. For the first time since I've been here time seems to be hanging heavily on my hands. To tell the truth, I've done all I can with the meditations for now. A whole week here, and almost four long weeks to go. The shadows lengthening, then shortening, then lengthening again. Three meals a day, a walk, another walk. Some listen to music on headsets for hours on end, others have come here with satchels of books, disregarding the guidelines that speak of bringing just the two books.

A few seem to be using the place like some poor man's resort, reading book after book, listening for hours to classical music through their headsets, and chowing down. But who knows? Others daily take pictures of the rugged landscape here, and one of the novices has already pieced together six or seven complex puzzles on a small side desk in the Reading Room. The worst for me just now is that I want to talk with someone and I can't, which has sent me back to my old borrowed book to read up on the incredible hardships of the early Jesuits in Abyssinia, Goa, the Straits of Ormuz, and the Spice Islands. I'm bored, but at least I'm not dying. Unlike these men, who died by the score, the cream of their generation, taken off by fever, drowning, or the sword. Witnesses to the end. Seed falling on rich soil. But the cost! The incredible cost. Surely there's a hard, vinegary lesson in there for me somewhere.

DAY 6: TUESDAY, JANUARY 11

8:20 A.M. Ten minutes to go before I see JJ. Up twice in the night with doubts about my decision to make the Long Retreat and—even worse—thoughts of writing about it. It's the old question, as Hopkins once said, of making capital out of the sacred. It looks as if this time the Enemy has gotten in through the Culvert of Boredom & Self-doubt, and all I can do is ask God's help in getting me through this one as well.

11:00 A.M. Told JJ of the boredom I'd experienced with the coming on of another long winter night. He listened, then read Paragraph 315 of the *Exercises,* the *Second Rule for the Discernment of Spirits.* "In the case of persons who are earnestly purging away their sins, and who are progressing from good to better in the service of God our Lord," he read aloud, "it is characteristic of the evil spirit to cause gnawing anxiety, to sadden, and to set up obstacles. In this way he unsettles these persons by false reasons aimed at preventing their progress." I could hardly believe what I was hearing. "How the hell did Ignatius learn all that?" I asked.

"Because he spent eleven months making the *Exercises,*" JJ answered. Eleven months in the isolation of Manresa. One could learn a lot about the human condition in that time. He went on:

> With persons on the right road, it is characteristic of the good spirit to stir up courage and strength, consolations, tears, inspirations, and tranquility. He makes things easier and eliminates all obstacles so that such persons may move forward in doing good.

And suddenly the whole weight of fatigue and fear dropped from my shoulders, and I found myself at peace. I do not know how this could have happened, but it did.

JJ talked about my progress, about the importance of honestly saying what was on my mind, as with the boredom that I had felt and that I was at first afraid of mentioning, thinking it would reflect badly on either JJ or on the *Exercises*—to say nothing of myself. The point, he said, was to try to bring whatever was on my plate, without editing, bowdlerizing, or putting a spin on it, insofar as I could. Then he gave me two new passages to meditate on. The first was from Isaiah, chapter 59, verses 1–21, the second from Matthew, chapter 18, verses 21–35. Both passages, he explained, dealt with God's forgiveness.

I am also to do the Fifth (and final) Exercise for the First Week: the meditation on Hell. The point here is to try to imagine Hell, though I hope to do better than James Joyce's Irish Jesuit father did in *A Portrait of the Artist as a Young Man* ("AND the walls of Hell are four thousand miles thick!"). I looked at the clock on JJ's desk. I'd gone over my allotted time by twenty minutes. Instead of time dragging on, it had begun to speed up. "Please ask Marcie to forgive me for making her wait," I said. As I got up to go, JJ mentioned that it was customary at the close of the First Week to make a general confession of one's sins. If I wanted, he said, I could go to him. Or I could make an appointment with one of the other priests. I told him I would be ready to have him hear my confession tomorrow morning.

I've spent the past hour here in Chapel, kneeling before the Blessed Sacrament. The sun has finally broken through the clouds and is streaming in through the southeast windows. I've read and reread the two passages JJ has given me. Both deal with the theme of God's forgiveness. Here's Isaiah first:

Your guilty deeds have made a gulf
between you and your God.
Your sins have made him hide his face from you

so as not to hear you,
since your hands are stained with blood
and your fingers with guilt;
your lips utter lies,
your tongues murmur wickedness.
No one makes upright accusations
or pleads sincerely.
All rely on empty words, utter falsehood,
conceive trouble and give birth to evil.

The passage from Matthew concerns the parable of the debtor who refused to forgive his debtors. Peter goes up to Jesus, the passage begins, and asks him, *Lord, how often must I forgive my brother if he wrongs me? As often as seven times?* And Jesus tells him, *Not seven, I tell you, but seventy-seven times.* Then, to drive the point home, he tells Peter a story:

> *The kingdom of heaven may be compared to a king who decided to settle accounts with his servants. When the reckoning came, they brought him a man who owed him ten thousand talents.* [That would be between sixty and seventy million dollars today.] *He had no means of paying, so his master gave orders that he should be sold, together with his wife and children and all his possessions, to meet the debt.*
>
> *At this, the servant threw himself down at his master's feet, with the words, "Be patient with me and I will pay the whole sum." And the servant's master felt so sorry for him that he let him go and cancelled the debt.*
>
> *Now, as this servant went out, he happened to meet a fellow-servant who owed him one hundred denarii* [about $200]. *And he seized him by the throat and began to throttle him, saying, "Pay what you owe me." His fellow-servant fell at his feet and appealed to him, saying, "Be patient with me and I will pay you."*

But the man won't listen. Instead, he has him thrown in jail until the debt can be paid. Naturally, the other servants who have witnessed this are distressed, and soon they've gone to the master to explain what they've seen. The master sends for the man. *You wicked servant,* he tells him, *I cancelled all that debt of yours when you appealed to me. Were you not bound, then, to have pity on your fellow-servant, just as I had pity on you?* And so he hands the man over to the torturers until he pays up every last penny. *And that,* Jesus says, *is how my heavenly Father will deal with you unless you each forgive your brother from your heart.*

Does Hell exist? Is it a place or a state of mind, and what—really—is the difference? Ignatius urges us to use all five senses to call up a vivid image of damnation. But try as I may, I can not get much beyond Michelangelo's *Last Judgment* in the Sistine Chapel, or Goya's *Chronos* devouring his son, each with their man-eating demons or the look of crazed anguish on the faces of the damned. I have tried imagining a pigsty, a toilet overflowing with waste, the charred bodies of the dead. But all this is forced. The deeper sense of Hell is only going to come later, in a manner I have no way now of gauging.

1:00 P.M. At half past eleven, I got up and went into the Reading Room, looking for something, though exactly what I didn't know. There on the front page of the *Boston Globe* I caught sight of a photograph of two C.E.O.s—lean, well groomed, all business, their hands raised in a victory clasp, though one hand, I noticed, dominated the other's. Both men were staring into the camera, both jubilant. Billions of dollars had just joined other billions. One more done deal, like countless others in the history of the species, from Sumeria and ancient China on through the Caesars to John D. Rockefeller, J. P. Morgan, Carnegie, Frick.

With Ramadan over, I see the Chechens are counterattacking. Twenty-six Russians have been killed in one assault, another thirty-three badly wounded, while at home Russian TV speaks only of mopping-up operations. But will the war be over even when Grozny falls? I think of the Greeks before Troy, Grant before Petersburg, the Somme offensive, Verdun, the hedgerows of Normandy. The killing goes on and on and on. The nightmare of history goes on.

4:00 P.M. Sitting here in the nearly empty dining hall, thinking. Early this afternoon, clouds began rolling in off the ocean, bringing with them the wind again, whipping up the ocean. Except for the houses, the seascape here could be Genesis all over again, the varying modulations of waves rolling in, no two breaking in exactly the same way. How little after all one gets down on paper, the infinite possibilities lost as one goes after first one thought and then another, trying to get it right. Two or three seagulls are soaring in the dying light. And now, suddenly, hundreds of them, a swarm: charred paper blowing in the wind, drifting to the left toward Niles Pond, fishing for something.

Fishing for something. It has just struck me what actually happened yesterday while I was making the *Triple Colloquy.* I see now that it was in bringing my petition before Mary and Christ and the Father that it was answered, not with words, but with a radical consolation that lifted the weight of my sins from me. I was looking for one thing, with my long list of failings, when the Father simply washed the whole damned burden away so quietly I didn't realize until now that He'd actually done it. Amazing! What's going on here anyway?

9:00 P.M. Someone placed a cut-glass bowl of fresh roses on the nightstand in front of the lectern at Mass tonight. Another bowl, this one on the altar table in the Main Room, is brimming with freesias—purple-speckled on a white background. How refreshing and right. After dinner, I called Eileen, relieved to hear her voice again. It rained heavily in New York yesterday, and the wind buffeted her Crown Victoria as she drove up to Montague with her aunt. Mark, good old dependable Mark, has attended to the chores I asked him to do. And I'll be seeing Eileen this Sunday at John's. Hoorah!

Afterward, I went down to Chapel to pray. The crazed wind romped and bit along the windows, but I felt peaceful and protected sitting there in the dark, illuminated by that single candle. Then back here to my room, where I've begun my final meditation on Hell. I thought of Fr. Maximilian Kolbe, the black-robed Franciscan, who traded his life for another prisoner's, lying there in his dark cell in the strangling heat of August 1941, the stench of the dying permeating the rancid air, as he and the others were systematically starved to death. Each day the Nazi prison doctor looked in on the prisoners until, finally, needing the space for yet other prisoners, he injected Kolbe with carbolic acid. That ended it.

I thought of Ieyasu, first of the Tokugawa shoguns of Japan, intent on rooting out Christianity, at last finding a suitable torture. This turned out to be hanging prisoners head down from a gallows and then easing them into a cesspool of dung and piss. To prolong the torture, the body was roped tightly to slow circulation and a vein in the forehead opened to lessen the chances of congestion to the brain, which would have caused the victim to lose consciousness. What's the point if the victim doesn't know what the enemy is doing to him?

When I ponder it, I'm amazed sometimes that I am still alive, still functioning. How many are already gone? Terrence, my mother, Ed Callahan, Bill Matthews. Classmates long gone, and colleagues. This too is hell: being separated forever from those you love. I remember sitting once alone in the dark, waiting for Eileen to get back from New York, the hours passing without a word, my heart sinking, fearing I'd never see her again. I thought of myself, left to live my grand thoughts alone forever. That too is what hell is.

DAY 7: WEDNESDAY, JANUARY 12

3:30 A.M. Awoke two hours ago, an ingrown toenail of all things bothering me, and trimmed it for some relief. Small things loom large in this silence. Down to Chapel. No one about, the room dark except for the flicker of the single candle in its large cut-glass vase and the shadows it casts on the stuccoed ceiling. I sat against the wall and tried meditating once more on Hell. Ignatius cautions us not to avert our face from the reality of the hell within or the hell without by thinking *"about pleasant or joyful things, such as heavenly glory, the Resurrection, and so forth."* The reason, he explains, is this: *"If we desire to experience pain, sorrow, and tears for our sins, any thought of happiness or joy will be an impediment. Instead, I should keep myself intent on experiencing sorrow and pain; and for this it is better to think about death and judgment."* The consolations will come in due time.

As I sat there, old wounds began rising mistlike to the surface of my consciousness. Images of Hutus hacking their Tutsi neighbors to death, caught on film. People dying in natural disasters, houses swept away in mudslides on squatters' hills. Trailer homes ripped apart by tornadoes each year in the South. Swiss banks collaborating with the Nazis to steal the property of Jewish victims, their lives apparently not enough. American tobacco companies creating killer cigarettes, then lying about it year after year, as the death toll from cancer mounts, my own mother among the statistics. The injustice of it all and of how we cover over these injustices. I thought of the Jews' deep passion for justice—Isaiah, Jeremiah, the Psalmist—refusing to let these things be swept away by a kind of selective amnesia. I thought of Jesus, one more Jew from the provinces, beaten half to death, then led out to die.

God Himself crying out against the sheer weight of the injustices against the poor, the defenseless, those who cannot afford adequate counsel. The lies, the false claims and counterclaims, legal systems opposing true justice. Cubans detained in American prisons long after they have served their time. Black slaves and Native Americans, long dead, whose basic human rights were abrogated time and time again. Reduced to chattel, the men beaten or killed, the women raped and discarded, their children auctioned on the block. The palpable, barely concealed rage of my writer friend, John Edgar Wideman, the weathered look of some residual pain etched into his face, the deep desire to lash out or strike back against a white society for having done so much harm to his people. I kept trying to see myself in all of this, as Ignatius counsels us to do, but a wave of revulsion kept washing over me.

Now, back here in my room, I am left only with a sense of helplessness and outrage, with nausea setting in again. The cries of the poor, the helpless, the marginalized. Well, it's the secret police, after all, and the authorities, the corrupt lawyers and court officials, the government informers and the two-bit spies who often seem destined to inherit the earth. Let it go and get some sleep. You'll be confessing your own sins in a few hours' time, God help you.

7:30 A.M. Awake for hours last night, unable to get back to sleep. Then falling asleep. Then an erotic dream, from which I awoke in the dark, trying to understand what was happening, and why this, now. Turned it over to God and finally fell asleep, awaking just before seven to a plum purple-red horizon.

1:00 P.M. At half past eight I began my general confession with JJ, going over my life year by year, sparing myself nothing. No sooner had I begun confessing than tears began welling up as I recounted the wrongs I'd done to others, the promise of reforming soured again and again. I thought of my son making his first vows as a young Jesuit a continent away in Los Angeles. One by one, kneeling before the Blessed Sacrament, flanked by other young Jesuits. A life of poverty, chastity, obedience. I thought again of my own transgressions, of taking what did not belong to me, turning myself into some sorry, two-bit god, and my heart broke and for a long minute I could not speak.

JJ listened kindly, without judgment. After I'd finished, he asked me if I saw any pattern in my behavior. Something I'd said interested him in particular because he thought it might hold a key. "Mariani," a colleague had said to me years ago. "Three quarters of the time humble. The other quarter God." And there it was: a willingness to wait until things came my way and then snatching at what was not mine. Forbidden fruit. I thought again of Satan, given so much, before whom God had flashed whole galaxies like apples, his for the taking, presuming to be what he could *not* be: God Himself.

Or Eve and Adam in the garden, snatching not merely at some apple, finally, but at the Godhead itself, forgetting their own creatureliness. The hiss of the serpent: *"You will be gods."*

The driven ego has wreaked ruin in every creature who has ever attempted to snatch at it all: every king or emperor or chancellor intent on making himself or herself an absolute despot, every C.E.O. intent on another major consolidation in a "hostile" takeover. Anyone who eats or drinks too much. Disorders—as the Buddha says—raging everywhere like brush fires, adding to the universal conflagration. Consider Christ, who emptied Himself of everything, including His own heart. Or was that merely a sign of what we did to the Father, when He gave us the will to choose, and we chose *anything* but Him? The crowd—any crowd—choosing a murderer over a good man.

When I'd finished, JJ offered me absolution in the name of a merciful God. For penance, he asked me to pray for all those—family, friends, students—whom I had hurt, pleading for their good and begging forgiveness, especially for those with whom I had lost contact. Only then did I realize I'd gone over my time by another twenty-five minutes, and when I came out, there was Marcie—bless her—looking out the windows in the Main Hall as I walked past, my eyes still wet. For forty minutes after, in Chapel, I stayed on my knees on the cold, tiled floor, doing what JJ had asked me to do: bringing to mind as many of those I had offended as I could, praying for them and for their good. When I was finished, it took a full half-minute to get up, my knees were that stiff. Well, there it is. The end of the First Week. JJ had said I might want to rest now, and indeed I felt very tired and lay down for half an hour and nodded off, feeling deeply at peace.

7:15 P.M. The rest of this strange, wonderful day has gone by in a kind of heady dream. There was a bright, bluster-sunny wind this afternoon, and I seized the chance to take a long walk north into East Gloucester. How delicious it felt to be out, strolling about in my new freedom. Everything seemed alive and beckoning—the houses, the boats in the harbor, the handful of people out and about. By the time I got back here the sun was sinking and the wind, strong all day, had begun howling through the trees. I think we're in for our first real snow of the season. The upside is that each afternoon—if you can call it that—another minute of light adds itself to the total. Three weeks deep into winter, ten to go.

Walking into town this afternoon, I noticed once again the different architectural styles: colonial houses along the streets; Victorian gingerbread homes rising dramatically on the bluffs; old wooden buildings clustered tightly together; new houses in small, upscale residential clusters along the harbor. Dozens of large pleasure craft covered with blue plastic tarps, tamped down for the winter. A replica of a Portuguese caravel docked at a pier. Plastic containers—Prestone, Clorox, ginger-ale bottles, orange juice containers—all sloshing in the ebb tide where two swans drifted. A man worked under the hood of an old Ford pickup. And there in the distance: Our Lady of Good Voyage blessing us all.

Bill Devine said Mass tonight. He has trouble with stairs and uses the little French-hotel-style one-man elevator in the Main Hall to get from the first floor to his room on the second. How dogged and steady he is, quick-witted, as if he were just about to make some quip. There's something about him that makes you trust him instinctively.

At the homily, Mary Boretti gave a touching reflection on the first reading, focusing on 1 Samuel 3: *During the time young Samuel was minister to the Lord under Eli, a revelation of the Lord was uncommon and vision infrequent.* How sad, she said, and wondered if we, too, sometimes felt as if the lamp of God were almost extinguished. And yet God did not forget His people, she went on, answering Hannah's prayers by giving her the son she wanted in her old age, a man who would become a prophet among his people.

She closed by telling the story of Mother Teresa's cleaning a lonely old man's rooms and lighting his lamp, a gesture that had given the man a glimmer of hope. And suddenly I saw that the two lamps Mary was speaking of—the one almost extinguished but which could still help the half-blind old prophet Eli to see by, and this other lamp Teresa had lit to brighten an old man's way—were the same lamp shedding the same Light of God on His people three thousand years apart. Something about the understated way Mary had matched the two images—so quietly and yet so effectively, like a gift lightly, graciously offered—struck an emotional chord in me and I began weeping quietly as the Mass resumed.

Roast pork, mashed potatoes, mixed vegetables, gravy and applesauce. Afterward I said my evening prayers, then spent a half hour reading the two passages JJ gave me for today: Luke 15:11–32 and Ephesians 3:14–19. The chapter in Luke closes with the story of the Prodigal Son. *A man had two sons,* Jesus tells his listeners.

> *The younger one said to his father, "Father, let me have the share of the estate that will come to me." So the father divided the property between them. A few days later, the son got together everything he had and left for a distant country where he squandered his money on a life of debauchery.*

When he had spent it all, the country experienced a great famine, and now he began to feel the pinch; so he hired himself out to one of the local inhabitants who put him on his farm to feed the pigs. And he would willingly have filled himself with the husks the pigs were eating but no one would let him have them. Then he came to his senses and said, "How many of my father's hired men have all the food they want and more, and here I am dying of hunger! I will leave this place and go to my father and say: 'Father, I have sinned against heaven and against you. I no longer deserve to be called your son. Treat me as one of your hired men.' " So he left the place and went back to his father.

While he was still a long way off, his father saw him and was moved with pity. He ran to the boy, clasped him in his arms and kissed him. Then his son said, "Father, I have sinned against heaven and against you. I no longer deserve to be called your son."

But the father said to his servants, "Quick! Bring out the best robe and put it on him; put a ring on his finger and sandals on his feet. Bring the calf we have been fattening, and kill it; we will celebrate by having a feast, because this son of mine was dead and has come back to life; he was lost and is found."

It's really a masterpiece of storytelling, which once again—as so often in the past—brought me to the brink of tears, tears which I managed to brush away this time. Yes, there's the older brother, self-righteous and upset with all this attention being paid to his squandering brother. But it's the prodigal I've always identified with. Him and his loving father. It's a story many artists have rendered, but none so touchingly, I think, as Rembrandt. A print of his painting still hangs over my bed, given to me by Fr. Corcoran two years ago when I was on retreat. It shows the son kneeling before the father. The son is famished and ill, his shoes broken, his head shaved like a criminal's. Still, his father's hands have come to rest on his shoulders. One of the hands is a man's, the other a woman's, gentle and caressing. How did Rembrandt's great heart learn the mystery of God's justice tempered by such mercy?

9:00 P.M. A brisk walk under a waning moon. The skies clear and bright, the beaked-leaved boughs etched against the darkness. I've been meditating on the passage from Ephesians JJ gave me to read. It contains Paul's prayer for us all, and JJ read it aloud to me this morning, as a coda to the First Week. It's a prayer that could fill volumes with commentary. If Luke's father seems as prodigal in his generosity and care as the son is prodigal in wasting his inheritance, this passage points to the reasons for God's prodigality:

> *In the abundance of his glory, may he, through his Spirit, enable you to grow firm in power with regard to your inner self, so that Christ may live in your hearts through faith, and then, planted in love and built on love, with all God's people you will have the strength to grasp the breadth and the length, the height and the depth, so that, knowing the love of Christ, which is beyond knowledge, you may be filled with the utter fullness of God.*

Isn't it love, after all, that God wants to lavish on us, if only we will give Him room enough to show it? Of course we have to prepare ourselves to see that this is, in fact, what is happening to us. And if we are loved this much, why not try to love in return? We love as we are able, as millions of husbands and wives and fathers and mothers and children have learned. That being the case, Lord, help me to love You as lavishly and generously as You have loved me. Come to me in Your own good time, but come, Lord. Surprise me again and again with Your love.

THE SECOND WEEK

Thy Kingdom Come

DAY 8: THURSDAY, JANUARY 13

12:30 A.M. So it begins, the Second Week, without so much as a good night's happy rest, without so much as a frozen daiquiri and dancing girls. It's getting to be a habit, this getting up in the middle of the night. A midwinter's tale. Oh how part of me would love to get seven hours of uninterrupted sleep. But there's something appealing about being alone with a great Mystery in the night hours, with the wind howling against the shaking window frame here in my room, and only a single lamp and the sea for company. How dark everything is. You can feel the first snowfall of the season gathering to begin the New England winter in earnest.

Question. How do I actually begin to move now from the emptying I've experienced this first week to what spiritual writers call the illuminative and unitive way? Week One gave me the Foundation on which I have come to understand my place in God's plan. It meant emptying a disordered self insofar as I could, and I do feel emptied, no question of it. These next three weeks Ignatius calls the Second Foundation, and their purpose will be "to stir up enthusiasm in ourselves, as well as generosity and a desire to follow Christ in love and to share in his saving mission." That means doing what I can to further the Kingdom Christ came to offer us: a Kingdom of Love and self-giving. Underline that and score it in blood.

Now too the focus shifts from the Father to the Son, though how can you finally separate the two? *I and the Father are one,* Jesus tells us. And so now—at this weird hour—I will begin with the events leading up to the birth of Jesus: the Incarnation of the Word, the coming of God's Son into the world to set the broken bones of the world. Ignatius begins by asking us to imagine Galilee and Judea as Jesus would have known them. And so I've been trying to recall what I can of Israel from my pilgrimage there with Eileen in the summer of '92, two of forty pilgrims led by Fr. Stephen Doyle, that knowledgeable Franciscan scholar.

Israel: a place the size of New Jersey, a green belt in the central highlands surrounded by desert. Nazareth and Capernaum, Mount Carmel and Cana, the Sea of Galilee and the Mount of Transfiguration all to the north. Then the trip down the Jordan Valley, Israeli soldiers guarding the border under a blazing sun. Then Jericho, the rock ruins of the Jewish community at Qumran, the Dead Sea and Herod's mountain fortress at Masada, with the outline of Roman fortifications still visible half a mile below, even now, two thousand years later. Then back to Jericho and on to Bethany and the Mount of Olives and Bethlehem and finally Jerusalem. The Palestinian orphans we visited. Israeli teenagers—men *and* women—in uniform with Uzis, sitting in cafes, or strolling through the squares of the old city. I can still see one young Israeli woman walking toward me, blond hair flowing. So gorgeous and self-possessed in her crisp army uniform she made my teeth hurt.

Much of what I'll be doing from now until the end of this retreat will be recreating scenes from Christ's life, what Ignatius calls composition of place: "to see with the eyes of the imagination the synagogues, villages, and castles through which Christ our Lord passed as he preached." A bit anachronistic in his quaint phrasing, but there you have it. He also asks us at this juncture to take our dreams of perfect service and offer them to Christ. And because Ignatius had a soldier's—even a Crusader's—mentality, he asks us to consider what it might be like to ally ourselves to a temporal king. Or for me, as an American, to ally myself to some great charismatic leader: a president, a natural leader, or doctor. Or perhaps some college president, like Fr. Bill Leahy at BC, who reminds me of U. S. Grant, intent on taking Richmond. And having found such a leader, shall we offer dutiful service, he asks, or will it be distinguished service?

Ignatius, of course, understood that Christ is *the* leader nonpareil, His mission nothing less than conquering the world for good and overcoming whatever is inimical to humankind. In undergoing human suffering to reach the glory of the resurrection, He also provided a model that demands the larger perspective of eternity if it is to make sense. Would Jesus' life have made sense, for instance, if he'd been executed and his bones scattered to the crows and dogs? Would I have ever even heard of him in the event? Hopkins speaks of the *affective* and *elective* wills, the affective will being what we tend toward by inclination—as, say, a compass needle naturally points north—while the elective will is what we as humans *choose* as the greater good. It's the elective will Ignatius is interested in here: choosing the higher good, even where it runs counter to my natural inclinations. Especially then, I would guess.

And, of course, Ignatius begins the week by upping the ante, asking me to listen for Christ's call and then making a free and—insofar as this possible—"total" offering of myself, "provided"—he adds—"that it is for the greater service and praise of God." Moreover, I am to ask God for the strength "to imitate Christ in bearing all injuries and affronts, as well as poverty—actual as well as spiritual—if the Lord desires to choose and receive one into such a life." But first, he insists, I have to recognize my total dependency on God before I can expect to make any spiritual progress whatever. No wonder Ignatius gave us the First Week, your basic boot camp, in order to steady us for the tougher battles over the self that lie ahead.

So, I am to ask for a genuine spirit of poverty, whether actual or spiritual: the ability to leave anything behind that might interfere with my growing intimacy with God. The very thought sticks in my throat. For myself, I'm willing to live in the *spirit* of poverty. But what is the proper approach to take toward those for whom I am primarily responsible, especially my wife and sons? Or my future grandchildren, when they come? Or am I merely equivocating even now by deflecting the fact that poverty has always meant for me the loss of power, as Lear discovered after he'd turned his kingdom over to his two miserable daughters? Here's the rub. I've worked hard for what I have. Am I going to give it all away now? But, then, that is *not* what Ignatius is asking of me. What he is asking is that I share what I've been blessed with, and share it generously.

But, come morning, is JJ going to ask me to empty my pockets and turn everything I've got over to God? It's a hard question, and isn't it just like Ignatius to throw down the goddamn gauntlet at the very beginning of the Second Week? But, then, isn't it really a question of that two percent I always hold back on? A twenty in my sock, just in case. But Christ never held back. Nor, for that matter, did Ignatius. Go the extra mile, Christ said. If they ask you to walk a mile with them, walk two. Nor does anyone who wants to make spiritual progress ever hold back, it seems, whether one is a Christian, Buddhist, Hindu, or Jew. When Christ's life was demanded, terrified though He was, did He not offer it freely to the Father? And did not the Father in turn open the gates of Heaven with both hands, all of us holding on to Christ's coattails, trying to scramble through, showing the seal on our hands to gain admission?

3:00 A.M. Still wide awake and trying to understand God's incredible condescension in becoming one of us. Here's Ignatius on round one, the First Day of the Second Week:

> Consider how the three Divine Persons gazed on the whole surface or circuit of the world, full of people; and how, seeing that they were all going down into hell, they decided in their eternity that the Second Person should become a human being in order to save the human race. And thus, when the fullness of time had come, they sent the angel St. Gabriel to Our Lady.

Rather pathetically, I've been trying to imagine the Incarnation through God's eyes, zooming in and down from the great Cosmos to a mote of a room in Nazareth, where a Jewish girl named Miriam—Mary—lives. Perhaps I'm trying too hard to evoke the divine discourse between the Father, Son, and Holy Spirit. In any event, everything I imagine seems so damned inadequate. Rather like George Burns trying to imagine himself as God in the film *Oh God.* Better, the director told him, you should think of yourself as George, George.

8:00 A.M. A huge front is moving in off the ocean this morning, blanketing everything in a monotonous gray. Now wisps of downy flakes, coming faster and faster. It's the first real snow of the season, and it's painting the rocks a monochromatic white, brushstroke by brushstroke. I'm exactly nowhere this morning, except in some comic strip sense, trying to imagine the Incarnation. I guess I thought the imagination was going to be my strong suit with the *Exercises.* Composition of place—isn't that what I've been doing in my own poems and biographies for twenty-five years now? Then, too, there's my long study of the Scriptures and my readings in ancient history.

But did I really think I was going to do the *Exercises* with a book of directions? Even Ignatius, using his own imagination to summon up the various places associated with the life of Jesus, can be unintentionally funny at times, with his talk of castles dotting the landscape in Jesus' time. But now, looking over the *Exercises* again, I see that Ignatius speaks of grasping these scenes from the life of Jesus *not* with the imagination, after all, but with what he calls *the knowledge of the heart.* The knowledge of the heart. That's something altogether different, isn't it? But how do I get there?

10:15 A.M. I told JJ this morning of my difficulties in grasping the immensity of the Incarnation. It was a gesture on God's part, I confessed, that seemed to make very little sense from a purely human perspective, especially after reading Darwin, Hegel, and Freud. Why, after all, should God care what these scurrying creatures on planet Earth had done? Why not just let the whole human race go its merry way to its own destruction? Why, with a billion galaxies out there to look after, should God care about our miserable speck of a planet? None of it made sense, I realized, except if one factored in Divine Love, the way parents will change their lives to care for their Down syndrome child. Why else would God have entered our world in the form of a needy infant? Do any of us really understand any of this, we who are usually deaf to any pain except our own? What, after all, do we really know of this God whom Jesus called *Abba,* Daddy?

JJ did not enter into a debate, as I half hoped he would. That is not his style. After all, I'm sure he's heard it all before. Trust him on this. Instead, he asked me to continue with my New Testament readings from Matthew and Luke, and to meditate on three events. First, on the Annunciation by the angel to Mary that she was to be the Mother of the Messiah. Second, on Mary's visit to her cousin, Elizabeth, six months' pregnant with John. And third, on the birth of the Messiah and that first Christmas.

When I left JJ's office—on time for once—Marcie was looking out at the snow, falling now in huge, thick, wet flakes. In fact, here in Chapel, I can see nothing outside but a few bare twigs of the cropped bush nestled against the east window. No lawn, no rocks. Just white light suffusing the room. I've been meditating for the past hour on the Incarnation, thinking of God's promise to the tiny remnant of Jews enslaved by the Babylonians that He would never forget His people. Of how He would return them to the Promised Land and in time would send a Messiah to be a beacon for all nations: a son in the line of David. After a thousand years, tiny Bethlehem would have its king again. Against the incredible odds, Jesus would turn it all around, because He could, and because he was God and because He was faithful.

But by Herod's time, all of this must have seemed no more than an old wive's tale. And so, when foreigners from the East arrived in Jerusalem, asking where the new King of Israel might be found, Herod had to ask his advisors where the so-called Messiah would be born. Bethlehem, came back the answer. David's city. Then he warned the Magi to report back to him, so he too could pay homage, when what he meant to do was nip this potential threat in the bud.

Over against the mighty Herod, a young Jewish girl from the poor hill country of Galilee is asked to participate in the work of saving the human race. The angel Gabriel has been sent with the glad tidings, and his first words to her, to us, are: *Rejoice! You, who enjoy God's favor! The Lord is with you.* Human salvation waits on Mary's Yes, and she gives it. And though it will cause her suffering such as few mothers have had to bear, hers is, finally, a great triumph, nothing less than the turn-about of the human race.

1:00 P.M. I'm just now beginning to get over the shock I experienced earlier today. At half past ten, having meditated as long as I could on the Incarnation, I returned to my room to unwind and read. As I was getting ready to go down to lunch, I heard voices rising from the main stairwell. It turned out—I discovered later—to be the Thirty-Day retreatants, together with the Eight-Dayers, who had all gathered in the Main Hall for the final Mass before this first group of Eight-Dayers return home. I noticed at lunch today that they ate in a room next to the front office, and that they were talking softly in there. What the hell was up? I asked myself, as I and the other long termers chewed our food in silence.

It was only after lunch that I noticed the sign announcing the change in time posted on the bulletin board at the entrance to the dining hall. It had been there, of course, for the past three days, and everyone—including the mailman and the deliveryman—must not only have seen it but memorized it, perhaps even setting it to music. I can't easily explain my sense of loss, except to say I was deeply disappointed, for a day without the Eucharist is like no day at all.

So, the Eight-Dayers are leaving, wiping the snow off their cars, starting engines, riding over the packed snow as more snow falls. And now they're out the gates and gone, disappearing in the heavy downfall. I remember when I myself left after my own Eight-Day retreat that afternoon in November of '84, bent on getting back home as soon as possible, wanting it, yet uncertain of my future. And yet how relieved I felt to be going home. Forty years. Forty years since I first laid eyes on Eileen, who was just eighteen then. And the poem I wrote for her seven years ago, after three days of talking with the poet Robert Bly about Rilke. A poem about her sitting in a chair across from me, intent on some *New Yorker* article. How beautiful she looked at that moment. How lucky, I remember thinking, to have found this woman at all:

Glint of mahogany, glint of those pulsing
neon lights, the far shadows in the barroom
buzzing, as he rehearsed the byzantine
stratagems by which he might address her,
afraid she too would fade like all the others. . . .

Scalloped hair, blue eyes, blossoming white blouse,
this brightness, this Proserpine glimpsed
for the first time thirty years ago. The night sky
clear for once above the streets of Mineola, with
here and there a star. His Beta Sigma brothers, to whom
he had just sworn eternal solidarity, off
in the next room already growing dimmer. . . .

She sits across the room from him, bifocals
intent upon her book, head bent as if weighted down,
this woman he has shared a life with. . . . Can he call her
back as she was then? Can he rewrite their tangled
history as he would have it, now the plot
draws nearer to its close? The mind, the aging mind,
which must one day see itself extinguished. . . .

Expecting nothing, he found her there, there
in a pub, on the corner of Williston & Jericho,
in quotidian Mineola, in the midst of Gaudelli,
Ritchie, Walsh, and all the other hearts,
on a Friday night in mid-December, at the dull end
of the Eisenhower years, his third semester over. . . .

How can such gifts be, he wonders, even
as he looks up from his book to catch sight
of the blossoms just outside his window:
great masses of late June blossoms, white
on white on white, flaring from the shagged catalpa
that seems dead half of every year, until against
the odds the very air around is turned to whiteness.

5:30 P.M. Snow all afternoon. I'm still troubled by having missed Mass, the only one to do so, it turns out. A taste, then, of what it must feel like to lose God. Here I am, questioning the reality of God taking human form, even as I inwardly sob at having missed a chance of taking Him into me in the form of bread. Go figure. To try and make up for what I'd missed, I spent an hour in Chapel, thinking and praying for those who cannot, for political or geographical reasons, receive the Eucharist. Thoughts of England and Ireland under the Tutors and Stuarts, of priests entering the country under pain of death to bring the sacraments to the faithful, being hunted down, imprisoned, executed. Bare ruined choirs. Roofs torn off, walls left to crumble, as I remember all over the Irish countryside.

After meditating, I kept busy helping the custodian shovel, communicating with him when necessary with hand signs. Two hours of it, clearing walks and removing snow from around cars, from mid-afternoon until dusk, when it became too dark to see anymore. And still the snow kept drifting through the pines and cedars and the great denuded maples. When at last I came in, the custodian thanked me for my help. "I thought we were getting one to four," I signed with my hands, for this storm did not look like it was going to let up any time soon. "Four to eight," he whispered. "They've just revised the accumulations upward. And since we're on the coast, we'll get the full eight." "Well, then," I signed, "I guess I'll be seeing you in the morning."

At half past four a cup of tea and some peanut butter and crackers, then a quick call home to make sure Eileen was O.K. Snow there too, she told me, delighted to hear from me. But sad news too. Josephine Rodriguez, whom we have known since she was a teenager, married now and the mother of three, has been operated on for a tumor wrapped around her inner ear. The doctors had worked on her for nine hours straight, and now, in recovery, spinal fluid was seeping from her nose so that she had to be operated on yet again. I told Eileen I would pray for Jo until the ordeal was over.

Afterward, I went down to chapel to meditate on the Annunciation and Mary's visit to Elizabeth, Luke 1:26–38 and then Luke again: 1:39–56. For each of the scripture readings, Ignatius's *Exercises* provide three points. For the Annunciation, he asks us to consider (1) that Mary would conceive a son who would be the Messiah—*Hail Mary, full of grace, the Lord is with you,* the opening of every Hail Mary ever said, all trillion of them. Then (2) the news that her cousin, Elizabeth, had conceived a son in her old age—John, who would become the Baptist. And (3) Mary's response to the angel: *Behold the handmaid of the Lord. Be it done to me according to your word.* Each of these points I mean to sift through the alembic of the imagination, turning each scriptural phrase to the light.

And so with the Visitation, three points: (1) the infant leaping for joy in Elizabeth's womb when Mary and Elizabeth greeted each other, Elizabeth saying the words that have also found their way into the Hail Mary: *Blessed are you among women, and blessed is the fruit of your womb.* (2) Mary's response in the *Magnificat,* beginning *My soul magnifies the Lord!* And (3) Mary's staying with Elizabeth three months before returning home to Nazareth.

So: two sons, who would meet again at the Jordan, when John would baptize Jesus at the beginning of Jesus' ministry. Two sons, both killed in their thirties, one beheaded in prison by Herod during a drunken party, the other crucified outside the city gates of Jerusalem on the eve of the Passover. And two women, one little more than a girl, the other a woman beyond the normal childbearing stage, both pregnant with sons, pregnant with hope for themselves and for their people. How lucky we are that God keeps His promises in spite of our infidelities. So, He had come as He'd promised, this time making the choice to take on our human nature, and, having made that choice, soldering us to Him once and for all. I have no doubt who got the better end of that deal. But is this true? Did the same God who created the universe actually condescend to come among us and die for us? From one perspective, I could see how our human nature might look like some useless appendage stuck to the Divine. From another, it means that our humanity has been utterly transformed, and we have become God-like and immortal, unlike anything we might have imagined.

9:40 P.M. The snow has stopped, though the wind is still whipping up drifts around the retainer walls and doors. For dinner, spaghetti and large shells filled with ricotta cheese, meatballs and sauce, a salad, topped off with Boston cream pie and coffee. For accompaniment, a piano concerto. Just us Thirty-Day retreatants tonight. The priests have gone out to eat and to take a well-deserved break, while the rest of us have lingered over dinner. I could see some of the novices from Chicago and Detroit, sitting together at their own table, signing among themselves and smiling.

Afterward, I went back into Chapel to meditate again on the Incarnation. Listening with my one ear half-cocked to the wind howling through the trees, I suddenly—and inexplicably—felt a tremendous warmth surging through me. If Christ did in fact take on human flesh, it meant something more than taking on human nature in some abstract fashion. What He had done was to take on *my* nature, take on hands like mine, and feet, and eyes and ears and a heart and a human brain, the whole shebang. What incredible, mind-boggling condescension: that He should become a man not only to redeem us, but to be *with* us and *like* us. Like the adult who wants to get down and play with his kids, as one of them. Or like wrestling with my boys when they were little so I could hold them tight, and roll with them in the autumn leaves, and—when they were babies—kiss their tummies.

But then we lost our innocence and one brother killed another and so it began, and now God's Son would enter the world to bring his straying charges back in line, and they would kill him. And God would have to take even that outrage into the equation, for—try as we may—killing God is beyond even our ability. A contradiction, then, and a sign. Our passion-plungèd giant risen, and the great mystery of God's *kenosis*—Christ's emptying of himself to become our servant. Instead of demanding what was his by right, Jesus emptied himself for us, even to dying on a cross. Then, in his paradoxical fashion, he would draw us after him. It is Love Himself who refuses to give up on us.

Then, in the midst of my meditation, I began thinking of Jo again, and of what she must have suffered. And suddenly I was pleading with the God who had come among us and suffered for us to help this particular human being among all the billions of others He must also look after. I no longer want to argue why God should hear my particular prayer, any more than a mother wants to argue with the doctor about why he should cure *her* baby. When the little one's mouth trembles in fear and pain, all such logic goes out the window, and all I could utter now was, *Please God, please God, please God,* knowing He would know what my deepest prayer was. After a long time I opened my eyes to find the chapel empty. I got up and went down to the dining hall to make myself some tea. I could see drifts across the pathways and felt the cold tensing. I went outside under the lights and shoveled for an hour, clearing out from around the cold cars, making paths, and praying over and over, "For Jo, Lord. Can you hear me? This is for Jo." Isn't this why you came among us, Lord? To share in our frail humanity, that we might share in your divinity? Quid pro quo?

DAY 9: FRIDAY, JANUARY 14

3:00 A.M. At half past one this morning I came down to Chapel to meditate on the Nativity, Luke: 2:1–14. And so the promise of the Incarnation, the Word growing in Mary's womb cell by cell, then the long, hard, uncomfortable journey once again for Mary from Nazareth down to Bethlehem. Mary approaching term, then giving birth to her son and wrapping him in swaddling, unnoticed, except for the heavenly hosts and the Cosmos, singing *Glory to God in the highest.*

Here, in the second contemplation on the Nativity, Ignatius enjoins us "to see Our Lady, Joseph, the maidservant, and the infant Jesus after his birth," the maidservant Ignatius's addition, perhaps recalling the peasant woman who nursed and brought him up after his mother's death. "I will make myself a poor, little, and unworthy slave," Ignatius writes, "gazing at them, contemplating them, and serving them in their needs, just as if I were there, with all possible respect and reverence. Then I will reflect upon myself to draw some profit." For an hour I prayed, going over the familiar, comforting, and strange scene again and again in my mind, at one point even nodding off. Then, thirsty, I walked down the dark corridor to the dining hall to get a cup of cold water. One of the retreatants, unable to sleep, was reading a book under a solitary lamp in the Reading Room.

8:00 A.M. Awoke to the sun transforming my room with fresh light. The storm window is completely frosted over on the inside, and the sun has turned the window blond. At breakfast, I could see steam rising off the ocean, reminding me just how cold it is. Still, the sun is crisping brightly, lighting a low bank of peach-purple-mauve clouds above the rippling slate-blue waters. How beautiful God's world is, needing only the beholder to see and marvel at it.

11:00 A.M. JJ told me to continue meditating today on the Infancy Narratives: the shepherds in the fields that first Christmas night—Christ's manifestation to the poor. Then Christ's manifestation to the Magi and the greater world beyond. And, finally, Herod's paranoia over the news of this usurper, this new king of the Jews, followed by Joseph's flight into Egypt with Mary to save their infant son. Also—JJ added—I was to read the sections in the *Exercises* on the *Discernment of Spirits for the First and Second Weeks.* To further complicate my day, he also suggested I read straight through Mark's short Gospel up to the Passion to get a sense of the narrative flow of Jesus' life. Then, as I was leaving, he asked if I would read at Mass this evening, and serve as Eucharistic minister, offering the cup. It's always an honor to serve Communion, for it gives me the chance to see the faces of the faithful as Christ must see them.

The passage I'm to read is from 1 Samuel 8, a story so powerful I found myself moved to tears. The elders among the Hebrews come to the prophet Samuel, grown old now, and tell him they want a king to lead them into battle. A king like the one the Egyptians, the Canaanites, and the Jebusites have: a human king, and not some prophet who learns from God what God's will is supposed to be and then passes it on. *Grant the people's every request,* God tells Samuel. *It is not you they are rejecting, but me, as their king.*

And so Samuel goes back to the elders and tells them what it is they are really asking for. *You want a king,* he says—and here, in essence, is what he tells them:

> Here is what a king will demand of you. He will take your sons and make soldiers of them, tank officers who will go into battle ahead of him. He will appoint other men with the power of life and death over your boys. It is your sons who will have to do the king's plowing and harvesting. They will make swords and spears and bombs and tanks and cruisers for him.
>
> As for your daughters, they will work in factories and assembly lines, as cooks and bakers for him. He will take for himself your best grapes and wheat and olive oil, and these he will give to his state officials who feed his war machine. He will tax you, taking a tenth of everything you have and use it to feed his eunuchs and hangers-on. Over time you will gradually become his slaves. When this happens, you will grumble to the Lord against the very king you ask for today, but the Lord will not answer you.

But the elders persist. They want a king who can win wars for them. And so Samuel goes back to the Lord and tells Him what they want. And the Lord says, simply: *Give them what they ask for. Appoint a king to rule them.* It breaks my heart to see God treated like this. Why is it that we always seem to hanker after what we know must fail us?

3:00 P.M. Finally, I'm beginning to glimmer some deeper understanding from the meditations for the Second Week. One insight in particular has stayed with me, for Luke is very subtle on this: the foreshadowing of the Eucharist in the way he describes the infant Jesus laid in his swaddling shroud in the manger. *And they laid him in a manger. Manger:* to eat. Christ's body, which will be broken for us that we might consume it, that we might have life. And there it is, a hint of the Eucharist there in the Infancy Narrative.

And this: that Jesus was born not in an inn, but in the only space available, in the humble home of one of Joseph's relatives still residing in Bethlehem, since many—forced by the census—would have descended on the tiny town where, a thousand years before, Israel's greatest king had been born. And the bother of this long census. For what? The better to collect Roman taxes more efficiently? And at such an inconvenient time, with Mary nearing term and the people told to get themselves counted not according to where they now lived, but in the town where their ancestors had hailed from. And so the long trek for Mary once again through hill country and down along the Jordan valley, avoiding Samaritan territory, passing Herod's fortresses dotting the way, and on down to Jericho. Then the long desert stretch up to Jerusalem, that lonely, alien road where our Palestinian-operated bus broke down.

And the baby born, needing to be fed and protected and changed and held and loved. The King of Kings, born in these humble surroundings. Joseph the carpenter doing what he could to make his wife and baby comfortable, some shepherds at the door. Subsistence farmers, hats in hands, with some incredible story of angels come with the news that the Messiah was now among them, then being admitted into the room and staring, as one, then the others, went down on their knees, mute, respectful, before the infant they'd been told they would find there.

Little Lamb, who made thee?

Already the lawn down to the water's edge lies in shadow. The tide's coming in again, and the boulders are a speckled tan, with touches of blue-white snow clinging to them. Hour by hour, scene by scene this Week is going to unfold, as I leaf through the recorded facts of Jesus' life. The Infancy Narratives first, and then—in another day or so—Jesus' three-year ministry, leading directly to his death. And now it's the Circumcision, when Jesus shed his first blood eight days after his birth, a ritual which would mark him as adhering to the Mosaic Law. The day too Joseph named him and so took the child for his own.

Jesus would learn his trade from Joseph, who would work with him from the time he could handle a hammer and nails. Here, in the ritual of Circumcision, the Lord of all Creation makes himself subject to the Law, which is to love God with one's whole heart, and one's neighbor as oneself. I think of Joseph and Mary wincing as the necessary cut was made on their infant son. Yeshua: Jesus: Hebrew for *Yahweh saves.* And the names Gabriel spoke to Mary: Emmanuel. *God is with us,* the two names complementing one another.

6:30 P.M. Leather jacket, gloves and hat, and out for a walk at four. A Siberian clipper has followed in the wake of yesterday's storm, so that it feels like twenty-five below. I walked along one of the wooded trails to keep out of the full force of the wind, even as I felt my face going numb. Ice on the walks, ice over Niles Pond. A lone gull caught in the flare of the dying sun, the tops of the tall pines gold and yellow-red. The ocean's edge has a film of broken ice, and the rocks have been transformed into giant ice balls.

At Mass tonight, as I read from Samuel, the sadness of God's voice once again became so palpable that I nearly broke down at the lectern. I had prepared against this very possibility by going over the passage three times earlier, but it was not—apparently—enough. I am very much moved, it seems, by the force of the Scriptures as I read them now. How often have I chosen something—anything—other than Him, and—even so—how gracious He has remained.

11:15 P.M. Exhausted, and still grappling with the sadness evoked by the passage from Samuel, I lay down after dinner, thinking to rest for a few minutes, and fell asleep. In the blink of an eye, it was nearly ten. If I can go back to sleep, I thought, I will. But the image of the Lord telling Samuel to give the people the king they had chosen instead of Him filled me with such love that my heart burned. I lay there in the dark, torn between staying with these feelings, and getting up to prepare for my next meditation.

I thought of the Jewish people, of how they had remained faithful to their Covenant in spite of the tremendous odds against them. Then I was thinking of how I had learned—some dozen years ago—about my own Jewish roots. The story of my mother's father, Harry Szymborski, who changed his name to Harry Green when his only child, my mother—Harriet—was born in 1923. A cavalryman stationed in Texas, crossing into Mexico after Pancho Villa, then later a sergeant with the American Expeditionary Force in France, where he'd been gassed in the trenches. Dead at thirty-six of complications of the gassing, leaving behind a nine-year-old daughter and an alcoholic wife.

I have my mother's cryptic comments about it, delivered over the years. But when, a few months before she died of lung cancer, I asked her point blank if she was in fact Jewish, she smiled that enigmatic smile of hers, thought a moment before answering, and shook her head. Still, there is the conversation I had with my father, when I flew down to be with him after his hip replacement last October. "Why didn't you tell me mom's father was Jewish?" I asked him. At which the old fox looked at me as he popped another of the big cookies I'd brought him into his mouth. "Because you'd write about it," he said.

"You seem to like the Jews a lot," the poet Phil Levine—one of my dearest friends—once told me. "Ever think of becoming one?" "In a heartbeat," I said. "But then I'd have to give up Christ, and I couldn't do that."

"No you wouldn't," he laughed.

I looked at him.

"Oh yeah, I guess you would."

A sign and a contradiction.

But I know too that even the word "Christian" has sent chills through many Jews: the ghettos, the Crusades, the Inquisition, the Marranos, the pogroms. What a sorry history when Christendom won out and became the approved state religion under Constantine (*In hoc signo vinces: In this sign you will conquer*). An underground religion, a cult, that had suffered at the hands of that same legal system for three hundred years, including the state-sanctioned crucifixion of its founder.

Compound that with the split—probably inevitable—between the Jewish Christians (or better, those Jews who followed the Way of Jesus) and the majority of the Jews, themselves a diverse lot, including the Essenes and Zealots who finally forced the Romans' hand. Then the destruction of Jerusalem in 70. Jews slaughtered, dispersed, sold into slavery, the Temple once again destroyed, its treasury carried off to Rome, as I saw for myself inscribed on the triumphal arch of Titus in the Roman Forum. Then the reformation of Judaism that followed the dispersion, shaped in part as a response to the growth of Christianity. I remember someone remarking once that the New Law of Christ had replaced the Old Law of Judaism, as if we Christians no longer needed our Jewish roots, when the truth is that Judaism is our foundation and our older brother, its history the necessary ground of our own history.

So: the great divide between Christians and Jews that goes back almost to the beginnings of the Church. Often I think of St. Paul, my namesake, who grew up Saul, a Pharisee, a man who once sat at the feet of the great Jewish teacher, Gamaliel, as I have become who I am because of teachers like Allen Mandelbaum and Irving Howe. Paul, who brought the Good News of Christ to Turkey, Crete, Macedonia, Greece, and Rome itself. And yet the man who labored among the Gentiles gloried first in being a Jew. Even as Christianity was being transformed, so too was Judaism, as it remade itself after the destruction of Jerusalem. Didn't Jesus repeatedly say that he had come to save his own people first and foremost? It was only by necessity that he opened his arms to others who also implored his help, since the suffering and despair he saw in his mission wore then as it wears now a universal face.

DAY 10: SATURDAY, JANUARY 15

4:00 A.M. Up at 2:45 A.M. Down to Chapel to meditate on the *Discernment of Spirits for Weeks One and Two,* Paragraphs 313–336. These are rules meant "to aid us toward perceiving and then coming to a better understanding of the various motions which are caused in the soul—the good motions that they may be received, and the bad that they may be rejected."

Here's one. "It is characteristic of the evil angel, who takes on the appearance of an angel of light," the Fourth Rule of the *Discernment of Spirits for the Second Week* reads, "to enter by going along the same way as the devout soul and then to exit by his own way with success for himself. That is, he brings good and holy thoughts attractive to such an upright soul and then strives little by little to get his own way, by enticing the soul over to his hidden deceits and evil intentions." Oh, how well I know this one: how subtle and vicious this seducing spirit can be, like a weed mimicking a fruitful plant to keep it from being ripped out by its roots. Or like the con man that has only a woman's best interest at heart as he leads her to his bed. Pray for discernment that you may not be snared. How quiet it is. What's out there?

7:40 A.M. Down to Chapel again at half past six to meditate on the story of the Magi come to Bethlehem to pay homage to the young King of the Jews. But who were these Magi, these Wise Men? I seem to be able to go forward with these meditations only as they make sense historically. But what of this story? What's behind it? And why is it found only in Matthew? Modern scholarship tends to read the episode symbolically as God's revealing Himself from the very outset to the Gentiles. Also as the Son's rejection not by the poor, in the figure of the shepherds, but by the religious leaders.

For two centuries astronomy has tried to calculate what confluence of heavenly bodies might have appeared in the Near East in the period between 6 and 4 B.C.E., without a convincing single answer. I remember taking the boys to a Christmas show at the Hayden Planetarium in New York when they were little and following the explanations offered there for the Star of Bethlehem. Most scriptural scholars would say that such an approach is fruitless, that this is another of those stars in ancient cultures that attend the birth of the god. I don't know, really. Perhaps the Magi were scholars associated with one of the royal courts of Arabia or Iraq, earnest seekers come to King Herod to ask where the infant King of the Jews might be found.

In any event, the old fox, jealous of this potential interloper, asks his counselors where such a king would be born. Bethlehem, they tell him. The same half-forgotten town south of Jerusalem where David had been born a thousand years earlier. I think it is that which has most stayed with me: the image of Gentiles looking to the Jews for guidance and wisdom but finding this time only the desolation and paranoia of an old man, whom they seem to have instinctively mistrusted.

And then the rising star again—whatever this light was—and the Magi, arriving in Bethlehem and finding the house where Mary and Joseph and the infant were living. Then kneeling and paying the baby homage, offering him the gifts one offers a king. There's a fairy-tale quality to all this that I find delightful. There must have been something inherently honest and dignified about these men, for they did not turn up their noses at the poor figures before them but recognized the baby for the king he was. Herod had urged the Magi to return and tell him what they had found, for he meant to have his soldiers remove the tiny interloper immediately. But now it is the Magi who are warned in a dream not to return to Herod. And so they leave by another route, disappearing forever from history.

And Joseph, likewise warned in a dream of the impending danger, gets up, takes the mother and child, and leaves Bethlehem, heading not north back to Nazareth (Herod's agents would search there too if they had the census lists, or go house to house asking questions) but south, through the desert, to Egypt. There the family would stay, like that other Joseph in exile Genesis speaks of, until Herod was dead and it was safe to return home.

10:30 A.M. When I asked JJ this morning if he saw any pattern in the way I was proceeding, he simply remarked that what *he* heard was someone who was looking hard, amid all the words, for Christ. But am I trying too hard to intellectualize the *Exercises*? Have I left room to listen? JJ wants me to spend today focusing again on the early years, before moving on tomorrow to Jesus' public ministry. In any event, Christ's entire mission seems to be contained in microcosm in the Infancy Narratives.

After seeing him, I went down to Chapel to meditate on Luke's account of Jesus' Presentation in the Temple forty days after his birth. It's the feast we celebrate each year on February 2, forty days after Christmas and so midway through winter. In that sense, it's a welcome promise of things to come, of light and more light now each day. After all, these feasts are geared toward the natural cycle of the seasons, as they are in the Jewish liturgical calendar as well. It would have been Jesus' first appearance in the Temple, where he would return so many times over his life, no doubt during the years when we have no record of his comings and goings. We know he was there when he was twelve, the coming of age for young Jewish males. And we know he went up to Jerusalem during his public ministry, and that it was in the shadow of the Temple that he would die.

The first-born male, the Jewish Law says, must be consecrated to the Lord, in part as a remembrance of God's sparing the first-born of the Hebrews when they were still slaves in Egypt. A pair of turtledoves or two young pigeons would have been sacrificed—the offering of the poor—and Joseph and Mary were surely among the poor. And then the two old people, Simeon and Anna, two of the faithful who had lived and prayed in the Temple precincts for decades, recognizing the baby for who he was: the Messiah, the Redeemer, the Deliverer.

How moving the old man's words are, how full of joy and expectation:

Now, Master, you are letting your servant go in peace
as you promised;
for my eyes have seen the salvation
which you have made ready in the sight of the nations;
a light of revelation for the gentiles
and glory for your people Israel.

No doubt Mary and Joseph were astounded that others should recognize their infant son, picking him out of a crowd of poor folk offering their humble sacrifices. This one, Simeon says, is *destined for the fall and rise of many in Israel,* a sign that had already been opposed and would be again, so that the *secret thoughts of many may be laid bare.* The yes of fishermen and tax collectors and prostitutes, of thieves and lepers and even of some of the Pharisees. And the no of those glutted with power, jealous for their prerogatives.

And when, really, was it ever any different?

3:30 P.M. For lunch today: pea soup, a cold cut sandwich, an orange, and coffee. The same democratic cuisine, day after day. Good, but no Julia Child surprises here. Followed by a fruitless and comic search in closets, even in the large kitchen, in the unfinished basement, everywhere, for a 100-watt bulb to replace the one that burned out as I was reading in my room this afternoon. I left a note for Brother Bill Spokesfield, saying I'd combed high and low in all the wrong places, and could he help me? An hour later, there was a 100-watt bulb outside my door, which he'd quietly left so as not to disturb me.

Spent a good part of the afternoon meditating on Jesus' coming to the Temple at the age of twelve. It's the only glimpse we have of him between the Infancy Narratives and his public ministry, which began around the time he was thirty, and is therefore a scene of extraordinary import. The retreatant, Ignatius explains, "will contemplate how the child Jesus was obedient to his parents at Nazareth, and next how they found him in the temple. After this will come the two repetitions and the application of the senses."

I fixed the scene in my mind, imagining myself with Jesus in the Temple, and then with Mary and Joseph, as they searched three days for their missing son. What—God forbid—if he were dead? Then the discovery that he was with the doctors of the Law, discussing the Torah, the little snot. Relieved to find him, yet deeply upset that he had put them through such torture, Mary asks her son why he had stayed behind like this, for surely he can see how worried she and his father are. It is at this point that Jesus has to remind them both who his real father is: *Didn't you know I'd be in my Father's house?* Twelve years old, and already the outline of his mission becoming clear to him.

A young man, already champing at the bit, anxious for the work that lay ahead, but subjecting himself to his parents' authority, living on in total obscurity for another eighteen years, no doubt learning patience from Joseph and Mary. And then, with Joseph dead and his cousin John preaching in the desert at the southern end of the Jordan River, he realizes that it is time to begin his mission. A whole new set of rulers now in Rome and Galilee and Judea, which is no longer under the jurisdiction of Herod's sons but a Roman prefect named Pilate. And under it all the same greed and arrogance at the helm, the same murderous will.

10:15 P.M. As the sun was setting, I took a break to clear my head by walking down one of the paths that crisscross the property here. How gorgeous the lavender-pink clouds were, brooding low on the horizon. And then the blaze of flame orange as the sun dropped below the horizon. The snow had turned shadow blue along the trail, and there were pools of frozen water at the base of Brace Rock. Far above, a half moon floated in the heavens.

Sitting in the Fireplace Room before Mass, I let the music wrap around me. Dixie gave the reflection, focusing on her rediscovery of God during her time at the Weston Jesuit School of Theology in Cambridge. She folded her story neatly in with this evening's Gospel, which relates the story of Jesus' calling Matthew the tax collector to follow him. If Peter had decided to leave Jesus, she pointed out, he could always have gone back to fishing. But Matthew? Where could he go? Surely not back to tax collecting. There was no going back once you gave up a job like that. Too many others would be waiting in the wings for *that* plum. It's a point worth remembering if you give up your job at UMass.

A dinner tonight of meatloaf, peas, tiny onions, and (alas) a baked potato that screamed for fifteen minutes more at 350 degrees. On the side table in the Main Room coming out of Mass I found a note card from Eileen showing two yellow crocuses lifting through snow, and proclaiming that new beginnings are always a gift of God. It's dated Thursday, 9:00 A.M., and is crammed with information catching me up on things back home. More snow is on the way, she told me when I called at eight. And that could make things difficult when she drives up to Newburyport tomorrow for our visit. Pray she makes it, for she's been on my mind the whole time I've been here, like some distant Christmas present I almost can't bear to think about, lest it turn out to be an illusion only. A retreat, when all is said and done, is not a home, but a way of returning home with the spirit replenished.

I've spent the last hour reading up on the Jesuits in the Far East in the two hundred fifty years after Ignatius first sent them out, and marvel at their staggering losses and their almost superhuman bravery in the face of terrible trials. How did they do it as they journeyed to Persia, Turkey, India, China, Japan, the Spice Islands, the Himalayas, even Tibet? Bento de Goes, Desideri, Grueber,

Ricci. The deaths from sea disasters, at the hands of pirates, deaths languishing in prisons, hangings, disembowelings, beheadings, starvings, exhaustion, the myriad sicknesses from diseases undergone, and all to spread the Good News. And, almost as a by-product, the discoveries they made: sea routes and mountain routes and desert routes charted for the first time in history. I thought of the work of other Jesuits in the Americas, from Peru and Brazil to the Canadian forests and the northern Mississippi, from the swamps of Florida to the deserts of California and New Mexico. All of it given without counting the cost. How in God's name did they do it? But isn't the answer there in the question? Good luck, son. Good luck, my boy.

DAY 11: SUNDAY, JANUARY 16: FIRST DAY OF REPOSE

9:00 A.M. Two hours of sleep, then up shortly after midnight. Down once more to Chapel to pray. I sat on the floor and let the meditations of the last three days wash over me, ending with Jesus in the Temple. Only the western retaining wall of the Temple complex—part of Herod's grand project—remains now, before which Eileen and I once prayed, men to the left, women to the right. A petition on a piece of paper shoved into one of the many niches between sections of the cut stone, a cardboard yarmulke on my head, a spiritual Jew among Jews. Already, as I prepare for the first day of repose—this necessary break from the intensity of the *Exercises*—I sense a renewed urgency about the work Jesus began, work he left for others like myself to carry on. But what is it, really, that He is leading me to do? What *is* His will? And—when I know what it is—will I have the courage to carry it out?

Back to sleep at two and up for the day at seven. I showered and shaved and made my bed, employing the nifty hospital tuck. French toast, bacon strips, sausage links, grapefruit, and coffee. Bless the cooks. Bless those who provide fresh flowers for the altar. And bless Fr. Frank for filling the milk machine this morning (skim and two percent), the same man who last evening consecrated the bread and wine that brought me such consolation.

The wind—that Johnny One-note—has begun howling and moaning again, blowing the snow wildly about. I'm worried about Eileen. Ever since her accident fifteen years ago, when a woman crossed the yellow line on Route 63 and hit her head on, she's been skittish in this kind of weather, as who wouldn't be? Paul, thank God, was in the backseat; otherwise he would have suffered more than chipped teeth and a bruised shin. And me in Amherst, having gone on ahead, waiting for Eileen in the outer office to begin our session with the marriage counselor. Then the counselor coming out of his office, grim-faced, to say there'd been an accident up on 63, and that Eileen had been taken to the hospital. And so now, of course, that voice in my ear, whispering, "Tsk, tsk. How *could* you leave your poor wife to go away to indulge yourself in a long retreat like this?"

Damn you. Better this way than the last time I was here. God will protect her.

11:00 P.M. Out and back, returning at nine, the wind thrashing the trees and surf pounding the rocks, worried that Eileen was out there somewhere in the dark alone, driving the 110 miles back home. Some of the Thirty-Day retreatants were chatting in the Fireplace Room before a roaring, welcoming fire, the monastic setting devolving into a resort weekend in Vermont. How strange to be talking this evening, when I thought silence would have been imposed on our return.

No one had told *them* there was silence, one of them said, and so I found myself joining in the low-toned conversation, waiting for enough time to pass so I could call home. "The phone is just down the corridor," I thought to myself, "and I will have to keep passing through here until I know she's safe." I made three calls, each time growing more and more concerned as I heard only my own recorded voice played back at me. Each time I came back to the fire for human contact. Then JJ coming downstairs in his undershirt, asking for silence. And indeed, hadn't two women from the new group of Eight-Day retreatants, who'd arrived in my absence, walked by in silence, staring at us? Red-faced, I bid the others good night and beat a hasty retreat.

I tried again. Still no answer. And then at 10:30 again. Again, no answer. Then it hit me: feeling the roads yawing under her wheels, she'd probably turned back to stay the night at John's. I called there, and—to my immense relief—heard her voice in the background and John saying she was safe. Then she was on the phone. She'd gone a few miles and decided to turn back. Tomorrow will be sunny and she can leave then, before she picks up again and drives down to Paterson to teach.

And the day itself. How did that go? Splendidly, tenderly, with an edge of sadness, as if I'd been granted a short reprieve, knowing I would have to return here without her. I got to my youngest son John's at 11:15, feeling light and free. He was still out shopping for lunch, and so Maria and I spent the time over coffee, catching up. How strange simply to be talking, as if I'd been in a country where no English was spoken, or on Mars, and now, suddenly, I was back in a strangely familiar place. Then John came in, arms filled with Italian bread, extra virgin olive oil, prosciutto, Parmesan cheese, mozzarella. We spoke of how the retreat was going, John looking to see if I had grown wings in the interval. I brought up the subject of women's ordination. Maybe, he said, it would be better if I stayed at his place until I recovered my senses.

At a quarter to one, Eileen pulled into the driveway, and I went down to greet her. How good just to see her again. Talk, family talk, repeated a million times around this earth of ours. The freshness and delight of merely being there, as I quietly gave thanks for my wife, my sons, and their wives. Then a lunch of Italian cold cuts and a glass of red wine. Eileen has brought me another packet of pens and two more blue journals, which—at the rate I'm going—I will undoubtedly fill up as well. Also the books I'd asked her to bring, and which I've already told JJ I will need for my Scripture meditations: Fr. John McKenzie's *Dictionary of the Bible,* as well as Fr. Raymond Brown's two-volume *The Death of the Messiah: A Commentary on the Passion Narratives in the Four Gospels,* and his *Introduction to the New Testament.*

In the short faux afternoon, John, Eileen, and I went for a long stroll down by the bay estuary. As we walked back to the car, the red ball of the sun flared against the bare trees on the low hills to the west. Then he drove us down some of the back roads, past schoolboys throwing snowballs and laughing.

Cheese and spinach ravioli with a red sauce for dinner, wine, fruit for dessert, the tail end of a football game. Eileen gave me a brick of Italian *torrone* nougat candy, a gift from her aunt to me. I broke off a small piece and gave the rest to Maria. Isn't that what gifts are for? Then it was time to go. Eileen pulled out of the driveway, made a right turn onto 1A, and was gone. I hugged John, got into my car, turned left, and began negotiating the deserted roads back to the interrupted silences of Eastern Point.

DAY 12: MONDAY, JANUARY 17: MARTIN LUTHER KING, JR., DAY

8:00 A.M. I feel like some teenager for having broken silence last night. What's the big deal, part of me says, while the other part reminds me that this is no children's game, no ascetic slumming. Someone last night said they'd spotted my name in *America* as the poetry editor there, and I had gone on about my work for the magazine. Better, really, to have simply said, yes, I did that, and then changed the subject before old friend Pride could lift his glossy head. Besides, what talk could measure up to the sublimity of silence here, my own spoken voice the most banal and annoying of all.

How quickly moral entropy sets in. And so today I mean to focus on obedience. As it turns out, it looks as if the readings for today's Mass might actually set the tone for doing just that. In 1 Samuel 15:16–23, Samuel—grown old now—tells Saul he has disobeyed God by not slaughtering all the enemy's sheep, as God has strictly ordered, but instead has let his soldiers make holocaust offerings with some of them. But Samuel sees through this sham. No, he tells him, you didn't do this for God. You did this to puff yourself up, so people might say, "Oh, what a good king Saul is. Look how generous he is. Look how he lets his people offer up sacrifices." But, Samuel reminds him, God gave Saul the victory so he could root out the virus of the enemy *and* all their goods. And what did you do? he chides Saul. You decided to do things *your* way. Which makes you no better than an idolater. And now you can no longer be king, for there can be one king only: the Lord.

10:00 A.M. I tried explaining to JJ this morning what had happened last night in the Fireplace Room, but he merely waved it away. Still, I felt I had to tell him what the incident had shown me about myself: how quickly I tend to go after what is not mine. It's the old problem of control all over again. Instead of simply walking away from the group, I had to join in, even though I somehow knew it was strange to be talking. JJ listened. He must have sensed there was something to what I said, for he told me to go back into Jesus' hidden life again to see what the example of his obedience and humility might have to say to me personally. And so, here in Chapel for the past half hour, I've been thinking about how the Son of God worked alongside Joseph, of the family sitting down to meals, of Jesus learning from his parents' poverty and selflessness, of Mary's willingness to help her neighbors as she'd helped Elizabeth.

I thought, too, of Joseph working long hours as my own working-class parents had, just to put bread on the table, of how he and Mary had passed on their skills to their son. Then of what Joseph must have learned from Mary and Jesus, just as I have learned so much from Eileen and my sons: patience, control, a caring for others. Joseph, growing day by day into his own sanctity, the life of chastity he lived because he understood that something profound had happened to Mary. In many ways a family like millions of other families, living close to subsistence level, day in and day out, giving of their small excess to those in even greater need. I thought, too, of Jesus learning to read the Torah, and digesting it—like his parents—along with his daily bread.

None of this, I know, is recorded, and so I have had to extrapolate from what I do know of the public Jesus to try to understand how he came to be the man he did. His parables, for instance, taken from the worlds of farming and fishing and history and domestic life. The comparisons he made to explain the Kingdom of God to us. At Ignatius's suggestion, I've thought about the off-color jokes and casual blasphemies and sexual innuendoes that seem to be part and parcel of the speech of laborers: Jesus' Father mocked, his name taken lightly, the cruelties to animals and people he and Joseph must have seen. And all the while, zeal for his Father's house consuming him.

In time, Jesus came to understand how the world operates: the arrogance of soldiers, governors, priests, tax collectors. He saw how people preen themselves over nothing, their words an empty beating of the gums. He must have felt keenly the need to get away, to be alone with the Father, to pray, to study the Scriptures. The beauty and depth of women must surely have moved him, for they were certainly attracted to him, but he knew that his own life's work lay elsewhere. There is, too, his obedience to the commandments, his eagerness to do away with suffering and hunger and ignorance as he attempted to reveal his Father's kingdom to the world. I thought of all this, and of how I wanted so much now to emulate this man.

I'm reading Ignatius on the Four States of Life: the priesthood, religious life, single life, and marriage. That order will work for Ignatius, but I see I will have to reverse these priorities for myself. What he asks us to consider at this point in the *Exercises* is how we will open "ourselves in order to come to perfection in whatever state of life God may grant us to elect." Well, it's marriage I've been intimately involved with now for the past thirty-six years. Of course I think often of my oldest son and the religious life he's chosen, knowing that his life like any life has its consolations and difficulties.

But it's my job to try to come to perfection in the life *I* have chosen, remembering always, of course, that *everything* I do and *everything* I have—including even my willingness to strive—is a gift from God, and that five minutes submerged in those icy waters sixty yards from this window would surely serve to remind me what a poor creature I'd be if I had to depend only on myself. But even more, it's a matter of renewed enthusiasm for the life I've chosen, of giving all that I am and have to others. As Jesus did, feeding the multitudes waiting along the edge of the Sea of Galilee to be filled not only with bread but with his very presence.

11:15 A.M. Went out to the laundry room a few minutes ago for the second time this morning to put my clothes in one of the two available dryers, and there was Tom Wilhelm, right on schedule, removing his clothes so I could put mine in. Small courtesies and attentions to others, one notices, do abound. Last night I might have spoken to him. Today I can only nod and smile in his direction. And so it comes home that we are in fact plunged back into silence, a silence that comes as a profound relief, revealing itself as the best way of getting in touch with the things of God. It's as if I were finally beginning to hear the Spirit moving over the waters as on the first day of Creation, whispering something into my ear.

Thinking again about obedience: an emptying of the ego to be filled with God's presence. Ignatius asks us at this point to meditate on opening ourselves to the beauty of poverty (greed, in short, *not* being good, regardless of what my broker friend tells me), especially if we are to become open to God's will. Ignatius speaks here of two kinds of poverty: actual poverty and spiritual poverty. One

Jesuit theologian defines poverty for Ignatius as a total emptying of the self before God, and of our conscious dependence on him for ANY AND ALL SPIRITUAL PROGRESS. This sounds to me rather like Wallace Stevens's poverty at nightfall, when we will be stripped to our essential selves. Or like Robert Lowell's poignant image of the wristwatch stripped from my wrist when I am laid out on the coroner's table. The point is to rid myself of whatever stands in the way of meeting God more fully. But let's face it, you who grew up with so very little: this emptying of the self is going to be very hard for you, isn't it?

And, on top of that: a meditation on humility, the *sine qua non* if we are ever to become obedient to the will of God. This buckling on of humility, Ignatius tells us, is the first step toward ANY AND ALL VIRTUES. So: poverty and humility. A twofold emptying of the self to await God's filling us with His own consolations. Like Jesus, like his disciples, I am going to have to learn to travel with the bare essentials, picking up what I need as I go, and giving away the rest to those who need it more than I do. But can I do this? Can I?

3:30 P.M. Just before noon, I went out into the driving cold to get my clothes from the laundry room. I sorted and folded them and put them in two small black plastic bags I found in the trash closet to the right of my room. How simple one's needs, really, when you think about it. Clean clothes, a slice of bread, a bowl of soup, a cup of coffee. The dining hall is busy today with the comings and goings of our group—the Veterans—plus our twenty new retreatants. A day of small chores between meditations. I even managed to iron two shirts, one frayed about the collar after much wear, a checkered yellow-blue-and-green shirt that has grown old with me, rather like Linus's ratty blanket. The things we come to love.

Down to Chapel after lunch for my third meditation of the day, this one on the Two Standards proposed by Ignatius. Under the first standard we find Christ with his army at Jerusalem. Under the second, Satan with his army on the plains of Babylon. Thinking of these two opposing cosmic forces, I found myself making the *Triple Colloquy* again, this time asking the Blessed Mother—in the courtly language of Ignatius—for the honor of being allowed to serve under her son's standard, and to do this with the most perfect spiritual poverty, emptying myself as much as I could in order to be filled with His presence. I asked her to help me live simply and not spend on myself anything more than I needed. I also asked her to allow me to be as generous as possible with others, as Eileen has so often been, quietly, unobtrusively.

I also asked—and this was harder—for real poverty for myself, if that was His wish, remembering that God was the only one I could fully trust in such matters. Afterward, I asked Mary to help me to be more humble and know myself for who I really was, and to learn from the reproaches and injuries of others toward me, if in so doing I could better imitate her son's obedience and humility. When I'd finished, I said a Hail Mary.

Then I walked down the corridor with her to meet her son. Both were smiling at me, but as I prayed, I began breathing more and more heavily, sighing almost, my hands cupped upward and my eyes shut tight. I recited the *Anima Christi* ("Soul of Christ, sanctify me / Body of Christ, save me / Blood of Christ, inebriate me"), saying it slowly and reverently, before going with Mary and her son to present myself to the Father, where, in the great hall of the imagination, I repeated my request a third time.

But who will take care of my wife and my children? I found myself asking. And suddenly there was Jesus on the cross, and I was looking down from above him, as if from the perspective of the Father looking on His dying Son, thinking of John of the Cross's drawing of Jesus, blood and sweat striking off him, the Son's knees bent, hands helpless now, and Jesus speaking to his mother with his last strength, *Here is your son.* And to the beloved disciple—any of us who follow him—*Here is your mother.* I took the scene to mean that Eileen would be taken care of if anything should happen to me. Then I gave myself over to God's will, and my heart nearly broke. I said an Our Father and then began to come out of a kind of half-sleep. I looked around, surprised to find three others in Chapel, all deep in prayer. It was half past two. I had been praying for well over an hour, though it had seemed like only a few moments.

Several editorials today on Martin Luther King, Jr. "I have a dream," he said, and when he spoke there was a magnetism in his voice and a light in his eyes that drew us to him. Cardinal O'Connor of New York at eighty, his face bloated by the treatments he has been receiving for cancer, managing to laugh as the congregation at St. Patrick's Cathedral sang happy birthday to him. Having reached the Church's mandatory age for retirement, he wonders if anyone out in the congregation has work for him. And Russian tanks are firing into Grozny once again, round after killing round. Two worlds, then. This one, where peace covers you like a blanket, and the larger world beyond, raging as ever.

8:45 P.M. "A public service announcement," Young Fr. Joe said just before he began Mass tonight. "Be careful if you're walking out by the tall pines on the loop. There's a crack down one of them, and with these winds blowing there's no telling what might happen." And indeed it is bitterly cold out, made more intense by the howling winds, so that we prayed this evening for those who will have to suffer through the cold tonight. Some of the retreatants, I can tell from the petitions, have had firsthand experience with sheltering the homeless.

After dinner, I went back down to Chapel to meditate again on Ignatius's Three Classes of Persons. Of course it's just like Ignatius to up the ante a second, third, and fourth time, asking us now to imagine three people, each with 10,000 ducats—in short, a considerable fortune. How, he asks, shall we dispose of this wealth and get rid of the burden money brings with it? By praying, he says, for the grace to choose whatever way is more to the glory of God and will best aid us in saving our souls. Three classes, then:

1. Those who think about doing some good, but never get around to doing it.
2. Those who are sure they have a better plan than God's, and keep importuning Him to come over to *their* way of thinking, rather than trying to discern His will for them.
3. Those who want to get rid of the burdens that come with wealth, but in such a way that there's no inclination either to keep the money or to dispose of it.

Fascinating, this last category, and wiser than just handing it over to the worthy poor, as if you knew who the worthy poor were and how you would deal with giving your money away. This third class desires to keep or dispose of money solely as the Lord moves them to choose. That is, according to what they discern to be the better way to serve and praise Him. Keep things in balance, shun whatever turns you away from God, embrace whatever brings you closer to Him. You understand this intellectually. But do you understand it with the heart?

10:30 P.M. Called Eileen in Paterson and spoke in passing of how hard our youngest, John, seems to be working just now. Afterward, I returned to Chapel to meditate on the Three Classes again. But I kept thinking of him, my mind going over and over various schemes to get his debts paid off. At the same time I wondered if I should even be thinking about such things. Then, just as I was about to ask the Blessed Mother for light on this problem, I found myself in a stately dance procession, like the one in my *Magnificat* of Fra Angelico's Last Judgment. In it the saints were dressed in peppermint-striped hats and flowing gowns, holding hands in a long dance line with their guardian angels.

In the middle, Thomas Aquinas and Peter Damian were discoursing on some great theological issue, while all around them the line dance wove on. Mary was part of the line, and she was smiling at me with the same soft radiance she had blessed me with a week ago, when, holding her son, her eyes had enveloped me. In fact, all the women were beautiful, and yet all traces of lust had been beaten out of the scene. Eileen was on my left, looking as she is now, a beautiful woman in her fifties. But she was also on my right, looking as she had when we were first married. Once again, I found myself wishing I could have been a more attentive husband. And yet, somehow, all had been reconciled.

It was a dance made up of joy and sadness as we wove our way. A couple was entering a radiant gate, and we were that couple. The gate of heaven, I thought, the gate beyond which we shed our mortality. A gate radiant with God's unending love. And all the while the music played on, until at last I opened my eyes to find I'd been crying again. So this is what Purgatory must be like, I thought, a dance toward the Light, even as the wind barked against the black windows like a rifle butt and the lone candle before the Tabernacle tore at its wick, trying to escape its confines.

DAY 13: TUESDAY, JANUARY 18

5:00 A.M. Up at four, my mind racing with thoughts of how to help my son. But is this concern intruding on sacred space, the Enemy up to one of his old tricks, stealing my peace from me? Ought I even to be thinking about this now? Or is there some deeper issue with security at work here? Worse, is this another one of those control issues, where I'm going to save the day with a check? What *is* going on here? But you do know the answer to this one, after all, don't you? It's the look on your son's face that day you walked out on the family and he stared at you in utter disbelief. Well, you will just have to carry this one to your grave, won't you? Here, lie down and get some rest. You'll need it for your talk with JJ in the morning.

10:30 A.M. Up again at 7:45, feeling completely drained. What *was* this demon troubling me? And what *did* one do if one had 10,000 ducats? "I hope you're ready, JJ," I warned him as I walked into his office, "because I don't know where the hell I am right now." What was I to do about this frenzied concern with my sons and this money issue? I couldn't just throw the whole thing up, like St. Francis stripping himself naked of his father's clothes and embracing total poverty. There were, after all, responsibilities.

"Of course," he said, listening.

Was I way off track? I asked him, half-pleading.

Could these money concerns be put aside for now, he wondered, to be looked at when I got back home? What he really wanted me to think about was what was *behind* my concerns. After all, it wasn't really about money, was it?

I had to admit it probably wasn't.

What, then? A feeling of insecurity?

Yes, that. But more than that. Having control over my own destiny.

And as soon as I said it, I realized what a terrible delusion such a desire was. Losing control of one's resources meant being at the mercy of others who might take advantage of you, as they'd done when I was young. As John had been, and my other sons, when I'd walked out. Losing control was like being strapped to an oxygen tank and having someone else regulate your intake of air. I thought of my father in his forties, hard-pressed, his marriage going sour, loaded down with debts, unable often to enjoy his kids. I thought of how he seemed to suck the air from any room he entered. I told JJ of the time when I was fifteen, how my father—himself trapped by economic exigencies—had insisted I work with him at the day camp where he was foreman, and how I'd been hired on for $100 for the eight-week summer season. Twelve fifty a week for a fifty-hour week, my job to machine-wash dishes and pots and pans for 750 day campers, sweep and hose down the dining hall, wash and scrub thirty garbage cans each day. A hundred bucks for my sixteenth summer: the price agreed upon by my father. But, I thought, when they see how hard I can work, surely the bosses, with their race horses and palominos, looking for all the world like Hollywood cowpokes, would pay me a fair wage.

But when I opened my paycheck for my first two weeks' work, and found it made out for something under $25 with taxes deducted, my heart sank, and I walked out to the swings under the clump of tall pines, and wept at the injustice of it all. It was Big Stella, the heavyset Jewish-Russian cook who often showed up for work smelling of vodka, who came to my rescue then. The only one to take pity on me, the only one to open her pockets and slip me something. How much was it? Ten dollars? Twenty? I don't remember, and the amount really doesn't matter now. How often I've dropped two or three hundred and more picking up the tab for dinner for friends and family and not batted an eyelash? But at fifteen I would have walked to the ends of the earth for her, simply because she had understood. Later, when her drinking became a problem, the bosses sacked her, good as she was. But to me she was the stuff of heroes, and I sing her memory here.

And what did I learn from that episode? That I would work and work hard and make money, and come to rely solely on myself, beholden to no one. No one was going to own me. No one. But have I come, perversely, to rely *too much* on myself, and on the power and prestige I could accrue, modest self-protestations to the contrary? And is not that the demon holding me now, so that I am still more like Ignatius's second type, the one who tells God he has a better way, and that God would do well to come over to *his* way of thinking? The thick, bittersweet molasses of money. The demon of lust: that one I have come to recognize. After all, we were lovers once. Unequal, but lovers. But this greenbacked demon, lurking in the thickets there. This one has surprised me by masquerading as concern for my family.

It's the immigrant laborers—Asian, Mexican, Russian—who work long hours to better themselves I most identify with. Didn't

I work hard to get out of the world I was born into, pulling my family up after me? Give it a rest. You're where you are because others helped you get there: Fr. Hagen, who quietly paid for your schooling out of his own modest stipend because he saw you had promise. Allen Mandelbaum, your mentor, who saw a diamond in the rough and polished it. Your wife and your in-laws, who supported you. Your mother, who made sure you got the best schooling she could—or couldn't—afford. Your father, for his tenacity in holding the family together.

But how had all this impacted on my spiritual journey? I asked JJ. What were the real costs to the psyche in pushing up from under, like a dandelion in a field littered with plaster and garbage? Here I am, nearly halfway through this retreat, believing I was making some progress. I should have known the journey was not going to work that way. No use faking it. For the first time since I've been here, I see now, I can't follow Ignatius's map. It feels like driving on some deserted road far from anyone and getting stuck in quicksand, my wheels spinning wildly, with night coming on. Something in me is churning, some disconnect, disorder, whatever.

JJ looked for something in his copy of the *Exercises*. "O.K.," he said finally, "read over Mark 6:14–46. That's the passage on the two banquets. Think of it as another version of the Two Standards you've been meditating on, and see what comes of that. Mark gives us Herod's birthday banquet, which ends with the death of the Baptist. Then he turns to Jesus feeding the multitudes."

He could see I was still unsettled. "Do you think God can help you with this one?" he asked.

"I hope so," I told him as I got up to leave. But this time I was afraid. Not of some demon but of my own selfish self, unmasked now, and smirking.

11:15 A.M. I've read over Mark several times here in Chapel, linking it—as JJ suggested—with the Two Standards: Satan's and Christ's. Take the first scene: a drunken party that quickly spirals out of control, Herod himself a pawn to his own fears and weaknesses. There's his obvious drunkenness, his lust for his own stepdaughter, and all the while he's aware that his officers are watching him carefully. His wife too whom he has stolen from his brother's bed, watches him. Herodias: there's a killer for you, another Lady Macbeth, angry that this John called the Baptist, this filthy desert prophet, has named her for what she is: an adulteress sleeping with her husband's brother. Yes, they've locked him in a cell in the bowels of the palace, but he's still alive, and as long as he's alive, he's a threat.

Enter Herodias's daughter, the teenaged Salome of the supple limbs, gyrating hips and half-closed, sultry eyes. A girl/woman playing her stepfather, until he makes his drunken boast to give her whatever she asks for, even to half his kingdom. There's a swift conferral between mother and daughter, and finally the shock of the request: the head of the Baptist. One more birthday for the rich and beautiful. Herod's brain suddenly clears with the enormous finality of the request, while the others watch to see how he will respond. But he is afraid, and so the command is given, and soon after, John's head and clot of hair are brought in on a platter. . . .

Now consider Jesus, inviting his disciples, fresh from their mission work, to come with him into the hill country to rest awhile. But the crowds have spotted him out in the boat, headed for the opposite shore, and now they're following after him around the lake's edge, so that by the time the boat lands, they're waiting for him, hungry for whatever he can give them. And though he is tired, seeing the crowd, he takes pity on them and begins teaching them. When he finishes, the disciples warn him to send them away so they can find something to eat. Feed them yourselves, he tells them. And someone—is it Judas, who held the purse strings and used to help himself to the money there?—demands to know how they're going to feed so many mouths. Eight months' wages, John's version tells us, to feed them.

And then the Eucharistic moment, as Jesus gathers up the five loaves and two fishes (all the crowd could come up with), raises his eyes to the Father, divides what he has and gives it to the disciples to share as the food begins miraculously to expand to feed everyone. If there were five loaves and two fish offered, were there more, hidden in those tunics, to feed oneself, if not the others? And was part of this mystery Jesus' invitation that we share with others the gifts we have been given? After the crowds are fed, Jesus tells his disciples to head for the shore opposite, where he will meet them. Then he dismisses the crowd and goes off to be alone with his Father.

Given these two examples, how could so many of us follow the murderous ostentations of a Herod? And yet, and yet, look at the millennium celebrations all over the world, the extravagance and waste and drunkenness and greed. Look at what we spend our money on—serious money and not just loose change—and then ask me again. And where was I when the call went out for food to share? One of those who hid his loaf of bread and broiled fish inside his cloak? Or was I big enough to share the little I had so it might be multiplied a thousandfold?

1:00 P.M. I could barely taste my lunch today and left the dining hall as quickly as I could, surprised and disappointed that I seem to be making no headway with whatever is troubling me. Part of it—a major part—seems to be that beneath my *Yes* to God there seems to be lurking some deeper *No.*

6:30 P.M. All afternoon I could taste my unhappiness, thinking how interminably long this retreat was going to be if I didn't make some kind of spiritual progress. Worse, there was nothing I could do to change the situation. I was who I was, and any sense that I could really change seemed more remote than ever. Too many determining factors were operating on me—my culture, my background, my own self-bent proclivities—to ever make any real spiritual progress. If I was going to get to the next step on my journey, something a lot bigger than myself was going to have to intervene.

At last, realizing I was getting exactly nowhere, and though it was still bitterly cold outside, I put on my coat and headed down one of the paths. Deep in the woods, where the path crossed another, someone had built a snowman with a grimacing face. My sentiments exactly, I thought. Then I began praying the *Triple Colloquy,* this time asking for consolation and enlightenment as I entered the thickets of self-doubt. *Selva oscura,* I thought, Dante's dark wood.

And then it hit me: that several times in *The Divine Comedy* Dante tells us he had to be lowered or lifted to the next level of the journey if he was going to make any further progress. And suddenly I understood that my mind was incapable of bridging certain psychic and spiritual divides by logic or reason alone. That, however bright and independent I might think I was, there were certain spiritual realities I could not get at by any human ladder and so had to learn patiently to wait to be lifted by God's grace alone.

At the same time, something seemed to be leading me onward. Then, in the midst of making my petition, I found the grace simply to surrender to Him, and with that the stumbling block that all that night and most of the day had balked me quietly vanished. The assent *could* be made, and now, as the light faded in the west, I could feel myself simply, unequivocally, saying Yes to Him, no holds barred, unconditionally. I would talk to Him as a Lover and He would talk to me. I would do all in my power to keep the channels of communication open, though even here I knew from hard experience that *He* would have to give me the grace to keep me at attention. After all, I was completely dependent on Him, for He had created me and knew me far better than I knew myself.

Who was it said life is what happens to us while we're making other plans? Isn't it God that happens to us while we make other plans? The point is to merge my will with His, so that the two eyes—the two I's—make one vision. What I could not do for myself was being done for me by a God who had taken pity on me, just as He had taken pity on the crowd, feeding them simply because they were hungry.

By now I'd reached the edge of the path that leads to the ocean. I scampered up onto the boulders and walked toward the jagged edge as the Atlantic crashed against the rocks below. A lone boat was trawling slowly across the waters, struggling to make it into harbor. So there it was. I would put the money issues aside until I returned home, having decided only on this: to be as generous as I could, no questions asked. Yes, I have said to this challenge. To whom else can I turn anyway, O Lord? Who more gracious and unassuming than You?

After a while I scrambled back down the rocks, walked across the frozen field and in through the entrance facing the ocean, then down to Chapel to pray. Just before five, I walked into the Fireplace Room to prepare for Mass. Music was already playing when JJ—in stole and vestments—and a woman I did not recognize came in and sat down beside the lectern. She was attractive, blond, self-possessed, and JJ introduced her as an instructor at the Weston School of Theology. She read the First Reading, about Samuel's anointing the young David as king. Then JJ read the passage in Mark about the disciples eating the heads of wheat on the Sabbath. There was a small stand in front of the lectern, on which a bowl of wheat stalks had been placed. Then the woman got up and offered a reflection.

As soon as Mass had started, tears had begun inexplicably streaming down my face. Sitting in the front row facing twenty-five people, I kept trying to brush them away as inconspicuously as I could. But nothing could stop the flow. Then the woman began speaking of her own father, a wheat farmer from Montana, and the way he would break the heads of wheat to taste them. She spoke, too, of how Jesus kept turning things on their heads, surprising everyone around him. As Yahweh had turned things upside down by choosing young David over his older, more accomplished brothers to be king.

She spoke too of the great Jubilee Year, of turning things on their heads by asking the rich nations to forgive the debts of the poor, and asking us to forgive those who had treated us unjustly. She spoke of Mother Teresa telling us to be kind, even when others questioned our motives. To be fair and honest, even if others cheated us. To be creative, even if everything we created were broken or destroyed tomorrow. After all, this wasn't between you and them anyway, was it? This was between you and God.

Between me and God. So *there* were the words I'd been waiting for. By now the salt tears were burning my eyes. As we moved into the Main Room, I tried to compose myself, keeping my eyes shut because those around me had suddenly become very beautiful. They seemed now to be dancing some stately dance, their voices chiming in chorus, like the dancers in Fra Angelico. At Communion, I joined the stately procession as we wound our way in a double file to receive the bread and wine. "No more sorrow. No more pain," the words of a song flowed on. "Cease your silence. Come, O rain." All those layers of ice that had formed over the years in the depths of my heart were melting now, the water finding its way out through my eyes in the form of tears.

DAY 14: WEDNESDAY, JANUARY 19

5:00 A.M. The seventh day of the Second Week. Woke up an hour ago, looked at my watch, and tried to go back to sleep. But as I lay there, a voice kept saying, "Get up and talk to me." I thought of young Samuel hearing God's voice in the night, not knowing who was talking to him. And then I remembered the lines from St. John of the Cross I'd translated years ago:

One dark night,
burning with love's deep hungers,
—oh happy happy chance!—
the whole house asleep at last,
I slipped away unnoticed.

In darkness, in safety,
disguised, down a secret ladder,
—oh happy happy chance!—
hidden by darkness,
the whole house asleep at last . . .

I got up and went down to Chapel. How dark and peaceful it was there. Something was stirring within me, something like a deep love of God. But would I remain faithful in the long dry season to follow, or when my health began to go, or when I was called on to make a return for all I had been given? Would I be willing to call on Him then?

11:00 A.M. Snow was swirling out my window when I got up this morning. Gray ocean, gray sky, and still very cold. My meeting with JJ lasted only thirty-five minutes today. A record for brevity. I reviewed with him my sense of desolation yesterday, my inability to give over my cares and concerns, and then the lightening of spirit that had come late in the afternoon. He had to have seen me crying at Mass, for I was sitting ten feet from him. But if he did, he said nothing about it. If the subject was going to come up, I was going to have to bring it up, and I didn't.

Set against Satan's kingdom, I told him, how vulnerable and ineffective Christ's kingdom often seemed, like a flower Satan might trample at any time. How impregnable the lords of this world appear, one learns: the courts, the police, the military, the C.E.O.s of any number of corporations, those, in short, who hold the power. I thought, too, of those who give themselves for others, quietly and without fanfare. Mothers, fathers, teachers, doctors: all those who put their lives on the line every day. Isn't it true that both Standards—Christ's and Satan's—exist in each of us? I see now that my first instinct in meditating on the Standards had been to protect myself by refusing to take sides, to view the *Exercises* from a distance. And yet, don't we smother—finally—inside our protective armor?

Once again, JJ asked me a simple and direct question. Did I see a pattern to the day's events?

I did.

And when, he asked, had I noticed a change in my spirit?

I thought a moment. Walking in the woods in late afternoon, I said finally. When I was heading through the thickets toward the openness of the sea. Looking back, those twelve hours I had spent without Christ's consoling presence had been about as much as I could bear. And when His consolation had returned, it had touched me to the very bone. This was something new, a current of life awakening within that went far deeper than anything my poor brain could concoct.

Listen for that life, JJ advised me, though it seemed to me that what he actually wanted to say was something like, "You haven't seen anything yet, pal." Instead, he simply asked me to meditate on the Beatitudes—Matthew 5—and to think of Jesus' teachings here as the same ones Mark says Jesus taught the crowds the day he fed them. "See what sticks to you," he said. Then he directed me to read the passage in Mark 6, where, after feeding the hungry and going off to pray, Jesus walks out on the waves toward the storm-tossed boat his disciples are in.

For an hour afterward, I meditated in Chapel on the passages assigned, noting especially Jesus' insistence on getting to the heart of the Mosaic Law: to love God with your whole being, and your neighbor as yourself. *Blessed are the poor in spirit,* the passage reads in part, *the kingdom of heaven is theirs. . . . Blessed are the merciful: they shall have mercy shown them.* And since Jesus interprets my neighbor as including everyone, even my worst enemy, it's going be no easy task putting this into practice. As for the Law, Jesus seems to have been intent on raising the bar by several notches, of purifying the Law until it transfigures us, brightening even the darkest recesses of our hearts.

I'm especially struck by the image of the disciples out at sea in the middle of a storm. At night, no less. "Steady," he tells us.

"Steady, I'm here. Don't be afraid." And it's true, in retrospect, that he has always been there when I needed Him. It's only the next time I'm afraid He won't be there. And then, of course, I'll discover that He *was* there, even at the hour we fear most: our deaths, or the deaths of those we cherish.

How peaceful that July day when Ed died in that hospital room at five in the afternoon. Only fifty-two, and surely one of the most vital human beings I've ever known. A C.E.O., an ex-Marine officer, raconteur, whose love of baseball used to astonish me. A man generous to a fault, a good man, lovable, who lay there comatose, his eyes open but no longer seeing. "My Father will look after me," he'd told his daughter months earlier, as cancer ravaged his body. And when she'd said, "But, Dad, you haven't been in touch with your father in years," he'd said, "No, my Father in heaven." Help me, Lord, I'd prayed, as I shut his eyes in death while his wife and daughters looked on. Take your son. Enfold him forever in your arms.

3:45 P.M. After lunch, I took a break and drove into Gloucester for a badly needed haircut. I parked the car at Walgreens and walked across the street to Ciula's Barbershop. The place was almost too good to be true: 1950s décor, right down to the pink floor tile and green walls. Several Norman Rockwell prints decorated the walls, one—naturally—showing a barbershop quartet. A rerun of a Technicolor Western, '50s vintage, was playing on the overhead TV. Even the chairs were vintage '50s, right down to the ashtrays in the armrests, a relic from a time when customers smoked while they were shaved.

The barber: a man in his late sixties, dapper in a faded sort of way. He faced me away from the mirror, which was just as well, as my hair began piling up on the green apron he'd placed over me. Oh, I thought. Then they still exist: the old "one style fits all" barber shops. I hadn't had a haircut like this—strop razor and all—in thirty-five years, and the feeling was one of bizarre exhilaration.

Well, I resigned myself, whatever he does, it should be pretty much grown out by the time I get back home. A tonsure perfect for purposes of mortification. "Little lamb, who sheared thee," I hummed to myself, afterward, as I proceeded up Main Street. Then back to Eastern Point. The sun was already low in the western sky and Niles Pond was still frozen solid. Twenty-two degrees by the dining hall thermometer, and getting colder.

9:30 P.M. After Mass and dinner, I read in Raymond Brown's *Introduction to the New Testament,* hungry for anything more I might glean about Jesus as teacher. Matthew's Jesus, for instance, does not dispense with the Mosaic Law but instead asks for an even deeper observance that gets to the reasons why the Law was given in the first place: that we might be *perfect as your heavenly Father is perfect.*

So Jesus forbids not only adultery but even entertaining adulterous thoughts. He forbids not only murder but even rage and assaultive language. At times, he even forbids what the Law allows, like divorce and the use of oaths. Or goes counter to the Law. Love those, he says, who would harm you. He seems to clarify the Law, simplifying it, getting to the heart of the matter, to see it as God originally intended before it was qualified and reinterpreted. He speaks with more confidence than any rabbi of his time, as if he had more authority even than Moses. In fact, he presents the Law to his followers as if he were its author.

Remember, he says, it's God we are talking to when we pray, and God alone. When you give alms, don't tell others about your charity. Don't let your right hand know what your left is doing. When you fast, don't parade the fact about. Shower, shave, go about as you normally would. Prayer is something intimate, something between you and God, not you and the secret admirers you have concocted in your imagination. After all, you're not on film.

Think of how Jesus himself prayed: going off to a quiet place to be with his Father, often through the entire night. Keep your prayers short and to the point, he tells us, for the Father already knows what you need. And ask the Father not to put you to the test. *Do not send us more than we can handle, O Lord, for You know us better than we know ourselves. You know we are houses built on soft sand, forever about to collapse into the yawning ocean.* I begin to see again just how profound and deep and fresh and of a piece Jesus' teachings are. He shows us a God who would be with us always, even as the Father and the Son and the Spirit are with each other always. After all, it is *their* life they would share with us, if only we would let them.

DAY 15: THURSDAY, JANUARY 20

2:30 A.M. Day Eight of the Second Week. Up shortly after midnight, with a powerful sense of God in the room with me. So vivid was the feeling that I got up and went down to Chapel to talk with Him. Moonlight silvered the sea, the lawn, even the ice on the flanks of Brace Rock. A single light, far out at sea, brightened and dimmed. I sat there, trying to compose myself, but could not feel again what I'd experienced on first swimming back into consciousness. Nor is it mine, I realize, to evoke or call into being. Instead, what the Lord offered me now was a sense of patience, as if to say, *I will come again as I did tonight. Wait and see.* The thought was like a new and deeper sense of what was actually possible. It was like a new reality.

11:30 A.M. "I see you got a haircut," JJ said with his best poker face when I walked into his office this morning. The meeting was even briefer than yesterday's. I read him a few passages from my journal, he nodding or laughing at something I'd written. He pointed out that Raymond Brown's commentaries seem to be helping me, that they may even be a consolation. When I told him I was meditating more in my room now, rather than in Chapel, he reminded me that God was there as well. Then he gave me two new passages to meditate on. Luke 7:36–50 (another banquet scene), the one about the woman washing Christ's feet first with her tears and then with an alabaster jar of ointment. And Matthew 10:1–16, in which Jesus sends his disciples out to preach. Betweentimes, JJ added, he wanted me to consider the Three Ways of Being Humble, which Ignatius outlines in Paragraphs 165–168, praying the *Triple Colloquy* as I did so. Afterward, I spent an hour and a half in Chapel meditating on the passages and on the Three Ways of Being Humble.

2:45 P.M. I returned to my room after lunch, just as it began snowing again, to meditate on the passage from Luke on the woman who anointed Jesus' feet with the ointment. Simon the Pharisee—in whose home this event occurred—comes to the hasty conclusion that Jesus cannot be a real prophet, for, if he were, he would *know* what kind of woman is touching him. But Jesus knows what Simon is thinking, and poses him a parable and a question. *There was once a creditor, who had two men in his debt,* he begins. *One owed him five hundred denarii, the other fifty. They were unable to pay, so he let them both off. Which of them will love him more?*

And Simon: *The one who was let off more, I suppose.*

Right, Jesus tells him. And then he adds, *You see this woman? I came into your house, and you poured no water over my feet, but she has poured out her tears over my feet and wiped them away with her hair. You gave me no kiss, but she has been covering my feet with kisses ever since I came in. You did not anoint my head with oil, but she has anointed my feet with ointment.* The woman has come seeking forgiveness, and Jesus does not disappoint her. Great as her sins are, he tells her, they are forgiven, because she has shown such great love. His comment stuns the table. *Who is this,* they ask, *that he even forgives sins?* Who but God can forgive sins? But instead of responding to them, Jesus turns to the woman. *You know who I am, don't you,* he seems to say with his gaze. *And that is why you had the courage to come in here. Well, you are healed now. Go in peace.*

After my meditation, I took a nap, then went down for a cup of hot chocolate in the dining hall. Then, standing by the window looking out, the full force of Luke's story suddenly hit me. Hadn't the woman humbled herself by coming into the house of a Pharisee, looking for Jesus? And finding it impossible to speak, hadn't she knelt down with her frowsy hair, her eyes blind with tears, as the Pharisees winked and smirked or were shocked (and who knew *their* secret lives?). And hadn't she—in the only way she knew, with an outrageously generous gesture—begged Jesus to forgive her, drawn to him by some instinct, knowing he was a kind man who had helped others?

At first I had a vivid sense of myself watching the scene along with the other men and judging her. And then suddenly it all changed, and *I* was the woman kissing Jesus' feet, pleading with him for forgiveness, brokenhearted. I knew these men, these politicians and magistrates and Pharisees, knew their real worth because I was also one of them. But now my attention was all on Jesus, and I was pleading with him to help me, and he was saying, *easy, easy, yes, your sins are forgiven, go in peace,* and it was all I could do to keep from crying again right there in the dining hall. All those woman-hating jokes I used to laugh at, thinking them harmless enough. The way I have bullied women or—worse—patronized them. Forgive me, Lord, forgive my smugness and bullshit righteousness and cowardice.

6:30 P.M. Evening prayers in Chapel, along with another meditation on the Three Ways of Being Humble. Humble, as that woman had humbled herself. Then Mass at five, with a reflection by Sister Mary Boretti on now being halfway through the *Exercises,* halfway home, halfway anywhere. We all waffle, she said, we're all afraid of our own inadequacies. And so: a reminder to call on Christ when the burden seems too heavy.

A card from Fr. Jim Martin at the Jesuit-run house that publishes *America* magazine, likewise noting that I've now reached the halfway mark. "By now," he guesses, "besides meditating on God's love for you, your own sinfulness, and Jesus' ministry, you've also done the following: clambered over the rocks at the shore (and have at least *once* worried about twisting an ankle), seen a rare bird or two, complained (at least inwardly) about what the Israelites called 'this wretched food,' and have enjoyed a nice wood fire in the cleverly named 'Fireplace Room.'"

More seriously, he hopes I've met God in a new way, and that God is meeting me in a new way too. That is surely so. "If you get bored occasionally, don't worry," he adds, "everyone does. They don't call it the 'Long Retreat' for nothing." But the truth is that only once or twice so far have I felt bored. Too much is happening in the vast inner spaces for boredom to set in. Besides, a great mercy has been granted that allows me to keep writing with an ease I've seldom felt, even if the writing itself seems rather like gathering my experiences in a colander, only to see the fullness of things flow out through the gaps between the words. Even on days when nothing seems to be happening, God's presence keeps brimming over with an infinite largess. And me, with only a cup to catch it all in.

DAY 16: FRIDAY, JANUARY 21

3:30 A.M. Night, night, and night. By the time Mass got underway, it was dark. It was dark in the dining hall with the snows swirling just beyond the window, where I caught my own dark reflection. Dark too when I fell asleep at 7:00, and dark when I awoke at half past eleven. By then the snow had stopped. At midnight I meditated once more on Matthew 10: Jesus' sending his disciples out to announce the Good News that the kingdom of heaven is here. It is what I must make clear to myself and others when I return to the world.

Afterward, I went down to the Reading Room to see if I could find anything on Jesus' first followers, only to discover how little we know about any of them. I pored over their names for clues, and the etymologies of those names—Didymus (Twin), Zealot—hoping in any way I could to make Jesus' first followers more real, more personal, though I see just how thoroughly their stories have been washed away by time. A ragtag body picked up by Jesus from around Galilee, in the weeks following his baptism in the Jordan, operating for a time not far from the group of Essenes, who—convinced the religious leadership had sold out—had sought refuge in the desert.

And what did Jesus offer his disciples? He would make them fishers of men, he told them. He offered them a kingdom of love and mercy. *Go out to the surrounding towns and villages,* he said. *Take nothing with you. No money, no wallet, no sandals, not even a staff. Just the clothes on your back. When you come to a town, look for a decent human being.* He knew people. He knew there would always be someone hungry for the truth, or else why come among us at all? Stay with that person, he said, until you were ready to leave. Bless the house where you stayed. And if it turned out the townspeople didn't want you there, then leave at once, being sure to shake even the dust of the place off your sandals. *Preach the good news, cure the sick, raise the dead, cleanse those with leprosy or virulent skin diseases, drive out the devils that sowed dissension, bring peace. And since you have received all of this freely, give it away freely.*

Feed the hungry, he told Peter. *Feed my sheep.*

And now they come flocking: images of all the students over all the years I've taught. A kind of instant blur, with certain faces rising to the fore, then falling back, like the ghosts in the *Odyssey,* come to drink at the well of memory. Thirty-six years of it: literature and poetry. The faces of poets receding as others take their place in the endless round of days. That is who I went out to teach, the names of students, the names of poets who occupied the better part of my life, and now the time will not come back again. And then, just when I was counting the days to my retirement—five, four, three, two, one—a new urgency—His, I must believe—sending me to Boston College, and then here for reasons I only dimly understand. What, after all, am I being sent to do? I don't know, any more than I suppose Mary or Joseph or Jesus knew what lay ahead, except to do His will, step by tentative step. Certainly there will be a new lease on things, and something more before it's over. Your servant, Lord. A bit exhausted at the moment, thank you. But trying to stand at attention.

11:30 A.M. "Take it easy," JJ advised me this morning. "You have this intense desire to come closer to Christ. But try to see when *He* comes to *you*. Do the prayers and meditations. But leave room for Him to talk to you." I nodded. Of course. Still, as with writing, don't you have to keep your hand limber, waiting for the Muse to visit? And yet, all you can do is be watchful, like the wise virgins in the parable, not knowing when the bridegroom will come, in the meantime keeping your lamp trimmed and ready. Well, He will come in His own good time. Trust Him.

JJ asked me yet again to meditate once more on the Three Stages of Humility (doesn't he think I get it?), then gave me two more Bible passages to meditate on. The first is from Matthew 17:1–8: the Transfiguration of Christ on the mountain. The second is from Matthew 15:21–28: the story of Jesus and the Canaanite woman. After I left him, I meditated on both passages for an hour, mulling them over, worrying them, praying for light. Then it was outside to get some exercise, shoveling the new snow away from the cars. It was frigid, gelid, finger-numbing cold, and the wind bit, though by then the sun was beginning to peep through the cloud cover.

On the driveway the custodian and another man—both in coveralls—were cutting down the tall pine with the crack down its center. Slowly the chainsaw whirred and snarled, ringing the tree as the men kept checking the direction of the wind. There was, it turned out, only one direction in which the tree could fall without taking down the electric wires, hitting a station wagon parked nearby, or propping itself at a forty-five degree angle against another tree. From time to time one of the men lubricated the blades, then made another cut. Finally, as I was clearing out my third car, I sensed the imminent death throe as the pine quivered a moment, like one of Homer's soldiers before the walls of windy Troy dealt a mortal blow. Then the tree toppled, hitting the ground with a muffled thud. Goliath, the smooth stone smashing into his forehead. All that anger and posturing and brag in an instant crumpling before a shepherd boy from Bethlehem. A lesson in humility.

4:00 P.M. White caps rolling sideways, spume whipping off the tops, six or seven contrary motions occurring at the same moment, so that concentrating on one you barely catch the others. A fitting analogue for the wondrous activity of God that goes on day after day, year after year, millennium after millennium. For much of the afternoon I've been meditating on Matthew's account of the Transfiguration. First Jesus tells his disciples that the conditions for following him are self-renunciation, the taking up of one's cross. *Anyone who wants to save his life will lose it,* he warns us. *But anyone who loses his life for my sake will find it.* Then he tells them that he is destined *to go to Jerusalem and suffer grievously at the hands of the elders and chief priests and scribes and to be put to death and raised up on the third day.*

When Peter hears this, he takes Jesus aside and tells him he mustn't talk like this. Surely there's a better way. But Jesus turns on him in what must have been one of the worst moments of Peter's life. *Get behind me, Satan!* Jesus shouts at him. *You are an obstacle in my path, because you are thinking not as God thinks but as human beings do.* Not as God thinks. So—really—all those nights in prayer have given Jesus a passage to the God he calls his Father. But death? And what did he mean that he would "be put to death AND be raised up on the third day"? How? By whom?

And then, following these passages, Matthew writes:

Six days later, Jesus took with him Peter and James and his brother John and led them up a high mountain by themselves. There in their presence he was transfigured: his face shone like the sun and his clothes became as dazzling as light. And suddenly Moses and Elijah appeared to them; they were talking with him. Then Peter spoke to Jesus. "Lord," he said, "it is wonderful for us to be here; if you want me to, I will make three shelters here, one for you, one for Moses and one for Elijah." He was still speaking when suddenly a bright cloud covered them with shadow, and suddenly from the cloud came a voice which said, "This is my Son, the Beloved; he enjoys my favor. Listen to him," When they heard this, the disciples fell on their faces, overcome with fear. But Jesus came up and touched them, saying, "Stand up, do not be afraid." And when they raised their eyes they saw no one but Jesus.

I think of those Arab drivers in black Mercedes-Benzes driving us pilgrims in groups of six up Mount Tabor that June day seven years ago, taking the hairpin curves at sixty miles an hour, up to the Franciscan Church of the Transfiguration at the summit. Those retainer walls from the thousand-year-old church I saw then were here when the Crusaders were here. I imagined Jesus taking three of the apostles with him: Simon Peter—the Rock—and the two brothers, James and John. Sons of Thunder he called them, playing on their father's reputation for shouting a point.

They've come here to pray. But then, suddenly, something of Christ's full power and glory is revealed to them, enough to nearly blind them with its radiance. Is this who Jesus of Nazareth, this carpenter's son, really is? Do we understand the full impact of what happened that day? In his day-to-day activities, wonderful as they are, Jesus is a man working among men and women, proclaiming the good news, lifting our spirits. It is what most people see. But for those who follow Him, loving and serving Him, He shows himself at the most unexpected moments in all His radiance.

Then the disciples down on their faces, terrified, and Jesus standing there, alone, saying, *Stand up, do not be afraid.* And then it's back to slogging it out as Jesus descends the mountain to be one among us, curing the sick and proclaiming the Good News. We will need new eyes and new ears, a new body really, if we are to live for more than an instant with such intense light. And that, I suppose, will be in the nature of the resurrection that awaits us.

8:00 P.M. Mass at five. The First Reading told the story of Saul's searching for David to kill him and going into a cave to defecate, unaware that David's men were hiding there, ready to kill him in turn. Fr. Mark, rising to the occasion, spoke of how God's grace comes to us in all of our humanness, including our most basic functions: eating and eliminating in a great gastrointestinal cycle. A retreat, he went on, is not a place to get away from our human condition but a time to thank God for human pleasures, as well as grow in spirit from the physical discomfiture which is likewise part of our human condition.

Perhaps he was in collusion with the cook, for it was fish-and-chips again for dinner. Another letter from Eileen. Her fourth, and each one a tonic. This one was written in her room at the Holiday Inn in Saddlebrook, New Jersey. It's dated 7:30 Wednesday morning, which means she had to get up even earlier than usual to find time to write. And her with a classroom of teachers—querulous, eager, defiant—coming through the doors in another hour. She speaks of dinner plans with some of the teachers, math manipulatives with the kids, exercise and popcorn in her room for dinner the previous night. "I picture you with the wind, waves, praying, writing, zeroing in on your relations with God. Rest assured yours with me are deep and strong. I love and miss you more than I want to think about." And I you, dearest. And I you.

I've been meditating here in my room tonight on Jesus and the Canaanite woman. It's an important passage, I see, because it represents Jesus' first reaching out beyond his own people to the Gentiles. That would be like an Israeli leader today reaching out to the Palestinians and Syrians and Iraqis around him. Or vice versa. Or a Catholic Irishman reaching out to a Protestant Irishman from Belfast. Or vice versa. In this passage, Jesus heads north into the region of Tyre and Sidon to get away, only to have a Canaanite woman confront him. That's what Matthew calls her, using the older term that would have been familiar to Moses and David. A Syro-Phoenician, Mark says. Whichever, a non-Jew, an outsider, a goy. Not one of the chosen whom Jesus has come to save.

But the woman needs help. Not so much for herself but for her daughter, and she is desperate enough to humble herself for that help. At first Jesus refuses even to speak to her. But she is persistent, clamoring and begging, until finally the disciples are pleading with him to do something to get the woman off their backs. Jesus looks at them. *I'm a Jew,* he seems to say. *You're all Jews. This woman is not a Jew. Why should we help her? What do you want me to do?*

It's a brilliant strategy, really. Had he addressed her, they would have been scandalized by his talking, first, with a woman, and—second—with a Gentile. *I was sent only to the lost sheep of the House of Israel,* he tells her. But the woman pleads. *Lord,* she begs him, *help me.*

It's not fair to take the children's food and throw it to little dogs, he says again, dogs being the way Jews in Jesus' time familiarly referred to Gentiles. Perhaps the epithet "little" takes some of the sting out of the rebuff. But not much.

And then her brilliant retort: *Ah yes, Lord; but even little dogs eat the scraps that fall from their masters' table.*

And Jesus' great heart melts. *Woman,* he tells her, *you have great faith. Let your desire be granted.* A king's words to a subject. From that hour, the Gospel tells us, the daughter was well again. And if one Gentile, why not ten? And if ten, why not a hundred, a thousand, a million? Being a Gentile myself from Massachusetts, I can only thank this woman for pushing Jesus my way.

DAY 17: SATURDAY, JANUARY 22

5:00 A.M. Day Ten. In Chapel for the past hour. As I walked down the darkened corridor I was struck by a square of moonlight with crossbars outlined on the floor. And there was the moon, lifting itself above the scudding clouds, brightening the snow and trees, transfiguring the scene below with a soft silver beauty. The Transfiguration. I sat against the far wall on the floor and meditated on the scene again, imagining myself as one of the disciples—John or James, not Peter.

Christ was talking with us, when, by degrees, he seemed to become incandescent. But who could do such a thing? Who was this Jesus? And yet all I could do was be there with him. Peter went on chattering away for a minute more, trying in that way to maintain a connection between the Jesus he knew and this figure of light, even as we felt ourselves melting into insignificance. Even *we* could see that Jesus' proper company was with the great ones of the Jewish dispensation: with Moses, who had talked with God on Mount Sinai and had led his people out of slavery into the Promised land. And Elijah the prophet, come back again to join the greatest of the prophets, Jesus.

Then a radiant cloud was dropping over the mountaintop, and God was saying how pleased He was with His Son. I fell forward, my face hitting the ground, terrified. Great as the moment was, I wanted it to pass, for who could last long in this Holy of Holies? Then Jesus was touching my shoulder, and he was as before, the carpenter from Nazareth, my teacher and friend, and he was telling me not to be afraid. Afterward we descended the mountain, where the crowds were waiting for him.

Mostly—thank God—Jesus comes to me as a friend, the one who walks beside me, a fellow traveler. But there are moments in my life—as when I entered St. Peter's in Rome, or Notre Dame in Paris, or St. Paul's in London, or the great mosque on the Mount in Jerusalem, or the towering synagogue on Fifth Avenue, when I have instantly felt dwarfed by a Presence greater than myself. The Falls at Niagara have done this for thousands. Mont Blanc, the Rockies, waves crashing onto the deck of a ship caught in a storm, earth seen from the moon. And for a moment we see ourselves for what we are: insignificant creatures scurrying from here to there like ants on a summer anthill. Then, mercifully, God walks among us again as a friend and we are our old self-important selves, jabbering like children about their day.

Only now do I understand the connection between the two passages I've been meditating on: Jesus transfigured, a man from Nazareth revealed as the Son of God. And then this same Jesus, this same Son of God, fully and irrevocably rooted in the Jewish covenant, moving out beyond the confines of Israel to minister to the world beyond. He shows us—as he showed his disciples—that the God of the Jews is also the God of the entire world, as He is surely the God of the Universe.

11:15 A.M. JJ gave me two new passages to meditate on this morning. Both deal with who people thought Jesus was. Was he a prophet, a revolutionary, a madman? Was he really the Messiah? The first is from Matthew 16:13–23, where Jesus asks his disciples who *they* think he is. The second is from John 9, where the Pharisees keep asking a blind man whom Jesus has cured who the man thinks Jesus is. And, of course, the real question that has haunted these meditations since the retreat began: *Who, Paul, do you say that I am?*

One thing seems clearer now as this Second Week draws to a close. True, it has not unfolded as I thought it would. But there's no big surprise there, for the whole retreat since Day One has taken on a life of its own. Still, I *had* thought the Second Week would unscroll as biography, a step-by-step unfolding of Jesus' life from his coming among us up to his Passion and death. Instead, at each point, the central question for me, in one form or another, has been: *Who do you say I am?* How I answer that will determine—no doubt about it—how I live the rest of my life. For, if the Incarnation has indeed happened, if God did move among us as a man, that shapes everything that has subsequently happened in history and casts a new light on all that preceded His coming. More, it means that God still moves among us. "For Christ plays in ten thousand places," Hopkins has it,

Lovely in limbs, and lovely in eyes not his
To the Father through the features of men's faces.

I wouldn't be here, I tell myself, if I didn't think Christ was central to my very existence, that He is in fact the Son of God, and therefore intimately God. No, the problem—as it turns out—is who God thinks *I am.* I was sitting in the webbed rocker in the alcove between the dining hall and the Main House, facing the morning sun and the ocean and meditating on all this, when suddenly a terrifying image rolled over me like a breaker.

I had been following behind Jesus as a group of us walked down a road, flanked on either side by rough-looking soldiers. As Jesus neared them, he remained undeterred, so that they made way for him and the others. Then, to my horror, the soldiers began laughing, for they knew an imposter when they saw one. In an instant, one of them grabbed me by the hair from behind, drew his knife across my throat, and severed my windpipe. I found myself gasping for air as I swam back into waking consciousness, shaken by the image. To compose myself, I opened the Bible on my lap and immediately came across this passage from the eighth chapter of John:

In truth I tell you,
everyone who commits sin is a slave.
Now a slave has no permanent standing in the household,
But a son belongs to it forever.
So, if the Son sets you free,
you will indeed be free.

Sin, then, as slavery. Oh, I knew that one! And then, just above that passage I found this:

If you make my word your home
you will indeed be my disciples;
you will come to know the truth,
and the truth will set you free.

If I am going to be His disciple, if I am going to make God central to my life, really central, if I am ever really going to be free, I am going to have to make His Word my home. No part-time Christian stuff, no psychic bifurcation. There it is. Do you understand? Do you?

4:00 P.M. January sunshine. Twelve degrees by the thermometer outside the dining hall, a strong wind blowing. After lunch and some letters this afternoon, I put on my jacket and walked down the path that leads to the ocean. Over and over, in my mind, a soldier kept swiping a blade across my throat. At the same time, the wind was blowing so hard that I finally had to turn around. As I did so, I caught the slant sunlight shining full force on a large maple, flaring against the trunk in the shape of a brilliant cross.

As I trudged on, I noticed that someone had finished the snowman begun three days before. Three small spruce cones made up its eyes and nose, and a twig had been bent upward into a frozen grin like some whited corpse. "Dear Mother," I began pleading now, as I began another *Triple Colloquy*, "please ask your son to take me on as one of His soldiers. Ask Him to help me to do His will and accept me under His standard. Ask Him—please!—to give me the courage to stand by Him until my soldiering is finally over. Help me overcome my habitual cowardice. Help me always to remember this moment and this rock and what I asked for here." Then she and I went to speak with her son, where she pleaded while I begged Him to enlist me, asking only for the strength and courage to serve Him faithfully.

The wind was blowing even harder now as I struggled up the

rock to face the vastness of the ocean. Then I turned—with Mary and her son—toward the Father of Creation, begging Him to accept my self-offering. As I did so, I stretched out my arms, terrified of slipping or twisting an ankle, yet feeling somehow as if I were twenty again, and turned 360 degrees, to catch the great Lord at all points, asking Him to accept me. A single gull hovered above, playing the big wind, and for a moment I was one with the gull and the waves and the rocks and my God.

It is a matter of spending yourself, is it not? Of breaking yourself like bread for others. Of going among the poor, those hungry for knowledge and understanding, as you were hungry for those things and were fed, and learned in time to feed others. Students coming to you for help, a few angry with you for not giving them the grade they thought was their birthright. Some obviously disliking you. But most coming to understand that you were there to help them. Perhaps I taught them to believe in themselves, to believe they could express themselves with startling effect. And didn't most of them improve? Didn't a few transform themselves so that I shook my head in disbelief, so far beyond my own expectations had they managed to soar. They would surprise me now, I'm sure. "The most important thing we can do for another," Eileen has told me over and over, "is to pay attention." *That* at least should be within my grasp to achieve.

Who do you say that I am, Jesus asks his disciples. And Peter: *You are the Christ, the Son of the Living God.* Knowing that only the Father could have given Peter this insight, Jesus blesses him, then tells him that from this time on he is no longer Simon, but Peter, the Rock, and that on *this* Rock he will build his church. And so, with Peter's new insight comes a new life and a new identity. Jesus has seen something in Peter and praises him for what he sees. But in raising Peter to a new level of spiritual importance, he also gives him a new charge: nothing less than caring for his people. This is how God seems to work in our lives. His Word does not return to Him empty. We are here to grace others.

I am particularly struck by Jesus' sharp rebuke of Peter—*Get behind me, Satan*—coming as it does immediately after he has praised Peter. Why did Jesus turn on Peter in this way? Because, hearing Jesus say for the first time that he would have to go up to Jerusalem and suffer at the hands of the authorities and be put to death, and rise, Peter instantly comes up with a better plan. *Look here,* he tells Jesus, *we can't let this happen to you. Live and let live. Don't rock the boat. Don't butt heads with the authorities. Teach, but teach with moderation. Look how many of these people love you. You've got a long life ahead of you. Crucifixion? God forbid.*

And for a moment, Jesus is tempted. We know Jesus struggled with God's plan for him up to the moment when it crossed over from the realm of future possibility to Judas's appearing there in the garden with the enemy and the plan took on an irreversible logic of its own. But now, as Jesus looks at Peter, he realizes that it is Satan tempting him in the solicitations of his closest friend. And so he has no alternative but to shout at Peter to get out of his way. That is how powerful the temptation of longevity and peaceful coexistence has been for him.

Paragraph 325 of the *Exercises* tell us that the Enemy sometimes conducts himself like a certain kind of woman: weak when confronted by firmness, but strong and insistent in the face of our acquiescence. If you begin to lose courage in the face of strong temptation, there is no beast on the face of the earth so fierce as Satan when he is intent on destroying you. *Get behind me, Satan,* Jesus shouts at poor, startled Peter. Which must have brought *that* little tête-à-tête to an abrupt close. Poor Peter. Poor Paul.

7:30 P.M. *Who do you say that I am?* And so, a meditation this evening on Jesus as the light of the world. In John's Gospel, Jesus cures a man born blind on the Sabbath. For the authorities—out to trip him up—Jesus has broken the law by working on the day of rest. The fact—it is almost comic, really—that the blind man can see is lost in the charade of legalism that follows. Who is this Jesus? He can't be a good man, they reason, because good men don't break the Sabbath. And yet, others point out, what he has done is certainly a good deed. The parents of the blind man are brought in. How is it, the authorities want to know, that their son can see now?

But the parents are not eager to cross the authorities. *How should we know how his sight was restored?* they counter. He's an adult. Let him tell you. So the man himself is brought before them. *You know this Jesus is a sinner,* don't you, they begin, *for curing on the Sabbath?*

Maybe so, he shrugs. All he knows for certain is that he was blind, and that now he can see.

How did this imposter do it? they demand.

I've already told you, the man answers. And then, exasperated: *What do you want? To become followers of this Jesus yourselves?*

But the Pharisees are in no mood for this kind of rebuff. *Who is this Jesus? We don't know where he comes from.*

So now it is the man who has to point out the illogic of their thinking. Who else, he asks, ever restored sight to someone born blind? Only God could be behind this act. Otherwise this Jesus could do nothing.

To be preached to like this, and by a miserable sinner! And with that they throw the man out.

Who do *you* say I AM? Jesus asks each of us, providing the answer in the very question He poses: I AM. The name God gave himself when he spoke to Moses in the Burning Bush. Cured, the blind man wants no part of the authorities' sterile quibbling. Only God could have done what this Jesus did. That's enough for him, as it has been for countless millions. The rest is logic, philosophy, theological hairsplitting to the one who can suddenly, actually, *see* something.

DAY 18: SUNDAY, JANUARY 23

10:30 A.M. Sunday morning. Day Eleven of the Second Week. Up long before dawn, thinking about the nature of evil: how it infects everything if allowed to go unchecked. Then back to bed, then up again for good at half past seven, the sun shining through some low clouds off to the west. A cheery six degrees by the outside thermometer. Showered, shaved, dressed, made my bed. Then downstairs, quietly bouncing, to greet the day. French toast, sausage, bacon, juice, and coffee. Low tide and a placid sea. Devon, strolling by on his way to breakfast, smiling. Rita, over by the coffee pot, drinking a cup of coffee. Like the others, translucent in the morning light.

I told JJ about making the *Triple Colloquy* yesterday. He seemed particularly struck by what I had to say about feeding those hungry for knowledge and understanding. Of course, he pointed out, this was, in fact, my election, the direction in which I had spent and would continue to spend my life and myself: by teaching. It's the answer to the question of Election that Ignatius inserts here, late in the Second Week, and I had not as yet spent a great deal of time thinking about it other than to try to discern God's will for me.

For many young Jesuits, the Election is about the choice to remain Jesuits—as I am sure it was for young Paul. But for me the choice was made forty-two years ago, on a soccer field in Beacon, New York, when—as a seventeen-year-old postulant preparing for the priesthood—I promised God that, if I left the religious life, I would give all my professional energies to teaching. So, what can be a racking soul-searching for others making the Thirty-Day passed by for me as easily as that. Yes, I told JJ, of course. Not some new vocation, then, but a validation—quietly, without fanfare—that what I'd done had been good, good for me, good for others. I praise God once more for His gift, this chance to serve others in this way.

Two new passages for today. The raising of Lazarus in John

11:1–44, and Matthew's account of Jesus at Bethany a week before his death (26:6–13). Both events—as Ignatius understands—will lead directly to Jesus' death, and so to the close of the Second Week. As I was getting ready to leave, JJ asked me how I'd felt *after* I'd made the *Triple Colloquy,* when I'd asked to serve under Christ's Standard. I stuttered some banality, because—to tell the truth—the question took me by surprise. I'd been thinking rather of what had led up to the *Colloquy,* not so much about what had followed. But thinking back on it here in Chapel, I feel as if my request had been accepted, and that thought gives me new courage. The nagging fear I have felt about my own unworthiness is gone, and in its place there's a new buoyancy, a contentment so much a part of me I didn't know it was there until now.

1:00 P.M. Back in my room after meditating on the passages JJ gave me, doing my wash, eating lunch, and walking about the grounds. Now for the second meditation of the day on the raising of Lazarus. I've been to enough funerals to have some idea of what Lazarus's sister, Martha—that tough, lovely realist—must have felt when she went out to meet Jesus, on his way—too late, it seemed—to console her. And I think I understand better now what Martha's quiet, contemplative sister, Mary, also felt, as well as the force behind her gentle reproach to Jesus. *If only you'd been here.* The same words Martha had uttered, for both sisters must have wondered why Jesus had tarried so long while their brother lay dying. If Jesus wept, he wept in part—I feel sure—because these women wept. Having buried my own mother, I think I understand something of their sorrow.

But now, with a deep sigh, knowing that what he is about to do will lead directly to his own death, Jesus walks out to the tomb. By now Martha and Mary have resigned themselves to their brother's death. Jesus, they think, has come only to pay his respects. Instead, he orders the stone rolled away. And now it is Martha who tries to stop him. *Lord,* she gasps. *By now he will smell; this is the fourth day since he died.* And now he looks at her. *Have I not told you that, if you believe, you will see the glory of God?* Sure, she thinks. In the general raising from the dead at the end of time. But Jesus tells her:

I am the resurrection.
Anyone who believes in me, even though that person dies, will live,
and whoever lives and believes in me
will never die.

And then, looking directly at me, he asks: *Do you believe this?* I see Martha's answer must be my answer too: *Yes, Lord. I believe that you are the Christ, the Son of God, the one who was to come into the world.* And now he calls on his Father to raise Lazarus, so that *they may believe it was you who sent me.* And with that he summons his friend from the tomb, telling the bystanders to *unbind him* and *let him go free.*

And what is the reaction to the raising of Lazarus? Mary sees and believes that Jesus is, in fact, the Son of the Living God. But others report what they've seen to the authorities. A meeting is held by the chief priests and Pharisees, the gist of which is this: if they let this itinerant preacher from the north go on like this, he is going to create a schism within the Jewish community and cause a major problem between themselves and the Roman military authority.

And then what? What little political freedom they have managed to retain under the Roman military machine will be quashed altogether. Pilate will move to close the Temple and suppress *their* religious authority. Caiaphas, the chief priest, puts it even more bluntly, *Don't you understand?* he tells them. *That it is better for one man to die for the people rather than that the whole nation should perish.* He is speaking in terms of political expediency. But the Evangelist understands the deeper significance to these words: that Jesus is both the high priest *and* the Paschal sacrifice who will suffer for us all.

From that day on, John's Gospel says, the authorities were determined to shut Jesus up for good. And so Jesus is forced to leave Jerusalem again, heading north this time into the desolation of the hill country, on the edge of the wilderness. Here he will stay in the weeks leading up to early April of the year 30. When he does return to Jerusalem, it will be to celebrate the Passover meal and to die. The Lamb of God is about to become the Passover sacrifice.

6:30 P.M. White-bearded Fr. John Kerdiejus began Mass by holding up a small branch. "Once," he began, "there was a sapling that grew into a great and mighty pine. But in time it too grew old and developed a great crack down its length, and so had to be cut down. This," he said, holding up the branch, "is a branch of that tree, which I will use now to sprinkle this gathering with the life-giving waters of Baptism. Out of death, then, new life." What drama these sacramentals hold if we but think about it: a candle, water, wine, bread, a branch from a felled pine.

The first reading this evening was the story of Jonah's flight from God. At the homily, Fr. John spoke of his own difficulties in giving himself over to God, for he had been a hotdog pilot during the Second World War, flying from the deck of the carrier *Essex,* preparing for combat that (thank God, he said) never came. But something was also calling him to another life. When he finally left the Navy, he took his plane up for one last flight and put it through everything it had, then brought it in as smooth as that, and never looked back. Afterward came the call to return to school and from there the call to the Jesuits and the priesthood. Every step of the way he had had to be led, always wondering if it was the right thing for him. Well, here he was, in his seventies, still trying to figure it out. And here I am—at fifty-nine—trying to do the same.

8:00 P.M. Tonight I've come back to the anointing of Jesus' feet at Bethany, and Judas's remark that the costly ointment might better have been sold and the money given to the poor. Certainly, on the surface of it, Judas's seems a laudable-enough sentiment. Except that it was Judas who kept the purse, from which John says he used to help himself. The anointing with a nard of that price proves too much for Judas, I suppose, in the same way that people object to the building of cathedrals in a world burdened with poverty. How strange and loopy this Jesus is, attracting to himself not the powerful but the wounded, the misfits, those willing to throw away three months' wages on some extravagant, useless gesture. As for Jesus, if raising Lazarus has not convinced Judas that he is the Son of God, nothing is going to change him. Or the authorities. Perhaps not even us. But the time for trying to prove to the skeptical who he is is now past. There is only one way he is going to change our cunning, unteachable human hearts, and it will take the form of a stunning, unbearable paradox. The King will die, and die a slave's death. If words and miracles won't do it, perhaps this gesture of total immolation will serve to show his and his Father's love for us.

DAY 19: MONDAY, JANUARY 24

2:30 A.M. Up for the past hour meditating here in my room on Jesus' imminent death. I can't help but think of my mother on the phone, telling me she had lung cancer. At first I refused to follow the logic of that comment, but in time the full import of her news came home to me: that I was going to lose her. So now, with time running out, Jesus takes his small band of disciples aside to prepare them for what is coming. Neither teaching nor healing, he knows, is ultimately going to convince them who he really is. Only the sign of Jonah is left him. They will kill him, he tells them again, and then he will rise from the dead.

Mary, the contemplative one, is the first to understand that Jesus has now—irrevocably—turned his face to Jerusalem and his own death. He will go up to Jerusalem with a plan to outwit the Evil One, who has always held death as his trump card. And so she prepares him for his death. Why hold back? Did her Master hold back?

1:15 P.M. Back to bed around three, then up again at seven. JJ gave me two final readings to meditate on for this, the close of the

Second Week: Matthew 21:1–12, Jesus' entry into Jerusalem on Palm Sunday, five days before his death, and Luke 19:45–48, Jesus' preaching in the Temple in the days immediately leading up to his arrest. Afterward, I spent an hour in Chapel. Then it was Mass at 11:15, after which the second wave of Eight-Day retreatants ate together and left for home. How different to have liturgy at midmorning, with the gray light bringing out the intricate grain of the wood and suffusing everything with a sense of God's presence. How gentle the sea seems just now, and how small a community we have suddenly become. Just the Veterans, facing the sea as we eat in silence.

I sat there, thinking of Jesus moving down the narrow, steep path from Bethany and Bethphage, seated on the back of a donkey, cloaks spread beneath the donkey's feet, palm branches hacked and strewn to greet the Son of David. Many were ready to follow him, shouting hosannas to the King as he entered the great city, come to proclaim a jubilee of peace and freedom from fear. That he had a following by then seems clear from his telling two of his disciples to go into the village, where they would find a tethered donkey and a colt ready. These they were to bring back to him.

Matthew, searching the scriptures decades later for a sign that the Messiah would enter Jerusalem seated on a donkey, points to a passage in Zechariah:

Rejoice for joy, daughter of Jerusalem!
Look, your king is approaching,
vindicated and victorious,
humble, and riding on a donkey,
on a colt, the foal of a donkey . . .
He will proclaim peace to the nations.

I am gentle and humble of heart, Jesus had told his followers. And *you will find rest for your souls.* Ah, sweet, sad, poignant, comic victory. A King come to call his own, a king with a price on his head, the chief priests watching his every move now, while Roman conscripts on the ramparts of the Antonia Fortress adjacent the Temple likewise watch, as this north-country Jewish prophet steers his donkey through the cobbled streets of Jerusalem.

The raising of Lazarus, the raising of Paul. In the cold cave of death and sin, Jesus calls to me as well: "Paul, come out!" And then, "Unbind him. Let him go free." If he was willing to pay with his own life to free Lazarus, he was also willing to pay the price to unbind me from whatever makes me a slave to sin and death.

5:00 P.M. This afternoon I went for a ride as a kind of breather before I enter Jesus' suffering and death. I drove up to Good Harbor Beach, just as I had two weeks ago, got out, and crossed the wooden footbridge to the beach. A young woman jogged by, while another tossed a ball to her black-and-white cocker spaniel that kept eyeing me, wondering if I was part of the fun. "You want the ball? You want the ball?" it yelped at me in a dog language only I could understand. Two sandpipers darted, bobbing and weaving, pecking their way along the wave line.

Then up Route 127 to Rockport, five miles to the north. Old houses, some going back more than two hundred years. Rockport itself was deserted, with huge piles of snow everywhere. I stopped in Tuck's Candy Shop (*Famous Since 1929,* the sign read) and bought Eileen a pound box of mixed milk chocolate for our visit on Wednesday, and then—as a treat—some dark chocolate for myself. Across the street was the imposing Congregational Church. On the lawn, half buried in snow, a small British cannon still hunkered down, captured by the Americans after a British landing party had abandoned it during the War of 1812.

Then it was back into Gloucester to shop for a couple of ballpoint pens. On Main Street I ran into Steve Hannafin, one of the Thirty-Dayers. He'd been to the Dogtown Bookstore, he told me, and had spotted the blue-covered uncorrected proofs for my Lowell biography. "Didn't buy it, though" he added.

"Good choice," I told him, and moved on, for we're still following the rule of silence, of course. I continued walking south along Main, then north up Rogers. Driving back into East Gloucester, I turned on the radio in time to hear that the Dow had just dropped 240 points and the NASDAQ another 140. I shook my head and turned off the radio. Ah, Dame Poverty. Closer than I thought.

An ice storm is rolling up the eastern seaboard, ravaging Alabama and Georgia in its wake. It has already knocked out power to some four hundred thousand customers and is expected to hit here Wednesday, the very day I'm scheduled to see Eileen. "Snow's on the way," the saleswoman in Tuck's had said.

"How much?" I asked.

"Some say five, six inches. Some say less. Some more. Some ain't so sure."

"Sounds like my weatherman back home," I said. "Thanks for the tip."

9:30 P.M. In those final days between his triumphal entry into the city and his arrest, Jesus taught in the Temple precincts, while *the people hung on his words.* The Pharisees keep questioning him, demanding to know by whose authority he teaches. Instead, he turns to the crowd and tells them a parable about the tenants of a vineyard. The people would know from Scripture that the tenants were the religious leaders and the vineyard Israel itself. The owner of the vineyard (for which read God) sends his servants (for which read the prophets) to collect what is his. Instead, the tenants throw them out or kill them. Finally, the owner sends his own son, and the tenants kill him, thinking the vineyard will now come into their hands. And what will the owner do to those tenants? Jesus asks. He will put an end to them and give the vineyard to others. And, he adds, the stone which the builders rejected has become the cornerstone. The authorities, who also know how to read the parable, respond in horror.

They try another tack. Is it lawful to pay tribute to Caesar or not, they ask, figuring they have him whether he says no (they can then turn him over to the Roman authorities for treason), or yes, in which case he will surely alienate his own people. Show me a coin, he says, and when they do, he asks, *Whose image is this?* Caesar's, they say, and he's got them. If the coin has Caesar's image on it, it must belong to Caesar. Therefore, he adds, *Give to Cacsar what belongs to Caesar, and to God what is God's.*

They try one more time. There were seven brothers who married the same woman, one after the other, they tell him, setting up a hypothetical situation. All seven died, without producing any children. Then the woman died. To whom will she be married in the coming resurrection?

You really don't understand the resurrection, do you, Jesus tells them, unhypothetically. Marriage and childbearing belong to *this* world, he explains. In the next life, there will be no marriage. There all will live as the angels do. Stymied, the questioners leave the field to Jesus, looking for another chance to trip him up. It will not be long.

My meditations for the evening finished, I sat by the fire to rest. I saw the toppled pine had now been cut into firewood to be used once it had been seasoned. Even the branches had been stripped and piled. As the shadows flickered along the walls, I thought of the raging beast on padded feet stalking Jesus in those last days, just as he had stalked him in the wilderness. Having three times tempted him and three times failed, he had departed, to bide his time. Now I could sense his return, knowing his hour had come round at last.

THE THIRD WEEK

Suffering and Death

DAY 20: TUESDAY, JANUARY 25

3:00 A.M. Two-thirds of the way through the *Exercises*. From the time I was a teenager, I've relived the events of Christ's suffering and death. Not only during Holy Week, but throughout the year. The ten-dollar first prize I won for my poem from the Sisters up in Beacon, New York, for a poem on the Scourging. Jim Bishop's *The Day Christ Died,* the first serious hardcover I ever bought out of my own pocket. Both when I was sixteen. For two millennia so many artists and poets and writers have dealt with Christ's suffering and death that you wonder if anything new can be said about it anymore. Besides, how can words ever equal the thing itself, the terrible eloquence of sharing in Christ's suffering? St. Francis, for instance, receiving the five wounds in his body? And why should the Father have so loved us that he let His only Son—His darling boy—fall into our wretched hands?

And so begin the meditations for this darkest of the four Weeks, now, at 3:00 A.M. on a midwinter's night, in the interstices between one day and the next, then and now, between a final meal and a death, between one world ending in violence and another world about to be born. "Consider," Ignatius writes—it is the Fourth

Point for the First Contemplation at Midnight—"what Christ our Lord suffers in his human nature, or desires to suffer, according to the passage being contemplated. Then one should begin here with much effort to bring oneself to grief, sorrow, and tears." So be it, then. So be it.

The Passion: a night and a day of finalities—the Last Supper, the First Eucharist, a betrayal and an arrest, a desertion, a badly handled trial, a savage beating with whips, a mock crowning, the carrying of a cross. All ending with a man spiked to a tree, struggling to hold down the panic of suffocation as his body sagged on the wood, lungs screaming for air in a world of air.

The terrible sacrifice of the Servant of Servants of whom Isaiah spoke six centuries earlier. The price paid for the expiation of sins, for our billionfold disobedience, and the opening of the doors of friendship between God and ourselves. The debt canceled by the one the Baptist had recognized at the outset as the Lamb of God, sacrificed now at the Passover by the only one who had enough capital to pay the price: God's only Son.

It was warm enough tonight, finally, to get the storm window unstuck and open for some fresh air. I opened the Bible to chapter 13 of John—Jesus' last meal—and was stunned by a verse I've read many times before, but which struck this time with the force of revelation. At Passover, John tells us, Jesus *passed over* from this world to the next, from this present enslavement (to sin and death) into the presence of the Father and the eternal Promised Land. The Passover, *Pesach*: the passing over of the angel of the Lord to spare the firstborn of the Hebrews. Moses' passing over the Sea with his people on the way to the Promised Land of Israel.

I've read this passage over the years a hundred times, but what struck me this time was the figure of Jesus, knowing his hour had come to *pass over* from this world to the Father, *having loved those who were his in the world, loved them to the end.* So there it is: the real motive behind all Jesus had been about, revealed now at the end. He had come—like Moses before him—to free us from our fundamental slavery to sin. It is a freedom that goes deeper even than political freedom, dear as that is, for if I carry my psychological baggage with me into the Promised Land, how have I really changed?

There's the sad truth too that the Promised Land on which Moses had looked longingly in the days before his death should subsequently be ravished by Egyptians, Assyrians, Babylonians, Persians, Greeks, and by the Romans. Sad too that, by Jesus' time, the Jewish leadership should have devolved from Moses and Samuel and David to self-servers like Annas and Caiaphas. Now, in what John calls the fullness of time, the Son himself has come to do his Father's bidding. Like Moses and the prophets, he too will be rejected. Now, Satan returns in a cosmic struggle for humankind, here in Jerusalem, at the Passover, in the year 30.

That is how John sets the scene. From a political perspective, it looks like business as usual, the way states have always silenced troublemakers these past five thousand years. A troublesome prophet from the hill country of Galilee must be silenced by the Jewish authorities, and quickly, before the Romans do it for them, further eroding their already tenuous base of power. Whatever Judas had in mind in betraying Jesus, in the end he too will become a pawn of the authorities. They will plop thirty pieces of silver into his hand—the price of a slave—for his services as an informant, and then toss him aside. From their perspective, Judas is merely a pawn, a dupe, the weak link in Jesus' inner circle.

Strange, now that I think about it, that we should think more about Judas—relatively speaking—than we do about most of the apostles and disciples, who did their work, gave their lives, and subsequently disappeared from history. At every Mass, I hear the words etched into the Consecration: "On the night he was betrayed, Jesus took bread and blessed it. . . ." Judas, then, linked forever in the Mass to the Son of God. Better to have been lost to time than to be remembered in this way.

But it's also true that, in John, Jesus allows himself to be taken by the authorities. It's as if part of Jesus were watching the necessary drama of his death and our salvation unfold at the same time, himself both high priest *and* sacrificial lamb. I remember staring at a ten-penny nail once, in the midst of some carpentry job, and thinking: *what would this feel like if it were slammed through my wrist?* It was Lent, I was young, I'd heard of young men in the Philippines who allowed themselves to be spiked to a cross for a time. I picked up the nail and pushed the point against the soft skin of my wrist and flinched. There's a huge difference between meditating on the crucifixion in the relative comfort of one's room, one realizes, and actually being crucified.

And yet Christ's passion and death have been recalled so often that it is only by sheer force of the will that we can regain the underlying electric horror of what Christ did for us. But why undergo this psychic death, unless there is some deep consolation to steady me in the face of my own death and dissolution? It is *that* consolation I must try to recover, here, beginning tonight.

Having given us his magnificent cosmic perspective in the prelude, what does John follow up with? With Jesus simply getting up from dinner as any of us might, taking off his outer garment, wrapping a towel around his waist, and washing his disciples' feet. It is the lesson he wishes to pass on to us: serve others, wash their feet, their sores, care for them, love them, even when they betray you. Imagine if I were to get up after giving my best lecture in years, then took off my jacket, filled a large bowl with soapy water, and proceeded to wash the feet of my students, especially the bored ones?

Do you understand what I am asking you to do? Jesus asks his class of slow learners. *Maybe later you will understand my words, but here is what I mean. Put others first, be there for them. And remember, no act is too menial. You are to give of yourself, as I will give of myself, even—if necessary—to giving up your life. Can you do this? If not, can you at least wash the feet of those I will entrust to your care?* We have references to slaves and drudges doing this sort of menial work, but none of kings. That is, until now. It is a gesture I don't think any of the disciples ever forgot, as they undertook their own ministries in the years to come. In fact, it's a gesture that, once experienced, none of us can easily forget: nurses emptying bedpans, mothers and fathers changing soiled diapers, as I did for my children, gladly. Or secretly holding a crucifix in my clenched hand and listening to the sorrows of others. My poor mother, for instance, calling from some godforsaken motel in Syracuse in midwinter, her words slurred, static falling like snow, telling me she'd left the family again.

Consider Peter's shocked response as Jesus kneels before him, then takes his foot in his hands to begin washing it. It is too much for the man, as it would be for me. *"Wash my feet? Never."* And then Jesus looking at him, looking at me. He has something to say, and he does not have much time now to say it. *If I do not wash you, you can have no share with me in my ministry, my kingdom, my glory.* In humbling himself, isn't Jesus following the lead of the Canaanite woman who humbled herself before him for her daughter's sake? Or what of that woman who washed his feet with her tears? Or Mary, who poured that Estée Lauder essence of nard over his feet?

An extravagant gesture, and one that certainly goes contrary to my overdeveloped sense of the practical, I—who used to stoop for a penny found in a parking lot. No wonder Judas objects. *But this ointment could have been sold and the money,* he says, *given to the poor.* But don't people use this argument all the time? Don't I? The thing is that the poor never see the money anyway. And besides, in another fifteen hours, Jesus' own feet will be smashed and swollen, a single spike driven first through one and then the other to save the expense of a nail.

To save the expense of a nail. Have I ever in my life made one extravagant gesture in the direction of this man, this Jesus, who poured himself out like a bottle broken at the neck to let the last drop fall for us?

5:00 A.M. Holy Thursday has always been a very special time for me, and—though I've never been able to stay up the entire night—I have wanted to spend the hours with Jesus as he goes through his last night on earth. And so, I have come down into the darkened chapel to meditate again on his washing of his friends' feet, asking for the grace to make the same gesture in my own life. I wrapped myself in a blanket there in the deserted chapel, for it was particularly cold tonight, and I could feel the cold entering deeply. I closed my eyes and thought of Jesus kneeling down to wash the feet of the others, knowing these same men would—in another two hours—desert him. And then the tears began. Such beautiful hands. Such beautiful feet. That great heart. Smashed. All smashed.

I stayed like that for some time, then got up and walked down the narrow corridor to the dining hall to get a drink of water. As I entered the hall, I caught sight of the statue of the Blessed Mother standing silently against the stone retaining wall there in the darkness, her hands extended in beseechment. To bring a son into the world and love him and raise him. For what? To die like this, like some criminal? How could she ever have given her yes to this? But then, how does any mother give her yes, knowing that her son or daughter will have to go out into this bleak and unforgiving world?

8:00 A.M. It's raining heavily now, the wind strong enough to keep pulling the storm door in the foyer open, as if some giant were tugging at it. There were only a handful of others in the dining hall when I went down at seven. I breakfasted on a single wrapped burrito that handled and tasted like plastic. For once food was the last thing on my mind.

Then back here to my room to meditate on Judas, even as Jesus shares a piece of bread with the man who is about to betray him. The story comes just before Jesus' final requests, requests that in John's Gospel turn out to be Jesus' last will and testament. He has chosen these men to reveal all he can about his Father's kingdom in words he must have hoped they—and we—could fathom. Words echoing down the ages, transforming so many of us, more or less, less or more.

Throughout the Passion, the Gospels make it clear that Jesus repeatedly evoked the Psalms. So here, now, in the upper room where he shared his last meal, it is Psalm 41 he echoes: words spoken by a man deserted by his friends, words recalling how one of David's closest associates had betrayed him. *Even my trusted friend, on whom I relied, the man who shared my table, takes advantage of me.*

One of you, he says now, *is going to betray me.* Simon looks at the beloved disciple and signs to him. Ask the Master who he means. It is the man who dips his bread into the bowl of bitter herbs with me, Jesus tells him. Bitter herbs: recalling the bitter yoke of slavery. And now Jesus dips his bread into the bowl and offers it to Judas. It is at this moment, John tells us, that Satan entered Judas's heart.

If Jesus knows anything, he knows the Enemy has been prowling about the shadows of the room and has already entered Judas. Now he tells Judas—and Satan—to depart, for he has something he must tell the others before it is too late. We know that they too, to their shame, will scramble like bleating sheep when the wolf suddenly drops into the fold. But they will recover, and they will be forgiven—as I have to believe Judas himself would have been forgiven had he sought forgiveness—and they will come at last to see what Jesus wanted of them: faithfulness to the end, even to the laying down of their lives.

9:30 A.M. "And what about the washing of your feet? Did you let Jesus do that for you?" JJ asked me this morning. An unexpected question, for which I had no ready answer for him, as yesterday I had no ready answer when he asked if I had thought of myself as Lazarus, come back from the dead. How many times has JJ surprised me by some simple question, a way of looking at some scriptural passage that had not crossed my mind? The truth is the question should have been obvious to me, but who ever accused me of seeing the obvious?

And of course what he asks me to see—gently, unobtrusively—must be the fruit of having given these *Exercises* many times over. In any event, I find myself listening hard whenever he does offer me a way into seeing something, for it usually takes me outside my intellectual self to ask the questions that really matter. Matters, I mean, of life and death. And so, here, now, in Chapel, I have tried to evoke once more the image of Jesus washing *my* feet. It was easier, of course, to think of Jesus washing Peter's feet, or anyone else's feet, for that matter. To do that takes no commitment on my part, really. But for Jesus to kneel down before me, and remove my shoes, and wash *my* feet?

When I was five, I scalded both my feet trying to take a bath in the kitchen sink and passed out with a scream as my grandmother hobbled into the bedroom to rouse my mother. The right foot—closest to the faucet—scarred a permanent angry red, and so now I winced as Jesus cradled that foot in his hands and washed it tenderly. And again my heart went out to him. Are we not all in some way broken creatures? Do we not need his tender mercies? The millionaire who loses her little girl to leukemia, the poor Indian woman who loses her little boy in a mudslide: have they not suffered irreversible losses? Shall I not weep for them both? How humbling to have someone—especially a friend—minister to you like that, especially a friend who is about to lay down his life for you. And then for you to abandon him besides. So it comes down to two choices: Either we have others serve us because we have the power. Or we serve others, not because we must, but because love calls out to us.

10:30 A.M. From this window in Mary Chapel I can see the rain turning to wet snow. It will be the devil to move. Several retreatants are sitting across from me, their eyes closed in contemplation. We are all of us, I sense, more at ease now with God, each as we have been graced, the heat overhead clicking on, then off, in one great inbreathing/outbreathing, as the great waves keep coming in, *barooom,* one after the other.

Today is the Feast of the Conversion of St. Paul. A Pharisee, a zealot for the Law, hunting down Jesus' followers. *And* my namesake. Acts tells us Paul was present at the murder of the first Christian martyr, Stephen. *Got what he deserved, the blasphemer,* Paul no doubt thought. And so he went after these Jewish adherents to the Way, and was on the road to Damascus to round up more members of the sect when he was knocked down by a light so powerful it blinded him. Blinded, that he might be given sight. Humbled, that he might rise. Afterward, he would go out into the desert as Jesus had before him and then he would come back strengthened, ready to go out to the Gentiles to bring the Good News.

Words. Page after page of this journal I've filled with words. But how can words capture what the heart feels? How can they clothe the sublimity of the naked sun? A tent of words. *Let us build three tents,* Peter muttered at the Transfiguration, dazed by Jesus' tremulous, translucent divinity. Did David really think he could house the Lord? Did he think he could ever build a temple large enough to do that? Help me, Lord, to share Your Word with others. Let my words fall gently, not like the swirling, busy snow on these waves, but rather like seed that falls on good ground.

1:45 P.M. Leftover corned beef, carrots, and cabbage for lunch. The cook's little daughter is happily, quietly, following her around, school having been cancelled because of the snow. A grace note, this child, to remind me of the larger world outside. After lunch I slept, awaking much refreshed, the room suffused in gray light. Then down to the dining hall for tea, before returning here to meditate on the next phase of the Passion. The institution of the Eucharist: Jesus' giving us Himself in the bread and wine.

John's is the only Gospel to pass over the Eucharist at the Last Supper in silence. Instead, he places that event earlier in Jesus' ministry, in Chapter 6:30–71. *I AM the bread of life,* Jesus says there: *No one who comes to me will ever hunger; no one who believes in me will ever thirst.* And again:

I AM the living bread come down from heaven.
Anyone who eats this bread will live forever,
And the bread that I shall give
Is my flesh, for the life of the world.

And yet again:

Whoever eats my flesh and drinks my blood lives in me
and I live in that person.

The mind boggles before the enormity of this reality: that God should come among us daily in the form of bread and wine, should become flesh of our flesh, blood of our blood.

From the beginning, the words spoken at the Consecration of the Mass seem to have been in place. So, for instance, the phrasing Paul uses as early as A.D. 57 in his letter to the Corinthians shows that he was quoting an even older tradition. *For the tradition I received from the Lord*—he means going back to Jesus—*and also handed on to you is that on the night he was betrayed the Lord Jesus took some bread, and after he had given thanks, he broke it, and he said, "This is my body, which is for you* [or broken for you]. *Do this in remembrance of me."*

And so with the cup after supper: *"This cup is the new covenant in my blood. Whenever you drink it, do this as a memorial of me."* And Paul adds: *Whenever you eat this bread, and drink this cup, you proclaim the Lord's death until he comes.* So the Eucharist, the meal intimately linked to the Passover supper that will be celebrated the following evening, will be validated by Christ's sacrifice. It is *His* sinless humanity that redeems our fallen humanity, because he was obedient to God to the very end. And because he was, he found an escape hatch at the bottom of the abyss of death. And how shall we ever pay him back?

6:30 P.M. I feel as if I were seeing the Gospel events now through new eyes, especially with the imminent loss of this man whose life I've been following for the past three weeks. It's like a loss *and* a recovery, something in me rising through the anxieties, confusions, and losses of my first days here. Am I not in a sacred space now very different from what my watch and my calendar tell me are the hour and the day? Isn't that why JJ has asked me at what time of the day or night I've noticed the greatest changes in myself, those times when God seems to enter my world? How beautiful and peaceful it is here, despite the driving snow and rain and ice, what T. S. Eliot once called the unimaginable Zero summer, when God's time intersects with ours.

Late this afternoon the snow began turning back to freezing rain. Tomorrow's the second and last Day of Repose, and Eileen and I had planned—in spite of the presidential primary going on in New Hampshire—to meet just south of the state line for the afternoon. But when I called earlier today to firm things up, we both realized there is no way she can make it there in this weather. I told her I'd drive home after Mass tomorrow, which should give me a few hours before I have to turn around and come back. Two hours out and two back. The question is *when* to leave here without violating the spirit of the retreat. I guess I'll just have to leave that up to JJ.

I spent an hour shoveling out cars, my own among them, then helped clear the main door and side path to the wing. This is one heavy snow, no question about it, each shovelful as cumbersome to move as wet cement. After Mass, I stopped JJ and asked if I might speak with him in his office. I explained my problem and suggested three options for getting back here by 10 P.M. But his suggestion was better. Leave after Mass, sleep at home tomorrow night, and return Thursday morning by ten. I called Eileen with the good news. "We'll have a real date, won't we?" she laughed. We surely will. The only trouble for the next sixteen hours is how to keep focused on Christ's Passion and death, so contrary to this sense of Eastering expectation, the joy of seeing her again.

7:45 P.M. This evening a meditation on Jesus' prayer in the Garden of Gethsemane, asking his Father if the suffering he was about to undergo might not be waived. I can still see the church there at Gethsemane, next to the grove of fifteen hundred-year-old gnarled olive trees that face east toward Jerusalem. So: after the Last Supper, the instructions, and the institution of the Eucharist, after Judas's leaving to alert the Temple authorities, after Peter's protestations that he would remain faithful to the end, Jesus and his disciples head down the steep stone steps leading away from the city, across the Kidron Valley, to come to rest among the olive trees, along with hundreds of pilgrims in Jerusalem for the Passover.

Once in the garden, Jesus tells his disciples to rest, then goes off with Peter, James, and John—the same three who had witnessed the Transfiguration on that windswept mountain in Galilee. Stay awake, he begs them, and then goes off by himself to pray. And now, Mark's Gospel tells us, Jesus begins to experience a terror so intense it threatens to suffocate him. He throws himself on the ground and begs, *Abba, Father. Please, if you can, don't make me drink this cup.* How utterly human to fear being nailed like a crow to a barn door as a warning. But then he catches himself. There is no way out of death except *through* death. And so he bows to his fate. *Let it be,* he says, *as you—not I—would have it.*

An hour passes. Jesus gets up and goes back to the three men, only to find them sleeping. *Stay awake,* he tells them, *and pray not to be put to the test.* It is very late now—long after midnight—and most of the other pilgrims must have been asleep, with first light less than five hours away. And now Jesus looks up to see torch-lights skimming the interstices of the olive trees, and one of his own coming toward him with a mob of soldiers.

Could you not watch one hour with me? Jesus asks us, as that night he asked his disciples. One hour. Which is why so many Christians have tried to give Him that hour, in monasteries, in churches, in hospitals, in ill-attended wards. Forty years ago, and yet how vivid the memory. My father signing up himself and my brother, Walter, and me for the monthly meeting of the Nocturnal Adoration Society, an organization popular back then in so many Catholic parishes. It met in the night hours, from ten on Saturday night until six Sunday morning. Groups of men on a rotating basis kneeling in pews before the altar to keep their one-hour watch.

I was in college then, and soon Walter would be off doing his stint with the Army as a radio operator along the demilitarized zone in "peacetime" Korea. Saturdays were the one night each week I had to see Eileen, and I would get home from a movie or a dance in Richmond Hill at one in the morning in a beat-up car I was never sure would make it. And then, after an hour or two of sleep: my father, standing over my bed in the dark, twisting my toe to get me up and over to Corpus Christi for our shift.

I won't go into how I felt about being awakened, but they were not kind thoughts. Turning over and going back to bed was unthinkable, and soon, groggily, I was out in the truck with the old man and on our way across town to the yet-to-be-dismantled yellow brick church. I can still see the men in the darkened foyer, thirty or so of them. World War II vets for the most part, preparing to relieve the group already in the pews kneeling before the blessed Sacrament. *If today you hear His voice,* I hear the men intoning the ancient Psalm, *harden not your hearts.*

How touching, really, to see them lining up in the hushed darkness, hands folded, waiting their turn. Irish, Italian, and German, mostly. A way of being there to make up for the time when no one had been there for Jesus, when—the Gospel says—he had sweated drops of blood, as now the full force of evil settled over him, choking him. "Consider," Ignatius says, "how his divinity hides itself; that is, how he could destroy his enemies but does not, and how he allows his most holy humanity to suffer so cruelly." From this point on, Jesus will effectively enter a retreat mode, one of silence, a shorn lamb. He will die like any of us, as a man.

9:30 P.M. Ran into JJ in the dining hall a few minutes ago. He has given me a later appointment for Thursday morning. Obviously I want to be with Eileen, but what a strange time in the retreat to be seeing her. Better if the Third Week were over, or I had seen her at the close of the Second. Ideally that is when we should have had our Day of Repose. But we're caught—we Long Retreatants—between the progress each of us is making (not that I suppose any two of us are exactly on the same page), and the comings and goings of the Eight-Day retreatants. And so the staff has had to settle on these ten-day units. So here I am, with Jesus on trial for his life. I wonder how this is going to work, this being between two worlds, happy about seeing one friend and lover, while another (with whom I've been living for weeks now) prepares to die.

Down to Chapel this evening to meditate on Jesus' arrest, his disciples scattering as it became clear that their leader was about to be taken prisoner. Peter draws his short sword and brings it down on the high priest's servant's ear, only to hear Jesus ordering him to stop. Then Jesus turns to the authorities and demands to know why they didn't arrest him when he was teaching in the Temple before the crowds in broad daylight. Why is it they have come out only now, he asks them, in the middle of the night, to seize him like some criminal?

But they have him now, and so they take him, roped and bound, back across the Kidron Valley and up to the high priest's compound. And in a short time he is standing before the real power behind the priesthood: the old man, Annas, now in his seventies. It is he who begins the cross-examination. What, he demands of Jesus, does he have to say about these teachings of his, teachings that fly in the face of Jewish tradition? And Jesus, responding as if he still had a chance in the world: *I have spoken openly for all the world to hear. I have always taught in the synagogue and in the Temple where all the Jews meet together. I have said nothing in secret. Why ask me? Ask the people what I taught. They know what I said.*

But that would mean witnesses. That would mean a legitimate trial. And what Annas has assembled in the predawn hours is more like a kangaroo court. Then one of the guards steps up to Jesus and slaps him hard across the face. And you know, suddenly, that you are on a new page in the life of Jesus. No one up to this moment would have dared strike this man. Once—in Nazareth—a crowd had taken him to the edge of a cliff, meaning to throw him from there for his alleged blasphemies in claiming kinship with the Father. And what had he done then? Simply turned and walked through the crowd, and none had dared to stop him.

But now he has placed himself in their hands. It is the first time he has actually been slapped. But it will not be the last. It is the classic coward's gesture, and meant to please Annas. Jesus, shaking off the pain, responds, *If there is some offense in what I said, point it out. But if not, why did you hit me?* He still acts as if he expected justice from this court, as in fact he should have had every reason to. It's like calling on the police, and suddenly realizing that the police themselves are out to silence you.

For his part, Annas has heard enough. And so he sends Jesus on to his son-in-law, Caiaphas, the current high priest, who will know what to do. Peter, out in the courtyard with the guards and servants, warming himself before a fire in a brazier, sees Jesus taken across the courtyard to Caiaphas's. He catches Jesus' eye as Jesus is led away, but neither man speaks to the other. It is the last time Peter will see Jesus alive. And now a young girl, one of the high priest's servants, spots Peter. *You,* she says, *weren't you in the garden with him?* And Peter—who had sworn that he at least would never desert Jesus—absolutely, unequivocally denies ever having known the man. And suddenly a cock crows a second time.

In spite of what is going to transpire over the next twelve hours—a trial, a beating, a crucifixion, a death—is it not also true that a glorious new day, the day we call *Good* Friday—is about to break? Think of it as a birthday, the day a broken king earned a kingdom for you.

DAY 21: WEDNESDAY, JANUARY 26: SECOND DAY OF REPOSE

3:45 A.M. Up for the last hour meditating again on Jesus' trial. The high priest Caiaphas's palace before first light. The Sanhedrin, probably made up of seventy-one members, including the chief priest, has been summoned to an emergency meeting. Since the regular meeting place in the Temple complex is closed at night by order of the Romans, the Sanhedrin gathers instead in Caiaphas's quarters. It arranges itself in a semicircle to hear the evidence for and against this Jesus of Nazareth. Those for acquittal speak first, and, having spoken, may not by law speak again. Then those against acquittal speak. Then a vote is taken by head count—for or against acquittal, beginning with the youngest. A majority of two will be needed to convict.

The majority of the Sanhedrin, Matthew's Gospel makes clear, are for conviction, which means there will have to be corroborating evidence by at least two witnesses. There are witnesses, but they keep contradicting each other. Finally, two step forward to say they have heard the Nazarene say *he has the power to destroy the temple of God and in three days raise it up again.* The Gospels make it clear that Jesus had been speaking metaphorically of himself as God's temple (ah, dangerous metaphor!), and so we are reminded that he is not the only one on trial here, that those judging him are also being judged in the balance. Finally, Caiaphas himself stands up and addresses Jesus directly. *I put you on oath,* he demands, *by the living God to tell us if you are the Christ, the Messiah, the Son of God.*

Rather than maintain a silence that might save him, Jesus answers. *It is you who say it. Yes,* Jesus basically answers the high priest. *And the words have come from your own mouth.* But he is not finished yet. *You will yet see,* he says, *the Son of Man seated at the right hand of the Power and coming on the clouds of heaven.* At last Jesus abandons his strategy of the messianic secret before the authorities. "Tell no one who I am," he had repeatedly enjoined his disciples. A necessary stratagem, one sees, because the people had come to expect a political Messiah who would free them from the yoke of Roman oppression, while Jesus had come to free them from spiritual bondage. Now that he has revealed who he is, he evokes the words of the prophet Daniel and his dream of the Son of Man, the exemplar of the Holy One:

I was gazing into the visions of the night,
when I saw, coming on the clouds of heaven,
as it were a son of man.
He came to the One most venerable
and was led into his presence.
On him was conferred rule,
honor and kingship,
and all the peoples, nations and languages became his servants.
His rule is everlasting. . . .

The assertion is too much for Caiaphas, who proceeds to tear his robe. It is a gesture that reinforces what he has suspected all along: that Jesus *is* guilty of blasphemy for having called himself the Son of God. Given that Jesus is their prisoner, standing before them bound as he is, such a claim seems especially ludicrous. There will be no further need of witnesses. Caiaphas turns to ask the Sanhedrin for their opinion, and the overwhelming cry comes back: *the man is guilty of death.* Having judged, they have also judged themselves.

And what about me? Would I have voted for condemnation or for acquittal? For three weeks Jesus has been asking me who I think he is, and now, in Caiaphas's house, a condemned man, he turns to me again. Standing among the Sanhedrin, where push has suddenly come to shove and my own life is on the line, would my own answer have been Peter's: *I don't know the man?* Fear. Isn't that what it comes down to? Especially now, as Jesus is turned over to the Temple guards to be roughed up. Up to now, they've been restrained by a show of legality. But now that Jesus has been condemned by the Sanhedrin, they are free to play cat and mouse with him. And so—like so many soldiers and policemen the world over for the past five thousand years—they toy with their prisoner. They blindfold him, spit in his face, and smash him with their fists, demanding that this so-called hill prophet prophesy who is hitting him now.

Remember the Church of St. Peter Gallicantu—Peter of the Cockcrow—south of the Temple complex in Jerusalem? Remember standing there one July day at the bottom of an empty cistern with the other pilgrims and staring at the ancient Greek crosses chiseled around the lip of the stone retainer fifteen feet above you? Was it not a stark reminder that this pit had been venerated at least since the fourth century, when the Emperor Constantine opened these Holy Land sites again? Here is where tradition says they held Jesus until morning, before they turned him over to Pilate. Here is where I broke down and wept to think of him alone, while Fr. Doyle recited Psalm 88, that song of utter desolation, as perhaps Jesus did that night. "In the limestone cistern," I wrote afterward,

beneath St. Peter Gallicantu
in Jerusalem, my back against
the wall, try as I might,
I could not keep from weeping.
I am a man gone down into the pit,
we listened to Fr. Doyle reading,
a man shorn of his strength,
one more among the dead,
among those You have forgotten.

And did he call upon the psalms
to warm him in his need?
The night before he died
they dragged him here to try him.
What answers he could give
lay shattered on the pavement.
Later his quizzers grew tired
and impatient. Let others try him
in the morning. Enough for now
to knot a rope across his chest
and drop him into darkness.

Hanging by his wrists, *Eli,*
he would cry out, *Eli,* and again
they would misread him, thinking
he was calling on Elijah.
As each of us will be: alone,
friends scattered to the winds.
Except for one out in the courtyard
growing cold, poised now to deny him.
Darkness, the psalmist ended.
The one companion left me.

Two evils have my people done, Jeremiah's God says. *They have forsaken me, the source of living waters; they have dug themselves cisterns, broken cisterns that hold no water.*

10:15 A.M. Slept from half past four to half past seven, and woke to stormy gray skies and towering waves. I made my bed, straightened my room, packed a small bag for the overnight home, and went down to the dining hall for coffee and breakfast. At eight, I saw JJ for half an hour, then went into the Fireplace Room to prepare for Mass at nine. As I waited, I read over today's Gospel, from Mark 4. *On one occasion,* the passage reads, *Jesus began to teach beside the lake. Such a huge crowd gathered around him that he went and sat in a boat on the water, while the crowd remained on the shore nearby.* My mind was already set on leaving right after Mass, when—out of nowhere—I had an image of Jesus standing in Peter's boat, patiently teaching about the kingdom of God to crowds hungry for the Good News.

Light was shining on the water, transforming him. I couldn't hear what he was saying, but what seemed important was the music. Fr. Frank Belcher was sitting up front in his vestments, waiting to begin Mass, when suddenly a spike was driven through Jesus' hand at the wrist, the same hand that had healed the sick and the blind and had built forms and tables and chairs and had blessed the bread and the wine. And then I was crying, caught completely by surprise by the force of my own feelings. *Please, Lord,* I begged. *Not now. Not in front of the others.* But the tears came anyway. Only at the Eucharist was I finally able to stop. And yet, how sweet they were, those tears, rinsing my heart of bitterness once again, and filling me with a new love for the man.

I thought of Ignatius weeping as he said Mass and asking the Lord—as I did now—to remove his too-human tears so that he could go on with the Mass. Ignatius says it was duty alone that called him away from those tears. Otherwise, he would gladly have stayed with the Lord like that all day. And so with me. As we left the room after Mass, Tom Wilhelm, who had been sitting on my right, put his hand on my shoulder to comfort me. I have stopped trying to guess *when* these moments of consolation will come and am just grateful that they do come. They will keep me warm, I think, against the cold in the coming months and years, when I will need their comfort.

10:00 P.M. I'm here in my study at home writing in my journal while Eileen watches a bit of TV. It's not easy making the shift from the spiritual drama of Christ's Passion to this domestic scene, and there's no doubt I feel strangely torn by the situation. Thank God Eileen understands where I am in all this. It took two hours to get here, with snow all along the shoulders of Route 2, the piles growing higher and higher the closer to home I got. It turns out to have been the heaviest snowstorm of the year by far. My neighbor had plowed our driveway during the night, but several inches of new snow had fallen since, and the two feet of snow on the walks had yet to be touched. Eileen was out when I got here, having gone food shopping once the snow had stopped, and I followed her boot tracks down the path like some ghost presence. How good to be home, to find the house still standing in good shape, filled with thirty years of memories.

I was shoveling a path when she returned and together we brought in the groceries. Then we had some of her delicious lentil stew and some twelve-grain bread, and talked about the retreat, where it was going, how the boys were, her parents, my father, our friends. Afterward, I did some bank business at my desk and answered as briefly as possible the most pressing of the emails I found stacked on my computer, explaining that I would get back to everyone just as soon as the retreat was over. At six we had a quiet dinner—pasta and wine—by candlelight, talking about the things wives and husbands, if they are fortunate, talk about.

DAY 22: THURSDAY, JANUARY 27

4:30 P.M. Fell asleep watching television with Eileen. She stayed up to find out what had happened to a propane truck that had jackknifed and flipped on its side on I-91, closing the Interstate for five hours. A woman—one car of the thousands that had to be rerouted—was interviewed on the news as saying she'd driven up from New York to Vermont to ski. And now this. "Where the hell *are* we anyway?" she wanted to know. It's one of those questions I find myself asking myself every day now.

Even though I thought I would sleep through the night now that I was back in my own bed, I found myself wide awake at three in the morning, the image of Jesus before Pilate hovering over me, making his imperious presence felt in Jerusalem during the combustible high holy days. Down in the dark kitchen, a glass of orange juice in my hand, I caught the waning half moon high in the night sky, silvering the snow and outlining the maples and hemlocks behind the house. How still and quiet everything was. Time for you to get some sleep too, I told myself. You'll need it for the trip back to Eastern Point. But all I could do once I'd pulled the covers over me was lie there, thinking of Jesus abandoned, until finally, at a quarter past four, I got up and went down into the kitchen again, this time to meditate.

How terrible and yet how comforting to think of Christ's sacrifice, how it changed everything forever, so that finally I was able to go back to sleep until Eileen woke me at half past six. I promised her I'd see her for good on the 7th, kissed her good-bye, then headed back to Gloucester, arriving here in time for my meeting with JJ. He seemed particularly struck that even on my Day of Repose I should have gotten up in the middle of the night to continue my meditations. Well, he needn't have been. The Passion has become so compelling now that I have little choice but to be swept up in its vortex.

The world with its seductions is passing away, St. John's First Letter reads, *but the man who does God's will endures forever.* And yet, how quickly the grinding wheels of the world pull one back into the maelstrom, especially in the left lane of Route 95, with eighteen-wheelers and rigs spooling down the highway, big fish after smaller. "Every day," the morning prayer for today's *Magnificat* reads, "offers a choice, what sort of reading, what sort of TV, what sort of conversation, what sort of friends we will choose to welcome into our home." And so I find myself eschewing television and radio altogether and craving instead beautiful walks, beautiful music, or—even better—the very beautiful and pregnant silence of Eastern Point.

The red ball of the sun is resting now just above the tree line, casting a red-gold light over the houses on the eastern horizon. The third and final group of Eight-Day retreatants arrived in my absence, rather like raw recruits among Veterans. When this group leaves, our time, too, will be nearly over. I've been meditating much of the afternoon once again on Jesus' trial, following the events in Raymond Brown's *The Death of the Messiah.* But why, I wonder, do I keep coming back to Jesus' trial? Is it because I feel *I* am the one on trial here, rather than him? Up until now Jesus has not claimed his spiritual kingship, waiving all such titles so as not to throw off his followers into thinking his mission here is to restore an earthly kingdom in one of the most politically destabilized corners of the earth. And yet, when Pilate asks him now, on Good Friday morning, *Are you the king?* he does not deny it. Now, with his life in the balance, when silence or repudiation of the title might have saved him, he tells Pilate that, yes, he *is* in fact a king. But he also makes it clear that his is a spiritual kingdom.

His answer seems to satisfy Pilate. After all, Pilate's interest is in preserving the peace. If this Jesus claims to be king of some other place, so be it. That's not his problem. Clearly the man is no threat to the *Pax Romana.* But note this. Not only does Jesus claim now to be the Messiah, but to be David's rightful heir as King as well. The King of the Jews, Pilate will mockingly assert, insisting that the words be written above the head of Jesus as he hangs on the cross. With that mocking gesture—meant to irritate the Jewish leaders who have forced his hand—Pilate will speak truer than he knows. And in truth, Jesus *is* the only King I am willing to acknowledge.

But, if he really *is* my King, how will I respond to what he asks of me?

7:30 P.M. Young Fr. Joe gave a fine homily this evening, focusing on the First Reading: David's decision to build a fitting temple for God. I especially liked the words he gave God: *And who the hell are you, my little man, to build me—the God of the universe—a house? Better to sit still and know how much you are loved.* And so with us. Sit still and wait for God to tell you how much He loves you.

At the closing hymn, one of the new retreatants, a man in his late thirties, asked if the piano worked. Tom Wilhelm replied that that depended on whether someone could play it, and with that the guy walked over and began pounding the keys with a force I don't think it has felt in years, adding little honky-tonk jazz riffs that brought smiles to our faces. Of such unexpected grace notes are our lives here now made up. Strange too that at the Eucharist tonight, the other retreatants—including the new group—seemed to open like a bouquet of flowers before my eyes. The soft light from the candles, and the peace: how different from the traffic and jackknifed trucks out on the highways. How good, how very good, to be here and to feel His love again.

What a strange, wonderful paradox, that I should feel this consolation, even as I begin meditating on Jesus' scourging this evening. I find myself returning to the images my friend Barry Moser etched in wood for his illustrated Bible, work that consumed him for four years. I'm thinking especially of his *Ecce Homo* and of the triptych he produced for the Crucifixion. Be careful, I told him, when he began to design and illustrate the Bible, work no individual has attempted since Gustave Doré a hundred and forty years ago. This book would prove different from his illustrations for Dante's *Commedia* or *Moby Dick* or *The Wonderful Wizard of Oz* or *Alice's Adventures in Wonderland.* This book would look back hard at him even as he looked hard at it. It might even change his life. It has surely changed mine. I remember him at Pinocchio's last November, over a risotto and a decent Chianti, this man who calls himself a reprobate, breaking down even as he spoke of his hide-and-seek game with God, wanting desperately to be found, so that all Eileen and I could do was to try and comfort him. How many years is it now that he has wrestled with his God, a God who has blessed him many times over?

If I had months, years, a lifetime, I do not think I could ever reach the bottom of the mystery of the Passion. Even Raymond

Brown, for all his years of meditating on Christ's Passion and death, knew he had not exhausted the subject. After all, it is the Passion—this radical emptying of the Godhead—that welds the Mystery together and throws God's relationship with us into a totally new light.

Pilate seems to have realized that the Jewish authorities—whom he distrusted—were setting Jesus up and that the political charges against him were bogus. And yet the authorities and the crowds will force Pilate to have the prisoner beaten and then crucified. At first, when he recalls that he has the power to release a prisoner as a good-will gesture during Passover, Pilate thinks he has outwitted his adversaries. So he has Barabbas summoned from prison. This Barabbas is a bandit and a seditionist, and Acts calls him, bluntly, a killer. Choose between Barabbas and this Jesus of Nazareth, Pilate tells the crowd. Which of these two shall I set free? And, of course, the mob chooses Barabbas. No doubt *anyone* Pilate had pitted against Jesus would have gone free that day. Is there not an irony here in Jesus' buying the life of one prisoner with his own and comforting yet another as he hung on the cross?

Barabbas's real name, tradition tells us, was also Jesus. How ironic that a man who hated Roman authority, who had stirred up strife in Jerusalem which had ended in bloodshed, should be chosen over someone who thought it a matter of serious concern even to call someone a fool, much less raise a hand against him. The countryside was filled with men like Barabbas, and Jesus himself speaks of them in the story of the Good Samaritan, of a man being robbed by brigands and left to die on the side of the road. But now the crowd makes its choice. *Give us Barabbas,* the shout goes up, a shout that will resound down the ages to our own condemnation, as Barabbas mingles with the crowd, to be lost forever to history.

9:30 P.M. Pilate has one final hand to play if he is going to free Jesus. It turns out that Herod is in Jerusalem for the high holy days, so why not turn Jesus over to him? After all, isn't this Jesus a

Galilean? And doesn't Herod have jurisdiction over Galilee? And so, for the last hour, I've been meditating on Jesus standing in chains before Herod, the son of the man who had tried to kill Jesus as an infant. *That fox,* Jesus had called the younger Herod.

Herod has wanted to meet Jesus for some time, in order to see some magic trick. But now, when he questions his prisoner, Jesus refuses even to speak to him. Yet, even with that rebuke, Herod seems unwilling to condemn him. Perhaps the psychic repercussions of silencing the Baptist have made him reluctant to kill the prophet John had once heralded. Instead, he dresses Jesus up in royal robes and sends him back to Pilate. Let Pilate kill him if he wants. Let him take the consequences, if consequences there are.

History tells us that Pilate had come up against Herod earlier, perhaps when the Roman governor had placed gold shields with images of the Emperor Augustus on the walls of the Fortress Antonia overlooking the Temple. That flagrant gesture had caused a riot that had been brutally quelled, and Herod had, of course, objected to the killing of Jews. But now Pilate is willing to read Herod's gesture as meaning let bygones be bygones. A game of chess: Pilate trying to outwit the authorities, the authorities outwitting Pilate, and now—it seems—Herod, too, outwitting Pilate. And Jesus caught in the middle. How clever this Herod is. But of course he did not rule Galilee for forty years by making political mistakes. And yet he strikes me finally as one more self-serving, ineffective, uxorious fool.

DAY 23: FRIDAY, JANUARY 28

3:30 A.M. Up meditating for the last hour on Jesus before Herod. If it weren't so comical, I'd say the way I'm going through the Scriptures now is the way I went about preparing for my oral defense for the Ph.D. thirty years ago. Give it a rest, I hear myself saying, but it must be that dollop of German I get from my mother's grandmother. Herr Professor, trying to take heaven by storm. Still,

I have no other way of proceeding, except to slog it out, until I'm there, wherever *there* is.

Luke is the only one of the Evangelists to include Jesus' appearance before Herod Antipas, and he may have had the information from several converts of high rank formerly in Herod's service. When Jesus was still down at Jericho, the Pharisees, eager to please Herod by shutting this Jesus up, had come to tell him that Herod was watching him closely. The message was clear: *Get out while you still can.* Instead, Jesus tells them, *I am going, but tell the fox this: Look, I cast out demons and perform cures today and tomorrow. On the third day I will finish. But it is necessary that today and tomorrow and the next day that I go on, for it is not possible that a prophet should perish outside Jerusalem.* Now Jesus *is* in Jerusalem and under arrest. It is the "third day," and nothing Herod says or does one way or the other is going to change the fact that Jesus is about to die.

8:00 A.M. Up again at first light, some internal alarm waking me. JJ had asked me yesterday to meet with him at seven this morning, as he has an early doctor's appointment. I went over the readings and meditations with him and shared with him the frustration I felt at seeing Jesus tossed like a rag doll from place to place, no one wanting to take the heat for executing him when there was no real evidence against him and no trial. Of course Pilate is nervous, especially as the sea of faces confronting them grows more and more irrational and insistent. Get a crowd together, and there will always be someone to toss a hand grenade into the mix.

I remember the time—I was seventeen then, just a few months out of the seminary—when the guys from Mineola went out looking for the guys from New Hyde Park. Big Tommy kept looking for someone outside a bar on Jericho Turnpike, and then a very tough-looking dude came out. Tommy and the guy were sizing each other up, when suddenly some poor skinny kid from New Hyde Park stepped behind Tommy, jerking his body as if to spring, his hands opening and shutting.

Stupidly, I shouted to Tommy to look out, even though the kid was too skinny to hurt anyone. Tommy turned and hit the kid and the kid went down, his jaw broken, whimpering, balled up in a fetal position. And then what? Did Tommy and the tough guy square off? No. It was decided that one blood sacrifice was enough for the night, and now the kid could be dropped off at his house for his worried parents to look after. And what about the rest of us? Didn't we silently pile back into our cars and go home? Even Tommy didn't feel up to bragging about *that* night's work. How great the glories of the world in which the innocent are sacrificed.

10:00 A.M. After my meeting with JJ, I came back to my room to meditate on Jesus' scourging. All four Gospels relate the incident. *After having Jesus scourged,* Matthew tells us, Pilate *handed him over to be crucified.* Since Jesus was not a Roman citizen, he could be beaten until those administering the beating were exhausted. The Evangelists give short shrift to this public debasement, as if anxious to get past the horror of it, but there was a calculus for beating someone who was about to be crucified—a punishment reserved for slaves and the lowest dregs of society. Roman citizens could be scourged for the most heinous of crimes, but no more than 39 lashes could be legally administered. If the number was exceeded, the one administering the beating could be beaten in turn. It was, of course, possible to beat a man to death, but Jesus' torturers knew they had to leave him enough strength to carry the crossbeam out to the site of execution so he could die there.

The scourge they used on Jesus consisted of a series of leather thongs with a handle at one end, and pieces of bone or lead or small spikes tied to the thongs, flaring out like a squid's tentacles. The skin would have split on contact, and small pieces of muscle and flesh would be torn off, leaving the bone exposed and the skin shredded like old wallpaper. The Shroud of Turin, which some think was the cloth that covered the body of the dead Jesus, shows fifty-six lashes, back and front, which would have been administered with clockwork efficiency by two men—one apparently shorter than the other—after the victim had been roped to a short pillar. One thinks of old photos of black slaves in the United States, showing scar tissue lacing the entire back.

Matthew speaks of the "whole cohort" joining in the savage fun of seeing Jesus humiliated. I taught New York City police officers long enough to know what a few of them were capable of doing to someone they didn't like. Perhaps five hundred soldiers, inside the Praetorium, may have watched this Jew from the north country savaged. The officers of the cohort would have been made up of Romans. But the common soldiers were probably Syro-Phoenician conscripts, since Jewish males were exempted from serving in the army on religious grounds, a concession Rome had had to make to maintain some semblance of order. Many of the soldiers stationed in Rome would therefore have been traditional enemies of the Jews. If Jesus was mocked by Caiaphas's guards and by Herod's soldiers as Messiah and prophet, now he will be mocked by these soldiers as a Jew and—worse—the beaten king of his People. At last the Enemy has penetrated to the very heart of David's city. When the soldiers finish their schoolboy's play, off comes the scarlet cloak and on goes Herod's royal robe once again, as Jesus is escorted back to Pilate.

Meditating on the Passion is beginning to seem unending, and I am still only in the midst of it. At moments I feel like the figure in Edward Munch's *The Scream.* Now, for instance, when Pilate himself seems caught between two opposing forces, one representing light, the other darkness. *I've done everything but kill the man,* he almost pleads with the Jewish authorities. *I've beaten him, I've virtually castrated him. He's offered no resistance, he's broken, his followers fled at the first breath of trouble. He's a joke. Let him off with his sorry life. He'll be no more trouble to you.* But it is too late. Events have taken on a life of their own, and Satan calls for the final debasement of death.

Pilate knows an insurrectionist when he sees one, and this Jesus is no insurrectionist. Even Caiaphas must know that. All this talk of messiahs means nothing to a Roman governor. That's a problem for the Jews to work out among themselves. And besides, these Pharisees and Sadducees always seem to be at each other's throats. But now the Jewish authorities play their trump card. This Jesus, they tell Pilate, purports to be "King of the Jews." If you let him go, you will be no "Friend of Caesar." And suddenly Pilate can feel the ground shifting under his feet, especially since he is well aware that these people have already made things tough for him in Rome with the Emperor's men. *Then what shall I do with this king of yours?* he snaps back, and in the very question he loses what little power he still has over the situation. For now the terrible answer comes roaring back: *We have no king but Caesar.*

3:30 P.M. Slept from one until three. I seem to be wading now through a curious kind of death time, as if I were trudging through blackstrap molasses. The whole Passion, from the agony in the garden until Jesus' expiration, lasted fifteen or sixteen hours. But I have been going through it now night and day for seventy-two hours, and it feels as if it were going to take at least that long again before I finish. Is it that time itself is unwinding, or that I am afraid to let him go? Is that it? All I know is that, as the actual crucifixion approaches, time seems to be slowing down by the square root of itself. I realize that the Passion Narratives are structured like this, but to actually experience it is like undergoing a kind of slow strangulation.

The Gospels are essentially narratives of the Passion and death of Jesus, his teachings having been added on afterward, and the Infancy Narratives added still later. It is the suffering and death of Christ that remains at the heart of the story, one enacted over and over throughout the centuries. But they are clearly more than just stories, for they are also transformative, demanding a response from us who hear them. Since for Christians this death changed everything forever, every scene, every word, every image takes on profound significance.

So now, with the figure of Simon of Cyrene, who, happening to be coming in from the countryside as Jesus was led out, was forced by the contingent guarding Jesus to hoist the crossbeam across his own shoulders. From that chance meeting, Simon's life will never be the same again. Was he a Cyrenian, from the capital city of Cyrenaica—modern-day Libya? A Hellenized Jew in Jerusalem for the holy days? Mark tells us pointedly that he was the father of Alexander and Rufus, both well known to the Christian community in Rome when he composed his Gospel. So, apparently, at least Simon's family—if not Simon himself—was changed by his encounter with Christ, the sons later becoming leaders of the early Church. Paul greets a certain Rufus and his mother in his letter to the Jewish-Christian community in Rome, thirty years *after* the crucifixion. That one act utterly transformed a family, then, forever, and the thought consoles me. Just when I thought I was being entombed in this bed and this room, facing the eternal sea, I feel as if I were being lifted out of myself again.

9:30 P.M. Out for a walk late this afternoon, the sun low on the horizon, transforming the trees with a reddish gold glow. Mass at five, dinner, then back to my room to meditate for an hour on Jesus' being led out to his execution along the *Via Dolorosa,* the Street of Sorrows. Then Raymond Brown on the crucifixion. The *crux immissa,* the elongated plus sign of a cross with the inscription INRI—*Jesus Nazarenus, Rex Iudaeorum*—above Jesus' head. Three spikes, the absence of a seat on which to rest to keep from choking to death as the arms grew tired and the body sank in on itself, preventing the victim from sucking in air. I thought of the wine, coarse and vinegary, lifted on a sponge and forced into Jesus' mouth as he cried out how thirsty he was, thirsty not for wine but some counter-response in us, in me.

Well, Lord, I offer you myself, here, now, exhausted with it all, as my own heart breaks.

DAY 24: SATURDAY, JANUARY 29

3:00 A.M. Up for the past hour meditating on the crucifixion. Those crowds taunting Jesus . . . why don't they just let him die? Leave him with some scrap of dignity, for God's sake. Though Jesus speaks from the cross seven times, if you take all four narratives together, in Mark's unrelenting telling he speaks only once. *Eli, Eli lema sabachthani:* he cries. *My God, my God, why have you forsaken me?* The words are from Psalm 22, which I have just read again, feeling its full power for the first time in my life. *The words of my groaning do nothing to save me,* the Psalmist cries out,

> *My God, I call by day but you do not answer,*
> *at night, but I find no respite.*
>
> *Yet you, the Holy One,*
> *who make your home in the praises of Israel,*
> *in you our ancestors put their trust,*
> *they trusted and you set them free.*
> *To you they called for help and were delivered;*
> *in you they trusted and were not put to shame.*
>
> *But I am a worm, not a man,*
> *scorn of mankind, contempt of the people;*
> *all who see me jeer at me,*
> *they sneer and wag their heads.*
> *"He trusted himself to Yahweh, let Yahweh set him free!*
> *Let him deliver him, as he took such delight in him."*

11:30 A.M. Back to bed at four, waking again as the sun rose over a low bank of clouds. I looked over at the old crucifix on the wall above my desk, at the corpus with its arms extended and its head bowed, and suddenly Hopkins's words burned in me:

AND the fire that breaks from thee then, a billion
Times told lovelier, more dangerous, O my chevalier. . . .

The fire of Christ's incredible buckling, emptying himself, swooping down to lift us up.

After breakfast, I went down to Chapel to meditate again on Psalm 22, then went in to see JJ. I read him some of what I had written over the past twenty-four hours, looking for some deeper pattern among the words. "A lot of history in there," he offered. It was difficult to catch the tone of his voice. Was this an observation, or a mild criticism? Was I avoiding something I needed to look at? I asked him.

"Your reading seems to bring you closer to Christ's suffering," he answered, then began leafing through his copy of the *Exercises,* looking for something. It turned out to be Paragraph 199:

> In the colloquies we ought to converse and beg according to the subject matter; that is, in accordance with whether I find myself tempted or consoled, desire to possess one virtue or another, or to dispose myself in one way or another, or to experience sorrow or joy over the matter I am contemplating.

The wording was different in my edition, but the essential point he was after was this: *What exactly was it I was looking for as I went through the* Exercises *for the Third Week?*

"To be closer to him," I said. "To understand something of what Christ went through." But even as I spoke the words, I realized my answer left too much unaccounted for. I thought harder. "I'm going through this," I tried a second time, "in order to feel more strongly the consolations offered by the Fourth Week, when I can finally turn to the Resurrection appearances. I want to feel a lightening, a lifting up, when the ordeal of the Week is over."

He asked about the image I'd had of wading through black molasses, as if something in me was holding back. "Is he up on the cross yet, Paul?" he surprised me by asking.

The question hit a nerve. Suddenly I realized that I was afraid to let Jesus go. I was still holding back, trying to stay on this side of Jesus' death, for how could I understand what the other side of the cataclysm held for him or for myself? Instead, I deflected the question and rattled off my list of to-do things. I explained how I'd pored over Raymond Brown on the details of the crucifixion. Today I would go through Jesus' last words as he hung on the cross. Then I would let Jesus go. It was just a matter of . . .

"Sometimes you just have to be there for him," JJ broke in quietly. "The way you might for a dying friend. Sometimes that's all you can really do."

"Oh sure, Father," I interrupted, trying to explain that it was just a matter of meditating on each of the last seven words. And then suddenly I broke down, my whole body heaving, and I was crying as I had cried only once before in my life, when I had walked into the dusky funeral parlor in a working-class section of Syracuse to see my mother lying in her casket, my poor mother, with so many strikes against her, and I had broken down before the finality of it all, and then my brother-in-law, Bobby, the ex–New York City cop, was holding me, and saying *there, there,* until I could steady myself once more.

"It's O.K.," JJ was saying quietly. "Let it go." And, as the tears rolled down my face, Jesus' head tilted to one side, my mother's face flickering and merging with his, and then both were at peace. When, finally, I could compose myself, JJ mentioned that sometime during the day I might want to think of Jesus' mother, of what she must have gone through that day as well. I said I would, and again the tears came, but lighter, and I thanked him, grasping his generous hand in both of mine for seeing me through this, and I got up to leave.

"I'll be praying for you, Paul," he said.

"Please, especially today." I smiled weakly, and then I was

climbing the hall stairs back to my room. I sat on my bed, ready to change and go for a walk. But the image of Jesus dead on the cross, and of Mary looking up at her lost son, and of the detachment of soldiers who had nailed him there going about their business proved too strong. Joseph gone, and now her only son. And Jesus on the cross, saying to his disciple, *"Behold your mother,"* and then to his mother, whom he was leaving behind, *"Behold your son."* And suddenly *I* was that disciple and, for the first time in my life, I put my arm around Mary's shoulder, one more bereaved mother who had lost her son, and I was doing what I could to comfort her. But it was she, strangely, who seemed to be comforting me. I sat in my chair looking out at the ocean and wept quietly, sensing her presence and her son's, consoled by the thought.

Perhaps because of my mother's erratic ways, her drinking, her sudden departures for weeks at a time, then returning and picking up her life again, then disappearing again, I had difficulty trusting her. But now I was ready to take her in again. I sat there, in no hurry to change anything. Finally, I got up and went down to Mary Chapel to pray. Afterward, I walked down to the vestibule between the Main House and the dining room and sat in the rocker facing the sun and closed my eyes as we took Jesus down from the cross and carried his broken body to the tomb.

One of the soldiers had probed with his short lance between Jesus' ribs, pushing in, until he had broken that great, magnanimous heart to make sure Jesus was dead, and blood and water had flowed from his side. And now, because Passover was almost upon us, we—the others and myself—cleaned the body as best we could, and then lay it on the linen shroud Joseph of Arimathea had bought, and spread the herbs and ointments over the body. Then we folded the top of the linen down over Jesus' head and feet and bound him, just as Mary had wrapped her son the night she'd brought him into the world. But now her son was dead, and I took her out of the tomb, and the men rolled a great stone over the entrance to the grave, and I took her home with me. When, finally, I opened my eyes again, the sun had shifted, and it was half past eleven and—because more people were coming and going—I knew it was time to leave. *Grief is the price we pay for loving and we gladly pay the price.*

4:00 P.M. Luke has one of the thieves crucified alongside Jesus rebuke the other for mocking Jesus with the taunt, *Are you not the Christ, the Messiah? Save yourself and us as well.* But the other thief tells the man to shut up, that they are paying the price for what they've done, but that this Jesus has done nothing to deserve this death. *Jesus,* he says, *remember me when you come into your kingdom. Today,* Jesus assures him, *you will be with me in paradise.* The first to follow Jesus into his Kingdom, then, turns out to have been a dead man walking. And so the mercies begin, even as Jesus' life hangs in the balance, emptied for others.

8:30 P.M. Fr. John K. said Mass again. Tonight, he explained at the homily, he would illuminate the Gospel reading, which tells of Jesus' calming the storm at sea, by comparing it with an episode from *The Perfect Storm.* After he'd spun out at some length the story of a near shipwreck, he asked us, "So then, what is the connection you are to draw here?" Silence, while we searched for the answer. "Well, *I* certainly don't know," he said. "You figure it out." I laughed out loud, a relief after all the signs I've been daily trying to understand for the past month.

Dinner at six. Roast chicken, wild rice, mixed vegetables, salad, a brownie. Afterward, I called Eileen, who sounded very much alone. I tried to cheer her up, and she was certainly game, but it's been a long time for me to be away, especially with the dreariness of midwinter. She talked about her plans to watch the Super Bowl tomorrow night—alone, as it turns out—before she drives to Providence to teach on Monday. We made a date to talk on Tuesday evening.

Tonight begins the transition to Week Four, the movement from Good Friday to the Resurrection. Part of me wants to push on to

Easter Sunday and the risen Christ, while another part keeps reminding me that I haven't adequately mourned Jesus' death. The *Exercises* themselves suggest that I recapitulate the Passion again as a whole tonight, and yet *again* after midnight. I think I understand the dynamic here—the necessity of leaving sufficient time to understand my loss—but I don't want to stay here in the tomb. I was always the first to rush back to my routine, to something I could understand. And yet, how much of my real life have I lost adjusting some knob while the sun sets and the moon rises majestically just out of eyeshot?

I've been thinking again of what JJ said: what is it I've been looking for as I make these *Exercises*? For one thing, I've been trying to answer the question Jesus asked Peter, and now seems to be asking me. *Who do you say I am?* One thing is clear. I've been trying to do with Jesus what I've done as a biographer with the lives of others: discover who the *real* Jesus is. But the mistake is to fully equate the *real* Jesus with the *historical* Jesus, a figure who can only be recovered—like any of us—to one degree or another. It's the same problem I've faced for the past thirty years trying to reconfigure the lives of poets like Hopkins, Williams, Berryman, Lowell, and Hart Crane. Try as I might, what I have come up with in each instance has been a necessary fiction. A fiction based on all the facts I could assemble, but a fiction nevertheless.

But there's a crucial difference this time. I can try to recover the historical Jesus, but that figure will always remain open to new interpretations, new archaeological and textual information, new ways of understanding. With Jesus as with any historical figure there is always the problem of uncertainty, indeterminacy, a figure stuck together, finally, with my own words and my own faulty understanding.

And then there's that other Jesus, the Christ of the Resurrection, transformed and transforming, the one who acts upon me and remakes the questioner, the pilgrim, the seeker. It is *this* Jesus I have spent these past weeks trying to approach. Isn't it true that—at the most unexpected moments—I have been touched by this Jesus, the one who cannot be contained by a house of names any more than the Temple David wanted to build could house the Lord? I need this Jesus to touch me. I don't think I'm afraid of being touched, though I see now that I have used words as much to hide from Him as to find Him. All I can really do at this point is wait for Him to reveal Himself in His own good time.

11:00 P.M. This evening I found myself going back again to Hopkins. Not to the poetry, but to the notes he kept for what turned out to be his final retreat, just months before his death. Somehow his words are as fresh now as they were when he wrote them a century ago. Of John the Baptist he writes: "Everything about himself is weak and ineffective, he and his instruments; everything about Christ strong." But isn't he talking as much about himself here as about the Baptist? Of his own ineffectiveness, and yet of what he might still do with Christ's help? So much of his life, like mine, like Jesus', seems a failure: his ineffectiveness as a teacher, his inability to get his work accepted, his failure to make converts, his failure to interest even his closest friends in what was of such vital spiritual importance to himself. In fact, he couldn't even interest his own family in the things that were closest to him. Not one of them followed him into the faith that had transformed him. Not one.

And yet, look at the profound impact he has had on so many others in the century since his death. He made the same *Exercises* I am making now. Somehow he learned to break himself over and over that Christ might fill him with His own Life. Has he not shaped me as much as anyone has—living or dead—for forty years now? Am I not here at Eastern Point because of his example, both in his poetry and—more—by his life? What would my own work be without him? Strangely—and it is surely a great and unlooked-for consolation—I feel his presence here in this room, guiding me now, this very evening.

Breaking oneself. There's much to be said for breaking oneself for Christ and for others, isn't there? Isn't that what it's all about? Breaking our own selfish wills for others the way Christ is broken each day at Mass? Isn't this the same Jesus who comes to me each day in the form of bread, of manna, so subtly and matter-of-factly you would think nothing had changed? When indeed everything has been changed by what He did. Forever.

THE FOURTH WEEK

He Is Risen. Alleluia!

When, in your troubles, you have had recourse to those who conduct you and they have been unable to supply the appropriate remedy, God requires that you should remain in a state of entire abandonment to his good pleasure, awaiting from his goodness the help you need, after the example of the multitude of people who had followed our Lord and who waited patiently for him to supply their wants without even troubling to expose them. You may, in fact, rest assured that God will not allow you to be tried beyond your strength. It is when men are powerless that he does all, and thereby manifests his power and goodness in a striking manner. Hence, like those people who followed Christ, you must confide in God to suffer so long as he pleases, as being the best thing for you, or to be freed from your trials in the manner he will judge best, without striving to secure rest by individual efforts, which will often prove fruitless.

—St. John Baptist de la Salle

Human language falls silent before the mystery of resurrection. Only one word remains to us: Alleluia!

—The Magnificat

DAY 25: SUNDAY, JANUARY 30

5:00 A.M. Last night, having finished my meditations for the Third Week, I went down to the Reading Room to read and relax before beginning the Fourth Week. Browsing through the shelves with an eye for something different, I spotted Stephen Mitchell's *The Gospel According to Jesus Christ*. I'd read his translations of Rilke and Job and admired them, and was intrigued to see that he'd tackled the Gospels. But coming as he does from a Judeo-Buddhist perspective—as he himself says—it turns out that he ignores nearly all of the Passion Narratives and rejects the Resurrection altogether, which I take it he believes is bogus piety added to the essential Greek tragedy of Jesus' life.

What's left over when these are stripped away is a Jesus closer to the great Confucian teachers or to Socrates, a tragic teacher in the rabbinical tradition. His narrative ends with the Teacher crucified, his final words a cry of utter abandonment. End of story. It is a Jesus that fits in very much with the figure of the historicist Jesus Seminars, which reject most of what the Gospels give us—the miracles, the Transfiguration (except as hallucination, perhaps), the resurrection—dismissing these as fictions, and leaving us with a tragic figure more problematic, truncated, and spare even than the portrait Mark provides.

But if this were all that Christ was—no Infancy Narrative, the cures reported as if they were myths generated by the great unwashed, the emphasis on an ethical teacher, Mitchell, in short, picking and choosing what he wanted—what you have is Thomas Jefferson's Jesus. In other words, a rationalist Enlightenment figure, with no Church in place to help the millions on millions of pilgrims who would come after, with no place for Paul's resurrection-suffused letters, no communion of saints. A Jewish ethicist, first century C.E., silenced like Socrates when he became a threat to the authorities, his kingdom secretly of this world or none, his message ending with his death.

But the whole thrust of what Ignatius was after—and Aquinas, and Paul, and Francis, and Teresa of Avila, and the early eyewitnesses—is something else: the risen Christ, the Eastering Jesus of the Resurrection appearances in Jerusalem, Emmaus, Galilee, and—considering Paul's conversion—Damascus. Then too there is the coming of the Holy Spirit to ponder, confirming with tongues of fire and heady inspiration all that Jesus had promised while he was still with us. It is the Jesus the Church Fathers, the Church Doctors, and scholars like Hans Urs von Balthasar and Karl Rahner and Raymond Brown, among others, have given us. And it is *this* Jesus I have chosen to follow as the only one who has made sense of my own deepest spiritual experience. And so, filled with a kind of hope and yearning, I found myself rising at four, ready to begin the final Week by reading through Ignatius's directives.

"Upon awakening," Ignatius's Fourth Note for the opening of the Fourth Week reads, "I will think of the contemplation I am about to make, and endeavor to feel joyful and happy over the great joy and happiness of Christ our Lord." And again, in the Sixth Note: "I will call into my memory and think about things which bring pleasure, happiness, and spiritual joy, such as those about heavenly glory."

But am I there yet? Or still somewhere in a limbo between Weeks Three and Four, between Good Friday and Easter Sunday, in the interminable hole of Holy Saturday, with Christ dead, the suffering past, but the Resurrection merely a dim hope on the dark horizon? Ignatius lists thirteen Resurrection Appearances—he calls them Apparitions—all of which I am to meditate on in the coming week. But already I've come up against my first stumbling block: Christ's appearance to His mother, which Ignatius insists on placing first. The problem is that I have nothing in the Bible to actually turn to, since this first appearance is nowhere mentioned there, and examining the Scriptures has been my method, my ladder, since Day One of this retreat.

Ignatius foresaw this problem, of course, so that I found myself amused by his gentle chiding that, "although this [appearance] is not stated in Scripture, still it is considered as understood by the statement that 'he appeared to many others.' For Scripture supposes that we have understanding, as it is written: 'Are even you without understanding?' [Matthew 15:16]." In other words, he says, don't *you,* pilgrim, get even *this* much? Of course it makes sense that the risen Jesus would come first to his mother, the one who had so intimately collaborated with God's plan of salvation, who had given birth to him and raised him and stayed by his side to the terrible end. But how will I ever really come to understand this appearance, I, who sail so close to the shores of historical events, hardly ever venturing out into the metaphysical depths?

7:45 A.M. Down to Chapel at 5:30 to try to imagine Jesus' descent into Hell, the place of the dead, unable of their own power to enter the Kingdom of God. He came, tradition tells us, that he might lead the souls of the just—from our first parents onward—into the presence of the Father. The Harrowing of Hell we call it: so dear to the medieval mind, and rendered again and again in paintings throughout Europe. "Consider," Ignatius enjoins, "how, after Christ died on the cross, his body remained separated from his soul, but always united with his divinity. His blessed soul, also united with his divinity, descended to hell. Then, releasing the souls of the just from there, returning from the sepulcher, and rising again, he appeared in body and soul to his Blessed Mother."

I've always imagined this scene as literary fiction, and now my imagination just won't go there, no matter how hard I try. Holy Saturday, with Jesus dead, remains for me a blank, a void, an abyss, a *Nada*, the time—whatever time means to the dead—between Christ's death and burial on Friday and his Resurrection on Sunday some kind of surrealistic holding pattern, an uncomfortable gray zone to be crossed over by the living as quickly as possible. Since four I've been straining, trying to inch forward, but this time I cannot get my imagination to budge, much less soar. Historical re-enactment is one thing; fleshing out a mythic landscape is another thing altogether. How did the spirit of Jesus—his *human* dimension—re-enter that battered body lying there in the tomb? I keep sitting here, praying and waiting for something to happen, for some light on the subject, but the immensity of what I am asking—to understand the reality of what it means to rise from the dead—has been *so* great that I finally went back to my room, defeated.

I turned out the light and looked out the window. Off to the east on the horizon I caught sight of a thin magenta band, and then a sliver of hollow hornlight above that, like the band of light I used to see taking the Red-Eye from New York City to London or Rome. A new day was dawning, the winter night giving way to daybreak. I lay under the covers, my face to the wall, and saw the wall begin to glow with the sun's reflected light. Finally, I turned and looked out the window again. The band of red was getting broader and broader. More light. More light. No doubt about it. A new dawn was coming, coming from out there, beyond me, giving form and definition to everything, without any effort on my part whatsoever. "So, You're up and working," I thought, as I began to untense, and soon I was asleep. When I awoke again a few minutes ago, white light was streaming into the room, a light so intense I had to close the curtain. Even so, there was light everywhere, an eastering light where before there had been darkness. "Is this how You are going to surprise me?" I smiled, as I got up to face the day.

11:15 A.M. I read passages from my journal to JJ this morning, looking for some direction. Was I pushing things again? I asked him. "Go back to Holy Saturday," he suggested, "and talk with Mary about her memories of her son. Console her and let her console you in turn, as you might do at a wake. Let the Resurrection happen when it happens. Just talk to her and watch as her son comes to her."

"That's the problem," I told him. "There's Mary Magdalene in the garden, and when she goes to touch Him, Jesus tell her, *'Noli me tangere,'* Don't touch me." What kind of a response is that? What would he have said to his mother?

"That's a bad translation," he answered. "The Latin really means something like 'Don't squeeze me so hard. Don't keep me here.'"

Well, that makes all the difference, doesn't it? Between *hands off* and *don't squeeze me so hard*. Now, sitting here in Chapel with my Jerusalem Bible, I see that the translation I have reads: *Do not cling to me, because I have not yet ascended to the Father. But go and find my brothers, and tell them: I am ascending to my Father and your Father, to my God and your God.* So then, Jesus already *was* with the Father—body and spirit—that first Easter Sunday. Is it not true that his Ascension into heaven forty days later merely signals the end of his time here with his disciples and friends, the human afterglow, as it were, fading, to be replaced by something far more brilliant and intense: the coming of the Holy Spirit in fire?

After my session and some time in Chapel, I walked down to the basement behind the kitchen and put my laundry in one of the empty washing machines. The place was cool, dark, and suffused with a pleasant stone dankness. A few minutes later, when I came out into the light shining off the open expanse of snow-covered lawn, I could feel the day already getting warmer. For a few minutes I stood there, taking in the sound of birds calling to one another. Suddenly, my eye was drawn to the play of strong light on the huge rhododendrons across the open expanse before me.

Weirdly, the rhododendrons themselves seemed to be beckoning. I crunched across the snow-covered lawn and, just past them, found—in among the pines and maples and birches—a scattering of small images attached to crosses, each one raised on a slender metal pole. I had just stumbled onto the Stations of the Cross. I began to follow them through the softer snow, imagining I was making Christ's journey to Calvary once more with his mother. Pilate, Simon of Cyrene, Veronica, the women of Jerusalem, the squad of soldiers, Joseph of Arimathea, the entombment: I prayed at each station as I came to it. Once I'd finished, I looked back across the field and saw Mary in my mind's eye there. She was laughing and playing with her little boy, then watching him as he set off as a man to do what he had come to do, work that led to his death. And now I saw her at the foot of the cross, her son dead now, and she was weeping, and there was nothing I could do but watch, my heart heavy with the sight.

1:00 P.M. I had thought I would sail into the Resurrection appearances like a hawk on a high current, especially after the storm-crossed winds of the Third Week. But so far it has been all very tentative. To my surprise, the risen Christ has barely touched me. And yet, I've been here at Eastern Point long enough to know that He *will* show himself in His own good time. Has He not, after all, been there most when I most needed Him? And just because the map says I should be getting there does not mean I am there.

"There is," Fr. Hopkins writes in his last retreat journal, in the dog-eared pages of the paperback JJ lent me, "a happiness, hope, the anticipation of happiness hereafter." But not now, he added, not yet. It was "as if one were dazzled by a spark or star in the dark, seeing it but not seeing by it." Yes, I can understand that, for that's where I am just now. And yet, three days later, he writes that he has been granted "ever so much light on the mystery . . . and the historical interpretation of the gospel." More light, he adds, "than I can easily put down." Well, I too will just have to trust that the light will come. Still, I know in my heart that, if I am ever going to come to understand what the Resurrection means, something bigger than my puny self is going to have to lift me to get me there.

6:45 P.M. Well, it has happened! Glory be to God. At three this afternoon, after meditating on Christ's resurrection appearance to His mother for the better part of the afternoon, I dressed, put on my boots, and went out to chop ice from the paths and driveway. It didn't take long to see that I was getting nowhere with that task as well. The sun was going to have to melt this ice when it was good and ready. Just so, it struck me, nothing was going to thaw whatever inner resistance I was up against, except God, who would likewise act in His own good time.

Then, walking down the main road with the sun setting over Niles Pond, and the packed ice underfoot threatening to send me sprawling, it came to me to try saying the *Triple Colloquy* again, as Ignatius suggests we do at all important crossroads in our life. And so, turning right on to the service road that loops back to the Main House, I called on Mary to give me the courage and proper disposition to be prepared for her meeting with her risen son. What, I asked her, had that been like? What had they said to each other? Then she and I went to talk with her son.

Two local women were walking along the service road toward me from the rocks along the ocean. They were obviously out for a Sunday stroll and were talking animatedly to each other, even though there were signs everywhere reminding visitors that a silent retreat was in progress. Their talk jarred me, like people speaking back and forth at a concert, disrupting the silence I so much needed just now. As they approached, I turned sharp right and began trekking across the snow-covered field behind the kitchen until their voices faded. I found myself standing in the same place I'd stood that morning, the Stations once again before me in blue shadow. How peaceful and quiet everything was, so much so that I had the sudden urge to kneel right there and beg for God's help in getting across the deep divide I felt. What stopped me was the thought that someone would see a grown man down on his knees in six inches of snow.

Instead, I began following the Stations again, stopping at each to say a prayer. When I reached the Ninth Station—where Jesus falls for the third time—I suddenly fell to my knees with a heavy thud, as if I'd been pushed. I did not try to get up. Instead, I begged God to help me go forward with my retreat, not even sure what *forward* meant under the present circumstances. After fifteen minutes or so, I got up and walked back out onto the snow-shagged lawn and down the icy path leading to the rocks. It was there that the question hit me. What, exactly, was I trying to do anyway? *Feel* the Resurrection? "Relax," I thought. "Who do you think you are, anyway, little man? Just follow Mary's lead. Talk to her. Let her guide you. When she goes to meet her son, follow her."

And that is exactly what I did. It turned out to be a very quiet encounter between a mother and her son: a sudden glimmer of light flickering in the darkness, Mary aware that someone was in the room with her, then realizing it was Him, as if He'd just come back from a trip rather than out of the maw of death. He was not radiant, but I think this was done as a courtesy to me, for God knows I was not yet ready for anything more brilliant than this twilight world of gray. Then Mary went up to her son and held Him gently. She seemed to understand that this was how it had to be after all, that, yes, He had had to be about His Father's business of bringing the Good News to all and that He would have to die for that, and that now, on the third day, she'd found Him again, as she'd found Him twenty years before in the Temple, a boy of twelve.

It is difficult to describe the tenderness these two showed for each other, Mary kissing her son's hands, which showed the marks of the nails through the wrists. But beautiful marks now, not at all grisly, lovescapes rather, and she kissed them gently, the way a mother will kiss her child's bruised hands. And though in my mind's eye the whole scene remained muted, I understood that its real colors were gold and radiance. I was in the hands of something very large and very holy now, and I knew that I would have to be readied before my eyes and heart could fully take in what was happening to them.

9:00 P.M. Fr. Mark said Mass tonight. "Open yourself," he told us, "and let God surprise you." As with those two women this afternoon. Who were they? And where were they headed? Emmaus? I find myself paying very close attention now, listening for any small sign, a movement of any sort, for life takes us by surprise in many ways, only a handful of which ever get recorded. At dinner, for instance, an old friend of mine, Dick Onofrey, here for the Eight-Day retreat, slipping me his business card. *Used Cars,* it reads. *Land. Whiskey. Manure. Nails. Fly Swatters. Dance Lessons. Bongos. Racing Forms. Advice. Light Bulbs. Repossessed Coffins. Used Sheet Music.* Repossessed Coffins! Grace comes in all shapes, including laughter, and just then I needed a laugh to lighten things up.

This evening it was a meditation on the Second Appearance, the one recounted in Mark. Early on the morning of that first Easter, three women, all of whom had been at the cross and had prepared Jesus' body for burial, return to the tomb. Intent only on anointing the mangled body of the dead Jesus, they are discussing who will help them roll back the stone from the entrance to the grave. But when they get there, they find the stone already pushed back. Inside, they find a young man in a white robe seated opposite the slab were Jesus lay. *No need to be amazed,* the angel says, as though the dead rose every day. *You are looking for Jesus of Nazareth, who was crucified. He has risen. He is not here.* Then he tells them to tell Peter and the others to return to Galilee, where they will see him. But the women are so terrified they say nothing to anyone. How, after all, do you explain the fact of a risen Jesus?

And who were these women who witnessed the Resurrection? All were from Galilee: Mary of Magdala, from whom Jesus had expelled seven demons. Mary, the mother of Joses and Jesus' disciple James, as well as the wife of Clopas. This Mary and Clopas were part of the Christian community in Rome when Mark wrote his Gospel there. And, finally, Salome, Zebedee's wife and the mother of John and James. A good woman, but full of chutzpah, the one who had asked Jesus to let her sons sit at his right and left hands when he came into his kingdom. It was a promise, he'd told her, not his to make. Besides, he'd come to bring salvation, not dole out benefices. Now, watching what Jesus' mother had gone through, even Salome must have realized the enormous implications of what she had asked for. If the kingdom Jesus had spoken of was ever going to be realized, it was going to cost his disciples—then as now—everything. Jesus had just seen to that.

DAY 26: MONDAY, JANUARY 31

2:00 A.M. For a culture of death like our own—and like the Romans—the idea of rising from the dead would sound absurd, if it did not touch some deep wellspring in us, some hope beyond words themselves, something to say that we don't, after all, enter oblivion. I suppose, too, the sheer brutality of Jesus' death would only have reinforced the fact and finality of his end.

So what *did* happen that first Easter Sunday? Was it a passing over from death into some kind of new life? Something had obviously happened at the tomb for the terrified disciples who had scattered like sheep to begin preaching so boldly as they did, and what was at the heart of what they preached was *Jesus crucified and risen.* Every page of Paul, who witnessed the risen Christ on the road to Damascus, shines with the certitude of that vision. Back to bed now. I'll come back to this in the morning, once I've rested.

3:30 A.M. How wonderfully strange! A short Alleluia refrain, like a trickle, has been quietly, insistently, playing through my head yesterday and today, when I've swum up from sleep into consciousness. The problem, I realize now, is that I've been tuned into some other frequency. No, it's not Handel's cosmic Alleluia, but the one I heard on the old upright piano at Mass the other evening. Funny how the fact should just now register. I wonder what else—despite or because of the plethora of words the mind keeps churning up—I've managed to miss during these weeks. It's like an inkling—this music—of another reality, altogether different from philosophy or theology. Something simpler, deeper, a strain of music touching me to the marrow.

Meditating for the past hour on the Third Appearance, Matthew 28:8–10. We know some of the women who followed Jesus—His mother among them—were there at the cross, witnessing Jesus' last hours. But what of the men? Where were they? No doubt the authorities had their names from Judas or from other informers and could move against them whenever they felt it necessary. But at the moment, with their leader hanging from a cross, it wasn't. These men were no threat now. This movement would soon go the way of countless other cults. Granted, Jesus had been a threat to the status quo, but now he was dead, his movement nipped in the bud.

From the cross, Jesus had looked down to see the women standing there. So why should he not comfort them now, on the third day, for their fidelity? No doubt they would have been frightened and confused to find the tomb empty. But what indescribable joy when the reality of the Resurrection at last sank in. On at least three occasions he had told his disciples that he would have to die, and that he would rise again on the third day. Could he? Could he have risen as he'd said he would? And now—early on the morning of that third day—a figure stands before them. At first they do not understand. But then, at a single word from His lips—*Greetings*—it begins to become wonderfully, ecstatically clear, and they fall to the ground to clasp His feet. It is the gesture of the shepherds and the Magi before an infant king repeated again at the close of the Gospel. A gesture not of fear and trembling, though, but rather one of awe and joy.

And He comforts them. In His own good time He comforts them. *Do not be afraid,* He tells them, even as the divine breaks in on them, like the sun from behind a cloud. *Go, and tell my brothers that they must leave for Galilee. There they will see me.* And yet it is right there in the upper room in Jerusalem that He will appear to Peter and the others that very evening, as if He could not wait to be with them. How many appearances were there, really? Were they all recorded? From the scattered evidence it does not appear so.

8:00 A.M. I'm beginning to understand just how powerful a tool this *Triple Colloquy* is, which has got me through several difficult moments on this Thirty-Day retreat and allowed me a way of approaching the ineffable. Once again I find myself bowing before the Mystery, like a child asking his father or mother to be carried up a mountain. At this level all the ladders of logic lie toppled, sprawled on the ground. Sure, you can climb for a while, but there's always more terrain above, and at some point the footholds fall away, and then you need Him to get to the next rock face. Even to get back down again you'd have to call on Him or freefall through space. Dante had it right. Virgil first, for the lower realms we inhabit most of the time, then Beatrice for the heights. And though I'm not there yet, I can feel Mary's help in getting her difficult, balky charge up the mountain. Funny, I thought the Fourth Week was going to be downhill after the starkness of the Third Week, but the Fourth has proven harder to work with than the others. Uncharted territory, this Resurrection business. *You know, Lord, I can't fake this,* I reminded God this morning. *Neither can I, Paul,* the answer came back. *Neither can I.*

11:00 A.M. The wind is howling and the ocean seems dizzy with threat. A driving rain has been washing away much of the ice and snow all morning. JJ gave me two more Resurrection passages for today: the appearance on the road to Emmaus, and the appearance to Mary Magdalene. Praying in Chapel this morning, that strange Alleluia chorus I heard last night began coursing through my head again. What began yesterday as a tiny rivulet has become a torrent, until I finally opened my eyes to look around, wondering if anyone else could hear it. *Al-lay-loooo-yah! Al-lay-loooo-yah! Al-laaay-loo-yaaaah!* I wish I could write music. What's more, the same gray light I saw when Mary went to embrace her son was actually suffusing the chapel.

Now, back in my room, I've been meditating on Luke's account of that first Easter. Two of the women are the same: Mary Magdalene and Mary the mother of James the Younger. But in place of Salome Luke gives us Joanna, the wife of Chuza, Herod's steward. Chuza may have been the official who came to Jesus while Jesus was at Cana and begged him to return with him to Capernaum, because his son was dying, only to have Jesus tell him his son was already cured. If the boy Jesus saved from death *was* Joanna's son, it would be reason enough for her to follow Jesus. What mother would not? Now it is these women who tell the men what they have seen. But, Luke adds, *their story seemed pure nonsense, and [the men] did not believe them.*

John tells us that Peter came out of hiding to investigate the rumor for himself, taking off at a run for the tomb. And Luke makes it clear that Peter did not go off alone, for one of the disciples on the road to Emmaus will report to the stranger walking beside him that *some of our friends went to the tomb and found everything exactly as the women had reported, but of him they saw nothing.* So it was Peter and John (or the unnamed beloved disciple), or all three, who went out to investigate. Perhaps others went out during the day as well. But Peter—as leader of the group—is the one specifically named: *He bent down and looked in and saw the linen [the shroud and the wrappings] but nothing else. Then he went back home, amazed at what had happened.*

The women's message must have reached the men early. Perhaps before six that morning. Then several of the men racing to the tomb to find it empty, the burial cloths still there. Surely it must have occurred to Peter that if someone had taken the body, why would they have unwrapped it before making off with it? But who would want to make off with the body? Certainly not the Jewish authorities. Nor the Roman guards sent to make sure Jesus' body was not disturbed. And certainly not the terrified disciples.

I remember once, some twenty years ago, being at a retreat house in New Hampshire one Easter morning, Eileen and the boys still asleep in the room. We'd been up late for the Easter Vigil services the night before, but now, on this Easter morning, the sun was streaming in through a crack in the curtains, and there was a small crowd out by the old cemetery on the hill across the way. "He is risen," Fr. Pat was proclaiming as I raced up the hill toward the group, alive with expectation. "He is risen and is not here," the words echoing among the budding maples and birches as my heart swelled to bursting. And now the retreat house gone, burned as the firefighters stood by helplessly and the old Shaker buildings collapsed. Those who were there then long scattered. And yet the promise as fresh now as it was then. He is risen. Alleluia!

2:15 P.M. Reading the *Boston Globe* after lunch today, I was struck by a photo of Senator John McCain hugging a Vietnam veteran. The pain in McCain's eyes touched me as I recalled some of the Vietnam vets I've taught over the past thirty years, many of whom brought the war back home with them, and who so desperately needed to be healed. I think of one veteran in particular, an ex-student of mine, recalling a fire fight in some rice paddy on the Mekong, his friend's head instantly exploding from a rifle shell as the two of them tried to get a third—wounded—back to a helicopter. Healing. How we all need that.

4:00 P.M. Meditated in my room this afternoon on John's account of that first Easter. Then, an hour ago, I took a break and walked out around Niles Pond and then north along the main road. Much of the ice on the blacktop has been washed away by this morning's rains, and—with the temperature hitting forty—what's left is navigable slush. The pond is pocked with pools of standing water. You can see great cracks and seams running through the ice cover. Out in the middle, gulls and ducks are once again congregating. I noticed striated sunlight off to the south, playing over Boston, like something out of El Greco.

John's Gospel speaks of Mary Magdalene remaining while Peter entered the empty tomb that first Easter. After the men had looked around and then left, she stooped down to look inside and saw two figures in white sitting there, one where the head would have been, the other at the feet. *Woman,* they ask her, *why are you weeping?* Because, she says, she doesn't know where they've put the body. Then she turns and sees through her tears a stranger standing there, who asks her the same question: *Woman, why are you weeping? Who are you looking for?* Thinking this must be the gardener, she pleads, *Sir, if you have taken him away, tell me where you have put him, and I will go and remove him.*

Then the figure calls her by name. *Mary!* He says, and in that naming, she knows at once who this is, so that she cries out in astonishment. *Go, and find my brothers,* He says to her, *and tell them: I am ascending to my Father, and your Father, to my God and your God.* No retribution. Full forgiveness. Obedient onto death, He has paid the price of Redemption. Now His Father has become my Father as well, a God of love opening everything to me, in spite of my many betrayals. How will I ever understand this? How will I ever be able to repay Him? But you can't, can you? All you can do is learn to accept the fact that, yes, you are loved.

9:30 P.M. Mass at five, followed by Irish stew for dinner, one of the lesser achievements of our stellar kitchen staff. To offset that, two letters from the outside world. One from Fr. Tom Shea in Springfield—an old friend, a model for me of what the priesthood is—keeping me in his prayers while I'm on this retreat. And the other from my dear, faithful Eileen, this one written on Saturday. "For 'historic' purposes," she begins. "'How many letters *did* she send him when he was on retreat?'" The biographer's wife winking at the biographer husband she knows like a book.

I've been meditating this evening on the Emmaus story, which Luke says happened on the evening of that first Easter. Two disciples (we have the name of only one of them: Cleopas) are returning to Emmaus, seven miles from Jerusalem. The two are busy discussing the disturbing, hopeful events they've heard about from the other disciples still in the city: about the empty tomb and some of the women seeing Jesus. A stranger traveling the same way as they comes up to them and asks what they've been talking about, and why they seem troubled. Cleopas is amazed at the question. Are you the only one in Jerusalem who doesn't know what has happened there these past three days? he asks.

"What things?" the stranger asks.

About Jesus of Nazareth, a prophet by what he said and did, handed over to the authorities on the eve of the Passover and crucified. The one they'd hoped would set Israel free. And now a report by some of the women that the tomb was empty, and some story about two men in white telling them that Jesus was alive! Then Peter and some of the other men going out to look for themselves, and likewise finding the tomb empty.

And then the stranger's response. Wasn't it necessary that the Messiah suffer before entering his glory? And then, using the Scriptures, He begins explaining the passages dealing with His mission. Then, arriving in Emmaus, the two invite Him into their home for a meal, still not recognizing who it is they've been talking with. Then, Luke says, the stranger *took the bread, said the blessing, broke the bread and handed it to them.* Only now do they understand who has actually been with them all along, even as the stranger vanishes from their sight.

Did not our hearts burn within us as he talked to us on the road and explained the Scriptures to us? the disciples ask each other. Unable any longer to contain the good news, they set out at a run—like Peter and the other disciple that morning—to return to Jerusalem. And isn't this the nature of the Good News: a wildfire, something to be shared, news that *stays* news? Once back in Jerusalem, they tell their story to the disciples, and how they recognized Jesus in the "breaking of the bread." A microcosm then of the Mass. First,

...ptures explained, then Christ giving Himself as bread to ... The essential gesture repeated down through the ages. The thing that sustains so many each waking day.

There are five of us in Chapel this evening, the room lit by the single candle that burns always beside the Blessed Sacrament. I breathed in and breathed out, mantralike, each word of the Hail Mary, slowly, concentrating on the words, tasting them, as Ignatius suggests we do from time to time, and nearly fell into a sweet dream, thinking of how much we are loved, if only we knew it. If this isn't peace, being here like this, what is? What happened to that intellectual and emotional resistance I felt only yesterday? How is it that He could steal in like this, in the space of a single day, transforming everything around me? How does He do it? How does He manage to comfort us like this, removing our deepest anxieties, until you feel you could lie down again like a small child, safe and protected in His care? Whatever lies ahead I feel I could accept—no matter what—if somehow I could just feel His presence as I do now.

DAY 27: TUESDAY, FEBRUARY 1

4:00 A.M. Up for the past hour writing a long, newsy letter to my old co-conspirator at UMass, Vince DiMarco, trying to give him some sense of what life here at Eastern Point has been like, insofar as you can get into a letter all the things you've gone through with someone who hasn't. The order of hours, meal times, liturgy, the quasi-monastic view of the North Atlantic: everything to please his great medieval apostate Catholic heart. And then there's what I've been able to pour into this account, knowing it can only be an approximation of the actual experience. How, after all, do you trace the wind on paper?

How quiet it is just now, the only sound besides the crash of waves a door opening and closing as someone on the corridor here heads down to Chapel. We must all be winding down, with only three days left to go. These Resurrection narratives have become a source of quiet consolation, what Hopkins called "a melting, a madrigal start." Having found peace of this order, one would like to stay here a long long time. Though I can't for a moment forget that to get to this place I first had to go crashing down on my knees in snow, like a medieval king kneeling outside the gates of some monastery, begging for entrance.

I've been thinking of Hopkins's great Eastering poem, "That Nature Is a Heraclitean Fire and of the Comfort of the Resurrection," which he wrote in the last year of his life. Having lived the Third Week during his five years in Dublin, he seems to have experienced the consolations of the Fourth Week there as well. Everything burns away, he wrote in this wonderful poem, as he watched the smoke of the world's passing figured in the re-forming clouds above him. Nothing lasted, not even the one watching the passing scene, whether in Dublin then or now at Eastern Point. Everything melted, spinning away into the Abyss. In the end, death alone seemed to reign.

Except, that is, for the Resurrection, that "heart's-clarion," Christ's telling us that we meant more to Him than mortal trash, that we are more than bone and ash. God's time—God, whose name is not I WAS, but I AM—is far more complex than either Darwin's or Einstein's notion. "I am all at once what Christ is," Hopkins ended, finding the *I am* of each of us embedded in the word d*iam*ond itself:

since he was what I am, and
This Jack, joke, poor potsherd, | patch, matchwood, immortal diamond,
Is immortal diamond.

In an instant, as on that first Easter morning, the whole leveling, tragic process reversed. We too will live on in Christ, Hopkins understood, as I do here, becoming what the Father has always destined us to be: His sons, His daughters.

5:30 A.M. In spite of this sense of profound peace I feel, I know there's much work to be done. Further explorations. Further testing. Even—I feel sure—further surprises. "Consider," Ignatius enjoins now, in the Fourth Point of the Third Prelude for Week Four, "how the divinity, which seemed hidden during the Passion, now appears and manifests itself so miraculously in this holy Resurrection, through its true and most holy effects."

And the Fifth Point, which follows: "Consider the office of consoler which Christ our Lord carries out, and compare it with the way friends console one another." Consider too the consolations he has shown me these last several weeks. What else can I say but *Praise Him!* and get back to meditating on the Resurrection appearances. The next is to His disciples that first Easter evening. John has Jesus appearing in the midst of the group, still huddled behind locked doors, still very much afraid. His first words to them are, as so often, *Shalom. Peace be with you.* And then, by way of proof that He is the same Jesus who had been with them all along—the same and transformed—He shows them what will forever mark Him: His wounds.

Luke says the disciples were afraid. John speaks of their joy. No doubt both emotions were present. And then He gives them their mission. *As the Father has sent me,* He tells them, *so now I am sending you.* To do what? To spread the Good News—His life promised to all who believe in His name. And then He breathes His life into them, confirming them, comforting, strengthening, giving them the power to lift the weight of another's sins from their shoulders, unbinding them in the name of the Lord, as He had done while He was still a man among us.

When I got up from my desk to shut the window a few minutes ago, I caught the sliver of the old moon rising late in the cold winter sky. I turned out the light and lay down under the covers to try and get some sleep. But He had another surprise for me. That haunting Alleluia began playing again, getting louder and more joyous, until it sounded like a chorus made up of hundreds—no, thousands—of voices singing the same refrain over and over again. How wonderful the music, how overwhelming and ecstatic. And now there were bells, hundreds of them, booming and ringing in earnest, bells of all sizes, from the small to the great, all sounding and resounding in St. Peter's Square, where I stood with my family, a young father again, all of us within the arms of Bernini's colonnades. Suddenly thousands of doves were ascending, flame-white, bellbright, all flashing in the brilliant morning sun like tongues of fire.

In a soft, comforting Italian, Vatican Radio was proclaiming the Jubilee. I stood there next to Eileen in her bright canary yellow dress suit she was wearing for the Easter services, as she had when she was twenty. Our sons were little boys again, dressed up in their Sunday jackets and short pants, all of us here to celebrate the Resurrection. And suddenly—like that—my failings and shortcomings (I could feel this) were being washed away in His Blood. Somehow, wonderfully, things were as they might have been before my failings had marred things, and I was laughing and pointing to something atop St. Peter's as Eileen and the boys turned now to see what I was pointing to. And even as I write this I am weeping quietly. Yet there were no tears in that great Eastering scene, where all tears had been washed away in Christ's gift of himself. Everything had been made new again, everything brilliant as in its first luster. Really, I understood, there was nothing to be afraid of anymore. Nothing at all. Not even death.

9:15 A.M. Toward first light I slipped down to Chapel to sit quietly with my eyes closed to give thanks. When, finally, I opened my eyes again, there was someone else in the room with me, like me deep in meditation. I closed my eyes again and breathed in the rich peace palpable in that room. When I opened them again, I caught sight of the morning star shimmering in the early light. Brace Rock stood sentry now like some empty Calvary.

I met with JJ as usual and read from my journal, describing the scene in St. Peter's Square. He seemed intrigued by my saying that I'd found myself pointing at something atop St. Peter's. What was it? he wondered. At first I wasn't sure, and it took a moment to recollect the scene and turn the image in my mind 180 degrees. Then I realized I must have been pointing to the marble figures atop the basilica—that is, to Christ and the apostles. "Why not spend some time today thinking about this communion of saints that makes up the Church," he suggested. "You've already called on several saints to help you through this retreat." Continue meditating on the Resurrection, he said, and then on Ignatius's *Contemplation for Attaining Love*. "And try to get some rest," he added, as I got up to leave.

1:00 P.M. And rest is what I did, returning to my room to sleep for an hour. I awoke refreshed, then went for a walk. Cold and clear and beautiful the salt air, the gulls mewing as they scanned the ocean for a bite to eat. Then down to the dining hall for a bite myself and a glance afterward at the papers, before returning to my room to meditate, this time on the story of Doubting Thomas, the disciple who had not been present when Christ had appeared to the disciples that first Easter evening, and so had—understandably—refused to believe that Jesus had risen.

And who among us hasn't at some moment doubted? Did I not doubt the whole necessary, implausible meeting between Mary and Jesus just two days ago? Hadn't Jesus himself trembled with fright the night before he died, asking his Father to remove the cup of his agony, if it were possible. Maybe Peter had been right. There had to be another way, without a crucifixion. But there hadn't. A Resurrection needs a death. Unless a grain of wheat fall into the ground . . .

He stands in for all of us, this Thomas, doesn't he? A skeptic who puts it as baldly as you can. *Unless I can see the holes the nails made in his hands, AND unless I can put my finger into the holes they made, and unless I can put my hand into his side, I will not believe.* This hard-nosed Thomas who, when Jesus had set his face toward Jerusalem and his oncoming death, had remarked, *Let us also go to die with him.* Thomas the fatalist. Thomas the realist.

Now, a week after Easter, the disciples are again gathered behind locked doors and this time Thomas is with them. Again Jesus appears in their midst. *Peace be with you,* he says. And then, turning directly to Thomas: *Here are my hands. Put your finger here [in the nail hole]. Now, give me your hand and put it into my side. Do not be unbelieving any more, but believe.* And with that, Thomas utters one of the most profound gestures of belief found anywhere in the Gospels. *My Lord,* he says. *And my God.* They are the words millions have said—and still say—whenever the host is raised at the Consecration. And Jesus' gentle rebuke: *You believe, Thomas, because you can see me. Blessed are those who have not seen and yet believe.*

Somehow we arrive at our yes or our no. Whether it be a single transformative moment or a lifetime of questioning, pray with all you have that it be yes. With Paul on the road to Damascus, the yes was sudden and unmistakable. With Augustine, on the road to Rome, it took decades. "Lord, change my heart," he once prayed. "But not yet." "With an anvil-ding," Hopkins sums it up in his great conversion ode, *The Wreck of the Deutschland:*

> *And with fire in him forge thy will*
> *Or rather, rather then, stealing as Spring*
> *Through him, melt him but master him still:*
> *Whether át ónce, as ónce at a crásh Pául,*
> *Or as Áustin, a língering-óut swéet skíll,*
> *Make mercy in all of us, out of us all*
> *Mástery, bút be adóred, bút be adóred Kíng.*

2:30 P.M. Q. So what is it, really, that sustains your spiritual life?

A. The goodness of others. My marriage. My sons and their

wives. My son's vocation. The loyalty of friends. The example of Christ as the Gospels reveal Him, a testament sealed in His blood. The sacraments of Eucharist and Reconciliation on a regular basis, as necessary as the bread I eat. My own response to the yes of the baptismal promises my parents made for me when I was an infant, even if they did not fully understand the import of those promises. Those same promises renewed hundreds of times by myself since then.

Q. And what about these thirty days? What have they contributed?

A. Consider this. Each time I have asked for His help, especially when I was at a loss as to how to move forward, He has come to my aid graciously. And not only here at Eastern Point, but over my entire life, beginning with the fact that I was not aborted by a frightened sixteen-year-old girl who found herself pregnant. Strange how you look back and the journey makes sense in hindsight. Whenever God enters the scene—whether in the guise of a messenger like Gabriel or with the angels at the tomb or when the risen Jesus enters through locked doors—His first words are: "Do not be afraid." Yes, He has been with me, as He said He would, always. Jesus curing ten lepers, and only one—a despised Samaritan—returning to thank him. *But where,* Jesus asks, *are the other nine?* And so now I turn back, retrace my steps, Lord, to thank you. From the bottom of my heart.

I've been thinking too of the Communion of Saints, the great body of those who preceded me on the journey, reminding me that I don't ever have to go it alone. I could never have gotten through this retreat without the help of those who keep this place going, from JJ and the staff to the cooks and the groundskeepers. Or without Eileen and the others who sent well wishes or said a silent prayer for me. Or the other retreatants. If I have remembered them in my prayers—as I have—have they not also remembered me, without a single word needing to pass between us?

Q. And who makes up this Communion of Saints?

A. Abraham and Moses, David, and Elijah and the other prophets, great and small, from Isaiah to Micah, each like one of that throng of bells I heard early this morning. Peter and Paul, Augustine, Francis, Dominic, Thomas Aquinas, Teresa of Avila, Ignatius, Francis Xavier, Matteo Ricci, Edmund Campion, Peter Claver. My beloved Hopkins. Isaac Jogues and Kateri Tekakwitha. The Jesuits in Brazil and Uruguay, who fought to save the indigenous peoples there. Thérèse of Lisieux, Mother Seton, Mother Cabrini, Edith Stein, Miguel Pro before a firing squad, Maximilian Kolbe. Those six Jesuit fathers killed in El Salvador. Oscar Romero, Dorothy Day, Mother Teresa of Calcutta, the African martyrs, Flannery O'Connor, Thomas Merton, Walker Percy, Andre Dubus.

And if these, why not others? Eileen. Eileen's grandmother and my poor Swedish grandmother, half-cocked often, but keeping her grandchildren together when the going got tough. Big-hearted Stella, handing a fifteen-year-old a small bonus to give him a sense of self-worth when he so desperately needed it. The work of God's presence among us goes on in a great round, ourselves the bells ringing out God's goodness. It goes on, the work. It goes on. Those who work with the hungry and those who cry out against the injustices of the world. *Do whatever he asks you,* Mary said at Cana, and for doing just that water was turned into wine. As here at Eastern Point, where the commonplace has a chance of being transformed into a brave new world.

4:00 P.M. A short walk around the pond, then back here to meditate on the Resurrection appearances in Galilee as John relates them. It's a strange episode—this Gospel passage—one that has all the reality of a vivid dream. Peter and six others have gone fishing on the Sea of Galilee all night and have come up empty. Returning to shore at daybreak, they notice a stranger standing on the beach calling out to them. Cast your net to starboard, the stranger says, and when they do, it is filled to breaking with fish.

And now the stranger invites the men to a breakfast of bread and fresh fish grilling over an open fire. No one, John says, dared ask who the stranger was, for they knew it had to be the Lord. How like a vivid dream, to see this man and wonder who he was, even as they understood that it had to be Jesus. It was the third time, John says, that Jesus revealed himself to them, each appearance marked by a Eucharistic meal of bread and fish.

And now Jesus turns to Peter. *Do you love me?* he asks the man who had denied him three times, the one he'd said he would build his church on. Love, he says, *agapo:* self-sacrificing love. And Peter answers, *You know that I love you,* though he qualifies it with the word *philo,* brotherly affection. Then feed my lambs, Jesus tells him. A second time Jesus asks him, and again he uses the word *agapo.* Again Peter holds back. *Philo,* he says, I love you like a brother. Then look after my sheep, Jesus tells him a second time. A third time Jesus asks him, but this time he uses the word *philo,* knowing it is all Peter can give in return at this point. Peter, do you love me, he asks, like a brother? And Peter: Yes, Lord, I love you. Like a brother. And Jesus: Then feed my sheep.

And yet, thirty-five years later, an old man and a prisoner in Rome, Peter will make the ascent. Now, as bishop of Rome, asked whether he is a disciple of this Jesus, he will give his yes, and then be crucified and buried where St. Peter's now rises. He will make one final request, a request so humble and gracious that it will undo all those years of bumbling: that he be allowed to be crucified upside down, as not worthy to die as his Master had. Yes, Lord, the gesture says. You know I love you. *Agapo* at last.

Do I need to spell it out? Do I need to say what the lesson for me is here? Not *philo,* Lord, not friendship, then—and I say it shaking—but love, *agapo*. An all-consuming, no-holds-barred, surrendering love.

7:00 P.M. This evening at Mass Fr. Tim Shepard accidentally spilled some of the consecrated wine over the altar cloth, and I found myself shaken by the accident. Nevertheless, there was much quiet activity—especially by Dixie and Mary—to make sure every drop was cleaned up reverently, efficiently, quietly, without fanfare. Even these gestures reveal in their own way the profound reverence with which the Sacrament is attended to.

After dinner I came back to my room to meditate on Matthew 28:16–20. The Eleven (Judas having hanged himself) have returned to Mt. Tabor in Galilee, "the mountain where Jesus had arranged to meet them," and where, tradition says, the Transfiguration had occurred. Some, Matthew reports, recognized him at once, though others hesitated. How strange and dreamlike for someone to point out a friend who has died and to say, "That's him. That's the same guy. Don't you recognize him?" A waking dream. Jesus the same and Jesus different.

And once He is lifted from our sight altogether, how will He touch us down the long corridors of history? With the physicality of the sacraments: with the water of Baptism, with the bread and wine of the Eucharist, with the tears that come with forgiveness, with the coming of the Holy Spirit in fire and wind and oil, in our lives together as husband and wife, with the priests and religious—the anointed ones—who serve as witnesses with lives of service, with the Lord for company on the last lonely leg of the journey through death, whether in a bed, on a road, at sea, in the air. Be with me, Lord, now and at the hour of my death.

Go, Jesus says now, *make disciples of all nations. Baptize them in the name of the Father and of the Son and of the Holy Spirit.* A formula established early on by the Church, beginning in Jerusalem. After all, Jesus told his followers, the Holy Spirit—the Paraclete, the Comforter—would come only when Jesus had returned to the Father, the caterpillar become at last a butterfly.

Paul's letter to the small community of Christians in Corinth in the year 57 is the oldest record we have to mention the Resurrection. The fledgling Christian community in the free-for-all port city of Corinth had come to accept many of Paul's teachings, but they'd balked when it came to the thought that a dead man could actually rise again. After all, the Greeks were rooted in a body/soul dichotomy and saw the body as trash, something to be sloughed off, like some spent rocket booster on its ascent into the world of spirit.

How then does Paul confront the Corinthians on this? By reminding them that Christ died for their sins, that he was buried, and that on the third day he was raised to life, in accordance with the Scriptures. Moreover, Paul is only quoting what had by then become the Church's credo. *If* you profess to be a Christian, Paul insists, you have already professed the Resurrection of Christ and therefore the resurrection of each one of us. It is the tradition, Paul says, that he himself received: that the risen Christ appeared first to Peter, as having primacy. Then to the other apostles. Afterward, he appeared to more than five hundred brothers at the same time, most of whom were still alive when he wrote his letter.

Then, Paul adds, Jesus appeared to James. This James, "brother of the Lord," was a relative of Jesus, and it was he, rather than Peter, who became the leader of the Jerusalem Church. James had already been martyred by the time Paul wrote, murdered by the religious authorities in Jerusalem fifteen years earlier. Had Jesus appeared to James to steady him in the face of opposition in Jerusalem, as he has steadied so many others?

Finally, Paul says, the risen Christ appeared to him, out of the "natural way." He makes no distinction between the Resurrection appearances to the Eleven and Christ's appearance to him. Whatever happened on the road to Damascus, it was enough to change him forever. Not for a month or two, but through beatings, floggings, multiple stonings, shipwreck, and finally death itself. You will have to take up your cross each day, Jesus reminds us, if you would follow me. It's worth remembering what this other Paul's witness cost him in his body the next time I burn the toast or call someone and am put on hold.

DAY 28: WEDNESDAY, FEBRUARY 2: FEAST OF THE PRESENTATION OF THE LORD

MIDNIGHT. Fell asleep at half past nine and awoke from a strong erotic dream an hour later, wondering where this one was coming from. Irony of ironies, it's that moment in the *Exercises* when Ignatius asks us to consider something far more important than the flash points of eros: the *Contemplation to Attain Love*. It's as if Christ had turned my face toward Him and away from all other distractions, however powerful they might otherwise be. In place of those He has given me a deep sense of peace. It is, I see, a great solace, and I thank Him for it.

The *Contemplation to Attain Love:* it's a keystone in the structure of the *Exercises,* love being the very thing upon which everything else depends. Ignatius is quick to point out here that "love ought to manifest itself more by deeds than by words." Love, he says, using a language the scientific medieval mind admired, is that which "consists in a mutual communication between two persons," the lover sharing oneself with the beloved, and vice versa. And so he asks me now to imagine myself as standing before God and the saints to beg specifically for an "interior knowledge of all the great good I have received, that, stirred to profound gratitude, I might be able to love and serve the Divine Majesty in all things." Strange how Ignatius's language holds one at arm's length here, perhaps so as not to intrude upon us or frighten us off, for I sense we are about to enter yet another gate into the Mystery of God now.

And so I have offered myself to God as fully as I can. But is this *agape* or *philo*? So far there's been no trombone crescendo, and, in fact, almost no emotional response whatever, even though I've been meditating on this act of self-surrender here in Chapel for the past hour. Certainly I would have liked this self-surrender to be attended by some great sigh of love, but so far it has had all the emotional force of signing some contract on the dotted line, the only sound the sober scratch of pen on paper. Still, I have made the offering as Ignatius presents it:

> Take, Lord, and receive all my liberty, my memory, my understanding and all my will—all that I have and possess. You, Lord, have given all that to me. I now give it back to you, O Lord. All of it is yours. Dispose of it according to your will. Give me love of yourself along with your grace, for that is enough for me.

I've also examined in detail the Second, Third, and Fourth points as well:

How God dwells in creatures at various levels, from the basic elements up through human intelligence.

How God labors for me in all His creation.

How all good things descend from above, filling and completing my limited goodness—my poor pence of power, justice, goodness, piety, mercy multiplied by His power, justice, goodness and mercy—in the process lifting and elevating me.

Quite by accident—though, as Ron Hansen warned me, there's very little that happens by accident during a retreat—I was reading Hopkins's notes on Suárez's *De Mysteriis Vitae Christi*. Suárez was once the foremost Jesuit commentator on Thomas Aquinas, and in Hopkins's time central to a Jesuit's formation. Hopkins speaks brilliantly here of how God's grace works on us. He calls the human tendency toward the natural good the *affective will,* the proclivity to follow our own affections and tendencies. Then he speaks of a corrective grace that leaves the will free to act as it chooses, but which stimulates it toward a more spiritual good. This he calls the *elective will*.

Finally, he speaks of a third kind of grace: an elevating grace, one that "lifts the receiver from one cleave [or spiritual plateau] of being to another, and to a vital connection with Christ." This grace, he explains, "is truly God's finger touching the very vein of personality, which nothing else can reach and man can respond to by no play whatever, by bare acknowledgment only, the counter stress which God alone can feel"—that is, my yes in answer to God's invitation. A breathing out, then, on God's part; a breathing in on ours. Then breathing out our own yes. Response and counter-response. What Ignatius, in short, calls love.

It is this elevating kind of grace I believe I've been privileged to taste again these past four weeks. It's like coming up against a mountain where all my spirit could do was groan, realizing that it could do nothing more on its own, except wait to be lifted—in God's good time—to the next level of spiritual understanding. And that, I see, had to come through Christ's emptying Himself as He was lifted up in death, in turn lifting all of us after Him. Call it a lifting to a new consciousness of our real spiritual potential. Admittedly, it's a potential few of us ever fully realize, though the possibility is always there for the earnest asking.

8:00 A.M. Fell asleep sometime after one this morning, rising for the day at seven, the sun hallooing through my window. Calm seas and a high tide. Ablutions, a breakfast of microwaved burrito, grapefruit, coffee. Sat in the rocker in the foyer and faced the sun, which seemed to burn the bush before me, even as it left it intact. Two meditations left on my list: the Ascension (Acts 1) and the Descent of the Holy Spirit (Acts 2).

I've been thinking that it's not the work I've managed to do that's important, finally. Others will decide what's of value there as they rummage through it, taking what they want and tossing aside the rest. Secondhand stuff, mostly, with a nugget, perhaps, here and there. Eileen has always said life is a matter of living each day we're blessed with. But for me it has mostly been some unidentified future I keep climbing toward. No wonder I find myself waking at night now and thinking about how fast it all goes, my boys grown and scattered to the wind, so many I loved or might have loved more deeply on the other side of the Great Divide. The books written, the teaching, the small, provincial accolades, the glitter: all these will have to fend for themselves when the man behind them is finally emptied.

11:00 A.M. A relaxed session with JJ this morning. Only two more meetings to go. We both sense, I think, that some major "breakthrough" has been made, that I'm wedded to these *Exercises* in some profound way for the rest of my life. I read him passages from my journal, looking for further patterns, further light. But it was to *The Contemplation to Attain Love* that JJ kept returning. I told him how I thought my contemplation had gone there: a low-keyed affair, unspectacular, done according to the text. Actually, he said, I'd been making pieces of the *Contemplation* all along. But now he asked me to return to it again. "It might still have something more to say to you," he added.

A meditation this morning on the Ascension, Acts 1:1–12. In the Resurrection appearances, Jesus reveals the Kingdom of God not only in words but by His very presence. Now, at the end of His time among us, He reminds His disciples that John the Baptist himself had spoken of a baptism by the Spirit. Very soon now, He reminds them, that Spirit is to come upon them. Yet even now some of the disciples *still* expect the messianic kingdom to be a return of David's kingdom: a kingdom of rods and acres. But that political reality is already too timebound, too tentative, a thing of the past. The kingdom Jesus is speaking of is something far bigger than Jerusalem or Judea or even all of Israel.

So now, when the disciples ask Jesus if He plans to restore the kingdom to Israel, He tells them simply that it is not for them to know times or dates. What else could He do? Would they have understood what lay before them, even if He'd tried to explain it to them? For the first quarter century or so after Jesus' death, the Church still thought in terms of the end times as something that might happen at any moment. It was, in fact, a radical failure of the imagination that would soon be corrected by, among others, St.

Paul, who would come to see that Christ had not said when He would return.

The truth is that the work of redemption would be enormous—the world being a lot bigger and more complex than the disciples (or anyone) had figured. Suppose Jesus had said, "Look, I want you to bring the Good News to New York and Los Angeles and Beijing and Sydney and Papua and Nagasaki and Kingston and Rio de Janeiro. Go forth." What would these fishermen from Galilee have thought? Better to tell them—as with children who want to know, "Are we there yet?"—that He'd let them know what was what in good time. In the meantime, He would send them the Holy Spirit, and then they would bear witness to His resurrection and to His teachings not only in Jerusalem but throughout Judea and Samaria. In fact, to the ends of the earth.

And so, having given His final instructions, He is lifted up. A cloud covers Him, and then He is gone. Two men in white hover there, as at the tomb that first Easter, and again they ask, as if no time had elapsed between Easter and the Ascension, *Why are you standing here looking into the sky? This Jesus who has been taken up into heaven will come back in the same way as you saw him go.* And when He comes *this* time, He will come in power and glory.

2:00 P.M. Broccoli soup and a sandwich. On the spur of the moment, I drove up to Rockport after lunch. The weather has been clear and cold, and the waves dazzled as I drove north along the Atlantic coast, past the old colonial houses and second-growth woods. Crazy-quilt clumps of frozen snow everywhere, along with standing patches of pond water and dead weeds, the first stirrings of New England spring still weeks off, though it is full Easter here in my heart. A time to think and pray and enjoy the fact of being alive, for a brief moment without a care in the world.

And so I drove up to Rockport to find the same candy store I'd visited two weeks earlier, where I bought Eileen a box of her favorite milk chocolates. All handpicked pieces, arranged in a satiny red Valentine's Day box. I also bought a pound of bridge mix (dark chocolate) in a more pedestrian bag for myself. A piece or two a day, I figured, by way of celebrating having weathered all these days of silence. The whole excursion took an hour—out and back—by which time I'd had enough of the world and its distractions for one day. And, miracle of miracles, I found my parking space on the loop waiting for me.

6:30 P.M. Fell into a deep, peaceful sleep this afternoon. When I awoke about four it was as if there were voices, childlike, insistent, sounding the way my sons used to sound on Christmas mornings thirty years ago, when they wanted to go downstairs to see what was under the Christmas tree. *Hurry!* the voices said. *Hurry! Get up, there's little time to lose!* The sun was setting, the lawn below already deep in blue shadow. I got up, put on my boots and jacket and ski cap, grabbed my copy of the *Exercises,* and headed for the path that leads to the ocean, as if led there by an unseen hand. The voices had stilled, but there was still a joyous sense of expectancy, a light leading me, as if whatever was waiting for me was out there by the rocks.

Because JJ had asked me this morning to meditate again on the *Contemplation to Attain Love,* I found myself reading over the points Ignatius makes there even as I walked toward the water. How God dwells in all creation, sustaining everything at the minutest subatomic level. How He is present in everything around me, in the very trees and the tangled bine stems behind and before me, in the ice and snow and rain, in the clouds, in the sunlight, in the very air I breathe. I thought of the Lord keeping all of His creation continually in existence, His very Being present in all of this.

Why? I asked myself. Why should He reveal Himself in matter? Why things? Why not just spirit? And then, in my mind's eye, I saw Christ's glorified body, like something out of Salvador Dali: a transparent, radiant torso, and light filling it. I thought of all he had done for me in bringing me to this point. I thought of Mary, a Jewish girl from Nazareth, who had said yes to the angel Gabriel's invitation, and given a human face to Love. It was a love that wanted to be part of our world, to visit it and yet leave it intact, free to respond or not as we wished, even as God had left Mary intact, even as her yes made it possible for her to be filled with God.

By now I'd reached the impasse of the rocks just as the sun set. I remembered what I'd learned in the woods before the Stations of the Cross, and began reciting the *Triple Colloquy* again, this time asking Mary for the grace to give myself to her son as the *Contemplation* asks us to do. "Take, Lord," I begged,

> and receive all my liberty, my memory, my understanding, and all my will—all that I have and possess. You, Lord, have given all that to me. I now give it back to you, O Lord. All of it is yours. Dispose of it according to your will. Give me love of yourself along with your grace, for that is enough for me.

A gift then of my liberty. For what was my freedom apart from my God? A gift too of my memory. For what would I want to remember apart from the memories He had rinsed with His holiness, transfusing, irradiating, lifting everything of worth to a new level of significance? A gift too of my understanding, so that it too might be cleansed to see the beauty and justness at the heart of the world. And finally the gift of my will, that it too might move in rhythm with my heart and my lungs. A receiving and a giving back again, where narcissism and self-interest were winnowed out in the sifting action of His great love.

Then suddenly I heard myself saying, "Hurry, please, Mother, for Mass is at five, and I want to take this request to your son," and we did, and I laid it all out before Him, such as it was, poor pence, but all I had. And I promised to give more, when I had more to give (and it struck me then that all I had I had because of Him, sixty years of it, every penny, every breath, every grace, Love falling like a gentle shower over my days). Then I turned into the flaming eye of the sun, low now—just over the thickets and brambles of the bushes along the coast—and prayed, "Receive it all, Father. Only give me your love and the grace to stay close to you always, and it will be enough."

I looked down at the rocks at my feet, broken, many of them, by the winds and the tides, and began staring at one fist-sized broken rock intently. A spiral of lighter colored mineral seemed to swirl downward through the middle of the rock: an intricate weaving within the darker hue, and I thought how I could have spent hours meditating on the quartz sparkles and delicate tan and brown and purple hues that seemed to form an expanding galaxy in this one rock alone.

I stooped down and picked up the rock next to it, and saw how it too had its own distinctive whorlings and tracings. And, beyond the rock I held in my hand, in the near distance, I caught sight of the intricate shadowtackle and interlacing of brambles in the cold February waning light. And beyond that, in the middle distance, stood the large rock to which I had been coming these past weeks. How subtle its curves and striations, nature artfully shaping over the last million years its Joseph coat of many colors.

And beyond that rock lay another and another. And beyond the rocks the intricacies of the waves crashing against these rocks, each wave distinctive, never to be repeated against this particular light. And beyond that the vast expanse of the ocean, with its translucent colors shifting from blues and greens to purples, a billion inscapes singing and laughing in all weathers and seasons, year after year, God working each splendid moment to give us such infinite variety, He whose own beauty and majesty are past change. And all I could do, all I could do was praise Him.

By then it was time to head back to the Main Hall for Mass. As I took off down the path, I heard the wind rising through the trees and felt the invigorating cold against my face and realized that one might spend an eternity praising this delicious Craftsman who had made all this and kept it all in existence. I thought too how very little of what was right here before my eyes I had ever really seen—

the peculiar, lovely, mesmerizing inscape of each thing, and I praised God—that subtle Maker—who had responded to my yes with the whole blooming Hallelujah chorus of creation. By now I'd reached a small clearing of dry soft needles beneath a pine tree, and suddenly I fell down on my knees again, this time giddy with joy. I prayed the Hail Mary and the *Anima Christi* and the Our Father to round out the *Triple Colloquy*, and understood in some profound way that my meager offering on this, the Feast of the Presentation, had been accepted, and that I was God's temple now, or one facet of it, rising there in a small clearing in the woods of Eastern Point.

9:00 P.M. Fr. John celebrated Mass this evening. The Presentation, the Purification, Candlemas: all names for the same feast, the day on which candles are traditionally blessed, recalling Simeon's hailing the infant Jesus in the Temple as "the light of the nations." It's also Groundhog Day, and—since I could see my shadow this morning, I suppose six more weeks of winter are in store. No matter, spring is coming, is already here in some real sense. No doubt about it: the days *are* getting longer. *Licht, mehr Licht!* You notice the modest increments of light each evening now at Mass. When I got here, the windows were pitch black when Mass began. Now, as I prepare to leave, there's a Matisse blue in the skies at the Consecration, and in the middle ground I can make out the damascene outline of oaks and maples.

One of the women making the Eight-Day retreat had put some chocolate bark out on the dining hall counter for whoever wanted it. Having been given the great gift I'd been given this afternoon, it seemed the least I could do was take the bridge mix I'd bought myself to squirrel away here in my room and share it with the others. And if I was going to share it, why not just give the whole damn thing away, the way He had given me His gift, without holding back. And so, next to the woman's candy and the note that read, "Energy for the Road to Emmaus," I poured out all that I had.

Finally got through to Eileen this evening. I'd tried getting her after dinner, but she'd been on the phone with her parents, who'd had a spat with one of the grandchildren. A small enough thing, but enough to send tremors through the circumscribed world of two aging parents, and so through a daughter who loves them, and so through me, who loves them all. We spoke briefly of friends, of tragic estrangements. And so prayers in Chapel for all of them, for all who feel hemmed in or confused or afraid as they approach the close of their journeys. Then I made the *Triple Colloquy* for peace in the lives of the elderly, knowing Eileen and I and everyone are heading down the same road, no two ways about it. Then a cup of tea, eight or nine of us in the Fireplace Room, Marcie finishing the baby blanket she's been working on, everyone looking very much at peace, myself at peace, a peace that nothing has disturbed.

I sat before the fire this evening, the crackle and pop of resin in the dry wood going up in flames in the great old fireplace, transforming the blazing scene in the grating to brilliant ember and gray-white ash. What is it about a fire that mesmerizes and comforts? Each night the wood appears, stacks of it, cured and dried, cut from fallen branches or from the trees felled by the storms that buffet this coast, as nature's great bonfire burns on. "All things," Hopkins wrote, "are charged with God and . . . give off sparks and take fire, yield drops and flow, ring and tell of him." Who but Love could have whispered this to him, as today Love whispered it to me?

DAY 29: THURSDAY, FEBRUARY 3

2:00 A.M. Up at one, thinking of the Holy Spirit descending on Mary and the disciples on that first Pentecost. A loud wind filling the room, then tongues of fire hovering above the heads of those present. It's Luke's way of describing a force each one felt, transforming them, giving them the voice to express their deepest desire: union with God, the very words transformed to music, syllables flying off, bubbling in the alembic of God's trembling love.

Now, suddenly, each finds himself speaking a new language. What did that mean, really? Luke says that, if at first the words sounded like babble, they were anything but, for the ancient curse of Babel had now been reversed. Language, which had hitherto divided one human being from another, has suddenly been transformed into a vehicle that unites. And now, all these devout Jews—assembled in Jerusalem from the great Diaspora that had sent them over the centuries to Iraq and Cyprus and Greece and Rome, Pontus and Asia, Phrygia and Pamphylia, Crete and Alexandria and the Libyan coast, in each place having to adapt to the languages of that place—hear the disciples speaking each in his own tongue.

I shall pour out my Spirit on all humanity, Peter tells the crowds, quoting the prophet Micah. *Your sons and daughters shall prophesy, your young people shall see visions, your old people dream dreams. On slaves too—men and women—I will pour out my Spirit.* Then he begins proclaiming Christ crucified and risen from the dead, quoting now from the Psalms: *You will not abandon me to Hades, / or allow your holy one to see corruption.* And who is this Holy One, Peter asks them, but Jesus. Jesus risen, as all those with him have witnessed. The same Jesus who *promised he would send the Holy Spirit; and what you see and hear now is the outpouring of that same Spirit.*

What can we do? the crestfallen assembly ask Peter. Pray for forgiveness, he tells them. Be baptized in the name of Jesus Christ. And then you will receive the Holy Spirit. It is the promise made for you and for your children first and then for the Gentiles. A promise offered to everyone whom God calls to Himself. That very day, Luke adds, three thousand were added to the infant Church. If this is not a transformative grammar, words capable of changing the very direction of one's life, I don't know what is. Truly, after yesterday, I didn't think there was anywhere else to go. And now, an insight into the further possibilities of language, a whole new way of communicating: through the Spirit.

7:30 A.M. Slept from three to half past six. Low purple clouds to the east, over deep blue-purple water, tints of blood orange and clotted cream. I knelt down the better to look through the opening in my storm window and watched as the sun, like some eighteenth-century French king—*le Roi Soleil*—stepped over the clouds so brilliantly I had to turn my eyes away. As I did, I caught the slant outline of my window frame shimmering orange on the wall over my bed, forming a series of Russian crosses. "Mornin', brother," the sun smiled, going about its business. "Mornin'," I answered.

Grapefruit, raisin bran, banana, milk. Ten of us at breakfast, all looking out on a calm blue sea to the faint music of seagulls, interrupted occasionally by the scold of crows. Here and there you can see one of the Eight-Day retreatants saying good-bye—a thank you, a hug for one of the directors, since they leave after lunch today. And then there will be just us, who have weathered the long one. You can see the finish line up ahead now. Shall we float there?

10:45 A.M. A terrific session with JJ this morning. I told him what had happened with the *Contemplation to Attain Love*. He suggested I go over my journals again, looking for evidence of Jesus as both giver and gift. He also urged me to do the General Examen each day, going over the day's events to see where Christ had sensibly entered my day (with this telephone conversation or talking with that student, with my time spent with Eileen, or with whatever the Lord surprised me with). He also urged me to do the Particular Examen as well, trying to root out this failing or that, then seeing how I had done by noon, and again how I'd fared by evening. I'm also to meditate on Paul's prayer in Ephesians 3:14–21, asking for continued strength to live out each day what I have learned on this retreat. And finally I am to pray for the wisdom to see how I might be failing even when I think I am succeeding. Thinking I am adorable, for instance, when I am simply being a jerk.

After my session, I walked down to the front office off the dining hall and turned in my evaluation of the Thirty Days to Deb Aiello, the secretary here. I'd spoken with her only once before, on the phone last October, when I called for an application to make the retreat. True, I'd seen her from time to time coming in and out of her office, but always before silence had intervened.

"How was it?" she asked.

"Like gold," I told her. "Pure gold."

"Yeah," she said. "I bet it was."

"You related to Danny Aiello?" I asked. I liked her instinctively.

"You think I'd be working here if I was?" she joked.

"Maybe," I said. "Why not?"

"Yeah," she said. "Maybe I would."

I ran into Dick Onofrey in the long corridor on the way to Chapel. He was already packed and ready to head home. "I'll be leaving soon," he whispered.

"I know," I whispered back. "Give me a hug, and my love to all the good souls in western Massachusetts."

1:00 P.M. Four of us in Chapel before Mass. "You will not abandon me, Lord," I read in my *Magnificat.* "But be there with me at all times, even to the end." Not to be abandoned. Ever. As I was as a boy. Such deep consolation in the thought. Fr. Bill Devine, robed in red vestments to remember a host of martyrs, gave a funny and impassioned homily. He noted that the retreat was ending now for the Eight-Day retreatants, and tomorrow for those who had been here for the past year. How much has happened in these thirty days.

After Mass there was the annual blessing of throats and other winter illnesses for this, the Feast of St. Blase. Three priests stood at their stations in the Fireplace Room holding crossed candles under our chins as we approached for the blessing. "A devotion that peaked in the sixteenth century," Bill quipped, "and which has never reached its former glory." And yet each year I stand in line for the blessing, my throat after all providing me with a good part of my livelihood.

Lunch for us Long Termers was eaten in silence while the others talked in the small room adjoining, after which they said their good-byes. By half past twelve, most of the cars were gone. Once again, there's that slight edge of sadness over everything. And, while part of me would like to be speeding home, another part knows this precious time will not return.

And now a meditation on Paul's prayer in Ephesians. *May the Lord enable you to grow in inner strength,* he prays, *so that Christ may live in your hearts. Then you will have the strength to grasp the breadth and length and height and depth and may be filled with the utter fullness of God. Glory to Him whose power, working in us, can do infinitely more than we can ask or even imagine.* It goes to the heart—doesn't it?—this prayer, especially now, as we prepare to enter the world once more.

7:00 P.M. Dropped off a donation for maintenance here at Eastern Point—a small enough gesture for all I've been given—and wrote my final letter to Eileen, telling her how much this place has meant to me, and how much I look forward to being with her again, always, forever. Around three I dozed off, thinking as I did so about the *Triple Colloquy* I want to make before the retreat is over. As I began to rehearse it, lying there on my bed, there was Mary again. And again she was a young mother and I a small boy playing with her. *Here I am,* I smiled, comforted, as I fell asleep.

At four I went out for a walk around Niles Pond, frozen hard again, patches of ice still sheening the roads. Then out to Eastern Point Boulevard and up Bemo Drive, before looping back here. I began making the *Colloquy* as I passed the broken snowman still lying there, just as he has these past two weeks. The groundskeeper had been trimming the branches of the tall pine that had been felled earlier, but he was gone now and no one else was around. The sun was already setting. I looked down the narrow tree-lined path leading to the ocean, almost expecting someone to appear. Finally, I finished the *Colloquy,* and still nothing had happened.

Well, I thought to myself, it was a terrific run with these colloquies while it lasted. We're all exhausted by now. Maybe even God, with all this clamoring of mine. Be still and let be.

I climbed up on the rocks to have a look around. A small boat was heading toward Gloucester Harbor. Otherwise, everything was very still. I turned to look back the way I'd come and saw a line of footprints embedded in the icy path, brambles and bushes off to either side. *Calvary,* I thought. *Golgotha. Skull Place.* As I turned back, my eye caught what looked like a dark sheen of liquid pooled in the rock upon which I was standing.

What's that? I asked myself.

Blood, came back the answer.

Whose? I asked, as it began to shimmer there.

Mine, he said.

Is that all there is?

That's all I have.

I thought of Mary and Dixie racing to wipe up the Precious Blood after it had spilled at Communion. *Such a small amount,* I said, *against the backdrop of all the pain in the world.*

It's all I had, he said.

But there are so many of us. And so much sin, and so much damage, I said. *Was it enough?*

Then came the answer. *It broke my Father's heart to see His Son's blood poured out like that. Whatever grievance He had against the human race He was willing to forgive when He accepted the price I paid.*

So, He made you pay the price? I said, more bitterly than I would have imagined. *Pay it with your life? What kind of father would demand his own son's blood?*

No, Paul, he said. *You have it wrong. It wasn't the price my Father demanded. He's too much the lover for that. It was the price* you *demanded before you'd turn back to Him. We both knew you'd demand nothing less than a total giving of ourselves before you'd be ready to respond. Isn't that so? Call it the price the inveterate human heart demands. True, it's not an awful lot of blood for all the blood that's been *spilled the world over. But it's all I had, and I emptied myself for you and the others in the only way you'd understand: with all I had to give.*

I was walking over the rocks now, heading back to the Main House. *What kind of God would do a thing like that? Give himself for us, who betray Him every minute of every day.*

Ah, Paul, he said. *You're finally beginning to get the point.*

9:00 P.M. I have to believe Fr. Hopkins has been with me yet again, for a poem of his that I do not often think of has been coming back to me all evening. It's a poem he wrote while on retreat in 1885, the year he wrote his heartbreaking sonnets. A few years earlier he'd been chaplain to a barracks full of soldiers, and so had no illusions about the lives such men lead. And yet he knew that even men with clay feet could rise to the call of duty. Hadn't his Lord slogged out His campaign against the darkness, and wasn't he himself one of Christ's soldiers? "Mark Christ our King," he wrote now,

> *He knows war, served this soldiering through;*
> *He of all can reeve a rope best. There he bides his bliss*
> *Now, and seeing somewhere some man do all that man can do,*
> *For love he leans forth, needs his neck must fall on, kiss,*
> *And cry "O Christ-done deed! So God-made-flesh does too:*
> *Were I come o'er again" cries Christ, "it should be this."*

Didn't he do all as a man he could do, this Jesus? Didn't he die like any of us, though more brutally than most? Didn't he show us the way, step by step, like any good line officer? And didn't he show us what, against the odds, could still be done? Pray to give back something while there's still time and still something left to give.

10:00 P.M. I have been thinking again of that image I had this afternoon, of Mary playing with her small son. Only this time it is the image of my mother as a young woman, still full of hope for her future and the future of her family. There's a photo of her in one of those cotton dresses, all dressed up, a beautiful woman, really. It's

1944. She's bent down on one knee, Walter on one arm, me on the other, and we're peering into the camera: The place is the public park on Fifty-first Street, overlooking the FDR Drive and the East River. Perhaps she's had the picture taken to send to my father, who's away in the army.

"Be my own good boy, dear Paulie," she ended those letters she wrote me each week I was in the seminary, letters I thought long ago destroyed, but which Eileen found recently in a drawer after all these years. News of the family, her struggles to find the money to buy me a new pair of shoes or a book, her firstborn gone from her. "Be my own good boy, dear Paulie," hoping the best for her Catholic son, she, who had been raised a Lutheran by her mother's family. Well, I'm trying, my dear one. Each day I try. Day by day, step by step. May you rest in peace now, having done what you could. This is my love letter to you, from your son who could not write you one while you were with us. But I write it out here, now, at the end of my long retreat.

DAY 30: FRIDAY, FEBRUARY 4

1:00 A.M. Up to rub lotion on my raw right foot—the one I scalded as a small boy, trying to give myself a bath in the kitchen sink of that old tenement over on East Fifty-ninth Street. Water so hot I went into shock and passed out. Both feet swaddled in bandages, the smell of sulfur medicine permeating the air. Last October, when I flew down to Maryland to be with my father after his operation, I asked him about this. "Yes," he told me, "I got the call at work and came racing to the hospital." What he doesn't want to repeat (and who can blame him) is that, if they hadn't discovered those sulfur drugs, gangrene would have set in and they would have had to cut both feet off at the ankles. Who was watching over me then?

A running leap off the roof of one tenement onto the roof of another, the dark alleyway five stories down. Is life an empty Mallarmean throw of the dice, pure chance behind it all, or does He send his ministering angels? Is it *Nada* or *Abba*? How many times have I called on Him, or simply groaned, and He was there, giving me, if the truth be known, better than I knew how to ask for? Coming from that background, how is it I ever got the education I got? Or became a writer? Or found a girl I didn't deserve, and sons I didn't deserve, if all were justice only?

A car crossing the divider on an ice road and smashing head on into my wife and son, the steering wheel bent, and yet both somehow escaping serious injury. Was there *ever* a time I called on Him that He didn't answer, sparing me even as my friends were taken? And why hasn't He demanded payment in return? Why does He seem to go on waiting at the door to be invited in? And if for me, then for others. But I can only read my own map, as others must read theirs.

And now, as I get ready to go back out into the world with a renewed sense of what I can do, I say Ignatius's prayer one more time, asking only for God's love to keep my goings graces:

To give and not to count the cost
To fight and not to heed the wounds
To toil and not to seek for rest
To labor and not to ask for any reward
Save knowing I do thy will.

Remember me, Lord, in the dark passes, a gimpy soldier bringing up the rear.

4:15 A.M. Restless sleep. Erotic dreams even now, at the end of the retreat. Get up, I told myself. No use lying here. Break it, and get on with it. There was a tenaciousness to this one, as if Satan, pimp that he is, was going to have the last laugh. But this one I broke in half by prayer. Is it my dogsbody craving a treat? Or something trying to snatch away my peace of mind? Better simply to turn the mind elsewhere, back into the lighted hall of the imagination and the things of God.

10:45 A.M. Had my final session with JJ this morning. He listened as I read bits and pieces, still looking for patterns, then made a final suggestion. Find a spiritual director to meet with once a month, he said, someone to talk over your progress and failures. He offered to talk with me these last couple of days if I felt the need. And then, like that, the session was over. We shook hands, and I gave him a hug, thanking him once again for all his help. He told me it had been a privilege to work with me. Well, it has been a privilege to work with you too, dear man. I thought of Fr. Corcoran writing me this past Christmas that what remained for me now was to break myself for others. We are, Andre Dubus wrote shortly before he died, poor broken vessels made whole enough by God to hold God in us. Most whole, it seems, when most broken. Broken himself and confined to a wheelchair in the last years of his life, he knew whereof he spoke.

Flurries this morning as I was praying in Mary Chapel. Mark Luedtke, one of the novices, was making multiple rubbings of the Russian cross that hangs in the chapel over the Tabernacle. Suddenly, I heard a crash, then muttering. He was still reassembling the cross when I left the room. How fitting that the Christ who has been putting us together these past weeks should be broken at the end once more. As He is each day at the Consecration, to make us whole. The still point of my turning world.

EPILOGUE

1:00 P.M. The retreat ended at noon today with Mass. Fr. Joe the Younger took the opportunity to remember his fellow Jesuits martyred in Asia in the seventeenth and eighteenth centuries, conflating them with John the Baptist's martyrdom, recalled in today's Gospel. During his homily he mentioned running into a woman he'd seen coming out of the woods with a bunch of forsythia branches she told him she was going to force. They were all bud now, tightly furled, but in time the branches would flower. And so with us, he said, as the fruits of this retreat continued to unfurl in the months and years to come. After all, he explained, the gifts we've received are not to be unwrapped here, but when we get back home, there to be shared with others.

5:30 P.M. How strange to be talking freely again. Many of the retreatants took off for a few hours, some to drive into Gloucester until dinner. After lunch, I went up to JJ in the Main Hall and asked him what he thought of my simply slipping away and going home. After all, the real work of the retreat is over now. But I could see from the way he looked at me that he hoped I'd reconsider, and I withdrew the suggestion at once. It's only now that I realize what really lay behind my request: the difficulty I've always had of saying good-bye.

Instead, I took a two-hour walk with Tom Wilhelm, the Augustinian priest; Bud Knight, a Franciscan brother back from leading retreats in Africa; and Mary O'Rourke, who holds a Ph.D. in chemistry from Harvard. We trekked about the ice-rutted roads outside the compound in the cold, crisp air, talking about the retreat and our own spiritual journeys. Everything seemed new, fresh, invigorating. Talking to them, it looks as though no two retreats were even remotely the same. Bud, for instance, told me he'd discovered God on this retreat as both mother and lover. And why shouldn't God come to us as we most need Him to come?

Laughter and jokes. Once, caught up in conversation, I slipped on the ice and fell flat on my face, my glasses tumbling into the snow. Well, no one ever said things were going to be any easier just because I made this retreat. When we got back to the retreat house, we joined a group in the dining hall and talked until the shadows had lengthened across the room, when some of us went down to Chapel, and some back to their rooms.

9:30 P.M. At half past seven we gathered in a large circle in the Fireplace Room to discuss how the "debriefings" of the next two days should proceed. There's such a different feeling to all of this. Until a few years ago, the Thirty-Dayers left right after lunch, like the Eight-Dayers now. In fact, one person did leave, quietly, without fanfare. But the staff here thought it might help if we went over the experience of the Thirty Days in four sessions—two on Saturday, two on Sunday—with some free time Saturday evening and a social hour Sunday evening, with everyone free to depart after Mass and breakfast Monday morning.

Fr. Frank began the meeting by explaining that there was no right or wrong way to make the *Spiritual Exercises,* that—despite the rigor of the outline—the *Exercises* were an encounter between oneself and God. It was, he said, a matter of remaining open to the Spirit, and so anyone who had done the *Exercises* honestly—even if he or she hadn't finished the Four Weeks in the prescribed time—had done them right. Having said this, he invited each of us to say something about what had particularly struck us during the making of the *Exercises.*

The first to go surprised me by the depth of her insight. What she had particularly noticed, she said, was the beauty of our faces, and how that beauty had manifested itself all the more as the weeks had progressed. Many good things were said in turn, but what each person said right off, first, was like a drawing off of the finest oil. Halfway around the circle came my turn. I found myself thanking the women especially for providing so many of the grace notes during the retreat: flowers on the altar, music at meals, the various small tapestries arranged over the lectern for Mass. Caring gestures, human touches.

Then two schedules for the weekend were presented and voted on. Here's the way the weekend will play itself out. On both days we'll break into three groups, a group to a room: the Main Chapel, the Reading Room, the Fireplace Room. Each day there'll be two periods for reflection and sharing, each ninety minutes long. One in the morning, one in the afternoon. Mass both days will be at 11:15, followed by lunch. I see I'll have just enough time tomorrow night to get up to Newburyport and back before they lock the doors to the Main House. Good. Now down to Chapel to drink in God's presence.

SATURDAY, FEBRUARY 5

9:00 A.M. Breakfast at half past eight, a walk along the ocean, then a visit to Chapel in thanksgiving for a retreat well made. Banter this morning over coffee, but I miss the silence, the intensity of my time with God. In truth, the place has the feel now of a party for Russian bureaucrats in Warsaw in the autumn of '45. This place, after all, was made for silence, and I think I could go on here in silence for a long long time. I almost wish JJ would come out and tell us to be quiet and listen to God again. And me the gregarious one. Have the Jesuits ruined me for life?

There are nine of us in Group One: six retreatants (three novices, a seminarian, two lay folk) and three staff members. There's Geoff Miller and Mark Luedtke, two of the Chicago/Detroit novices. Mark's the can-do guy, who does the driving, reads the maps, and stokes the fire each night. It was Mark who pieced together every jigsaw puzzle he could get his hands on around here, laying them out on a small desk one after the other in the Reading Room, day after day and night after night. But he was also the one who made some of the most diverse and imaginative petitions at Mass, his concerns ranging from those of his Jesuit community to what was happening in the world around us.

And Geoff's the scholar: the novice who seemed to take to the retreat in the old ascetic manner. I never saw him sign at meals, and now—since we can talk—the other novices have been kidding him about his intensity. I did notice how he separated himself out from the others to go about the business of the retreat as intensely as I did, perhaps more so, which brought a smile to my face, for he reminded me of my younger self.

This morning, after I mentioned some passage in the Scriptures, he lent me his copy of the Greek New Testament, which he's been studying these past thirty days. I took it back to my room to compare the Greek and English, looked at it briefly in despair, and realized how much of the Greek I'd learned in college has vanished over the past forty years. All I have left, in fact, is one ancient Greek drinking song I memorized when I was his age, figuring I'd make a hit at frat parties up in the Bronx. By contrast, Geoff has Mark and Paul down in the original. I have wasted my life.

Then there's Devon, the one new Jesuit from all of Jamaica. He wants to be a brother and serve among the poor. It's clear he's seen his share of tragedy and mayhem in the slums of Kingston, just blocks from the picture-perfect tourist beaches. There's a purity and forthrightness about him I find delicious and refreshing, and I love talking to him whenever I can.

Then Vinnie Schifano, from Rockville Center, Long Island, who will be ordained this summer. His room was only two down from mine, so I saw more of him coming and going than I did most of the others. He tells me he is shocked that I—a fellow Italian—could actually *like* the food they serve here. There were times, he tells me now, that he drove into Gloucester to get an Italian meal. At the diocesan seminary, after all, he says, they have three first-rate Italian cooks. His facial expressions speak volumes. He's like the guys I grew up with on the Island forty years ago, only younger.

Then there's Rita Jensen, the retired schoolteacher from Lawrence, who made an Eight-Day retreat here last year and wanted to do the Long Retreat under the direction of that stand-up comedian, Fr. Tim Shepard. A single woman, a Navy veteran, wracked by pain daily, she told us, from operations she had years ago, a pain she handles admirably. Often I've seen see her in the dining hall, early, having a cup of coffee, looking out to sea, thinking.

Then the two Jesuit fathers, Mark and JJ. Also: Dixie Burden, with the Weston School of Theology connection, whose stories about her family and life in New York so resonate for me. A kind woman who pays exquisite attention when you speak.

And then there's myself.

11:00 P.M. Mass at 11:15, lunch, a walk about Niles Pond, then back to the Fireplace Room at half past three for our afternoon session. The sharing is useful, though I noticed that JJ and Fr. Mark mostly listen. Dixie, on the other hand, is willing to share her story with us. There's the occasional surprise comment by someone—something refreshingly frank said, some observation about the nature of the retreat, something that chimes with my own experience, or illuminates a new direction for me to explore. Still, I've found nothing as intense as what I experienced alone in the silence of God. One thing is sure. I'll be living off the insights of the Thirty Days for years to come.

The afternoon session lasted until five, and revisited the First Week. We were all asked to meditate on Ezekiel 36:23–28: *I shall give you a new heart, and put a new spirit in you. I shall remove the heart of stone from your bodies and give you a heart of flesh instead.* I was tempted to look again at the failings of my younger years. But the deeper problem here is that I have too often snatched at the gifts God has given me as if I were their only begetter, rather than seeing them as gifts I might have shared more freely and unstintingly with others. It looks like the old *non serviam* syndrome—I will NOT serve—forgetting that I am a child of God only, and not God.

At half past five, in ice and darkness, I left Eastern Point and drove up to Newbury along 1A to have dinner with John and Maria. Fr. Tom Faiola, the Capuchin priest who married them eighteen months ago, was already at the apartment when I got there. John put wine and freshly cooked shrimp out on the table for us while we talked. I felt like the most contented man in the world listening to the others talk shop. Maria's third-graders, psychological testing and counseling, the Red Sox and the Yankees.

At seven we drove into Newburyport to an Italian restaurant up on the third floor of a Federalist brick building. Decent food, decent wine, good company. I made it back to Eastern Point just as JJ, dressed in an old undershirt and looking tired, locked the main door and shuffled on. Luckily one of the novices heard me rapping on the dining hall window and let me in. It's a strange feeling to have your spiritual director lock you out, like some angel in his undershirt blocking the path back into Eden.

Winter and darkness and the disappearance of the self. After calling Eileen, I joined a small group around the fire. As much as I enjoy the talk, there's someone else I need to listen to just now. There's so little time, I begin to see now, to come in contact with this other reality that surrounds us, yet which we hardly ever see. At its best, poetry does this for me. And prayer. What is this exquisite thing, this chord, this cello note that dissolves me to tears? Unattended moments in and out of time when you brush up against it and it whispers back, *I AM.*

Tonight, for instance, when John walked me to my car and watched as I drove out of the parking lot. Or Maria ordering a coffee-to-go for me, to help keep me alert as I drove the icy roads back to

Eastern Point alone. Simple gestures of attention, signifying everything. Driving back, I turned on the radio and listened to some talk show. The banter was smooth, sophisticated, yet careful to reveal nothing of substance, so unlike the talks I've had with Him these thirty days. How was it? my friends will ask. How the hell did you keep silence all that time? How to explain, really, what I've gone through? What words will ever tell the story? How will I ever remember, much less sing, this otherworldly symphony? Winter storm and winter sunlight, a moon waxing over a cove, a single candle flickering in the night reaches, and a weather-beaten rock where I have heard Him calling.

How much time does one have? Who knows? Who ever knows? As now, thinking of my youngest son, preoccupied as he must be with his own world, as surely I was at his age. A son who took the time tonight to wait under a street lamp surrounded by winter darkness, as his father turned left, then right, then down a ramp, right light blinking, heading into darkness until he must have seemed to disappear.

•

SUNDAY, FEBRUARY 6

9:00 A.M. Up early to begin my morning meditation. Here's Thomas Merton in *Seasons of Celebration,* for my sixtieth birthday, three weeks away. "We have found him in the abyss of our own poverty—not in a horrible night, not in a tragic immolation, but simply in the ordinary, uninteresting actuality of our everyday life." And yet how Christ makes the quotidian shine, the stones as well as the sea in all its moods. In their agony and in their calm they sing, they sing.

Breakfast at eight with Father John and several others. I asked him about his time in the Navy, flying F4F Hellcats. That plane was like a tank, he says. Had a top speed of 410 knots, and could chew right through the wing of a Japanese Zero. Once, he confessed, he somehow managed to bomb Cape Cod.

1:00 P.M. A short reflection this morning by Fr. Tim on the long Second Week. Then back to my room to meditate on what Christ asks of us, with an emphasis on service, on using ourselves up for others. Then we gathered in our small groups and spoke of our renewed commitment to serve others. My heart went out to the young men here, who are trying to discern the nature of the religious life they feel called to. My own youthful experience in a religious order and the numbers of those who stay the course in religious life remind me that some of these novices will probably leave the Order, though which ones I have no way of knowing. I think of Paul's commitment to the Jesuits, still strong after ten years.

The others here will go on with their lives, as I will with mine, teaching at UMass or, come fall, at Boston College. Our elections—our sense of what God's will is for us—seem to have been relatively easy for some, hard for others. After all, some of us are already retired, and I've put in nearly forty years of teaching, starting back at Colgate as an English instructor the same fall Jack Kennedy was shot. Teaching and writing. What else is there for an old war-horse like me to do? Besides, it still excites me each waking day. I actually get paid for doing what I love. How many can say that?

We spoke among ourselves in our small circle until eleven, then prepared for Mass. I was struck by the first reading, taken from the Book of Job. How stark Job's lament, how different from what I myself have felt this past week, though—as I've said—I've been where Job was too:

> *Is not man's life on earth a drudgery? Are not his days those of hirelings? He is a slave who longs for the shade, a hireling who waits for his wages. So I have been assigned months of misery, and troubled nights have been allotted to me. If in bed I say, "When shall I arise?" then the night drags on; I am filled with restlessness until the dawn.*

Now *there's* a sentiment as dark as anything in Beckett. I smiled to myself, hearing Job's words about sleepless nights. And yet, how many graces have come to me in the night watches.

5:45 P.M. This afternoon a short reflection by young Fr. Joe on the Third and Fourth Weeks. Then back to our rooms to reflect, followed by forty-five minutes of sharing. I kept looking up, watching the shadows lengthen across the room, knowing it was my last afternoon here.

Afterward, a photo-op. Several people took group photos in the Main Hall: on the landing, the stairs, around the altar table. Mary took a picture of JJ and me, which she promises to send.

10:00 P.M. Steak and swordfish for dinner tonight. The very best served last, I see. I ran into several retreatants and staff talking in the hall outside my room after dinner. In fact, small groups fall easily into conversation now whenever we meet. Fr. Frank invited me down to his study, where we spoke of many things, including Boston College. He wished me well and thought it would be a good move for the Jesuits as well as for myself. I hope so. I dearly hope so.

Then back to my room to begin packing for the trip home tomorrow morning. I put my books and journals into boxes and packed my clothes. Then I cleaned my room and vacuumed the rug. All of this by way of a dry run, a way of leaving by incremental stages. A final call to Eileen to say I'd be home by noon. Then we gathered in the dining hall for our social hour. Beer, wine, trays of snacks, a chance to talk for the last time together.

And did we not brush up against some great Mystery together here? Did we not speak here as the angels speak, in a language beyond words? Did we not hear God singing to us? What can compare to that, really? We walked about talking and exchanging addresses, and the room echoed with laughter. A laughter laced perhaps with sadness, knowing this time will not come again. Unless of course the time itself has been redeemed, so that in memory we will replay this time, all of us, as we weave together with the angels, as in a painting by Fra Angelico.

MONDAY, FEBRUARY 7

7:15 A.M. Down to Chapel this morning to thank God for His many blessings. I packed the last of my things, stripped the bed, and fitted it with clean sheets, as we were asked to do. Mass begins in fifteen minutes. After that, breakfast, followed by all those hearty, awkward good-byes. And then I'll get up from the table and walk out through the same doors I walked in through when I arrived here, get in my car, start the engine, drive down the tree-lined driveway, circle left around Niles Pond, and head for home.

8:45 A.M. But of course there *was* one last surprise. It was Fr. Tom Wilhelm who celebrated this morning's Mass, the only time he's done so since we've been here. It took me by surprise seeing him in chasuble and stole. He and Marcie and Steve Hannafin worked together on this liturgy, and, in fact, Tom asked me yesterday if I would read today, though I thought he was arranging the liturgy for one of the other priests. The reading was from the First Book of Kings, the passage where the elders bring the Ark of the Lord's convenant up to Jerusalem to place it in the Temple Solomon has prepared for it. After the priests leave, God takes up residence there in the form of a cloud. It's a sign that He intends to dwell there with His people. How happy Solomon must have been. May God abide here at Eastern Point as well, and in my heart. Forever.

Just before the Gospel, Steve sat down at the piano and played the Celtic Alleluia that has been haunting me night and day for the past week. I'd asked him how I might find that Alleluia, and by trial and error—and with me singing off-key for him and Marcie and Tom—they managed to find it. Now the music I've heard all week in my head was actually filling the room. The Word made flesh again. I caught Tom's eye as he approached the lectern to proclaim the Gospel. He looked back and winked.

How I shall miss the stately presence of my fellow pilgrims here. Already they're scattering to the wind, some to catch trains and planes, others in their cars, ready to move on to whatever lies ahead. It all changes, doesn't it? Like the sea that keeps crashing in, as it will when other pilgrims replace us, and others in time replace them. And yet, how many lovely surprises still lie ahead, like belated Christmas gifts the Lord has blessed us with, and which we shall unwrap, one by one by one, in the days and years to come.

AFTERWORD

What I have offered in the preceding pages is a story of sin and grace, one man's spiritual failures and victories, and the intimate knowledge of God's love operating day by day not only in his life, but in the lives of his family and friends. It is also a story—one of millions—about the profound consolations offered by the *Spiritual Exercises* of St. Ignatius of Loyola. It is the story too of the impact of the *Exercises* on a particular individual at a particular moment and in a particular place. Yet the Thirty-Day retreat recorded here was not the end but only the beginning of a healing, which has turned out to have ongoing implications, both in its desolations as well as in its deeper consolations.

In one sense the story is private and is being shared in the hope that it might resonate with what is most important to its readers, who must of course go their own journeys. As important as this book has been to me, it is the retreat itself and the ongoing fruits of the retreat that remain uppermost in my mind and heart. That is as it must and should be. In truth, I have relived portions of this retreat each time I have sat down to go over what happened during those thirty days. No doubt I have benefited from the experience spiritually and—because it is a book I wrote under contract—financially as well. That much must be said to help set the record straight. But, as Ignatius enjoins, I have tried to remain indifferent to the book's ultimate fate and trust only that those who read it will benefit from it and perhaps even be encouraged to undertake the *Exercises* for themselves. In any event, may what has been written here ultimately be *ad majorem Dei gloriam:* for the greater glory of God.

Praise Him.

ACKNOWLEDGMENTS

Where to begin? I suppose with my agent, Tom Grady, and Janet Goldstein and the staff at Viking, who came up with the idea of my writing about the actual experience of making the Ignatian Thirty-Day retreat. In the nearly half millennium since St. Ignatius of Loyola put together a version of the *Spiritual Exercises* in the solitude of Manresa, there have been hundreds of commentaries and guides meant for the one who gives the exercises. Practical advice, for the most part, or explanations—spiritual and psychological—into this or that aspect of the *Exercises.* Hundreds of thousands over the centuries and from all over the world have made either the Thirty-Day or its offspring, the annual Eight-Day retreat. Every Jesuit, and thousands of other religious who base their spirituality on the Ignatian model, has made the Long Retreat. In fact, every Jesuit is required to make the *Exercises* not once but twice over a lifetime: the first time on entering the order, and again during Tertianship, or the third year of formation, which characteristically comes some eight to ten years after a Jesuit makes final vows. Since their inception, the Jesuits have offered the *Exercises*—or versions of them—to men and women from all walks of life, from kings and queens to teachers, students, bus drivers, doctors, lawyers, teamsters, scientists, artists, soldiers, policemen, government officials, and businessmen.

Eighty-five years ago, James Joyce fictionalized a segment of the *Exercises* in *A Portrait of the Artist as a Young Man.* There young Stephen Dedalus is enjoined by his Irish Jesuit retreat master to consider the physical pangs of hell and winds up retching in the boys' bathroom. But that is only one view of the *Exercises,* and a jaundiced one. *Thirty Days* is, it appears, the first book to follow an individual retreatant through the entire arc of the Long Retreat.

And so, thanks to all those who made this book a reality. Thanks especially to the staff at Eastern Point, whom I have named in the book itself, and especially to Fr. John "JJ" Bresnahan, S.J., for guiding me through the thirty days. Thanks to the others, too, for their example in making the retreat with me and bolstering me by their example. Thanks to three other Jesuits who took me on the journey at various times: Fr. Larry Corcoran and the late Frs. William Sheehan and Brian Duffy. Thanks, too, to Fr. Rich Meehan, who twenty-five years ago steered me through the Nineteenth Annotation in weekly sessions over a two-and-a-half-year period, until I began at last to "get it right." Thanks, too, to so many priests and religious—women and men—who have sustained my faith over six decades.

Thanks especially to my editor, Janet Goldstein, who took me through the whole experience again with her voluminous and brilliant questions until I began to understand the *Exercises* on a whole new level. Thanks too to those who read the manuscript early on, in multiple versions—especially Ron Hansen, Tom Grady, and Fr. Jim Martin, S.J., at America House. Again and again their suggestions and support made all the difference.

A word of thanks too to Eileen, my wife, lover, and friend, and to my three sons, Paul, Mark, and John, my closest companions on this life's journey. They know better than any how they have been there for me and for each other in so many ways and for so many years. My debt to the living dead—to Ignatius and Hopkins and so many other Jesuits, as well as to the voices of so many writers and poets—is immense. And if anyone has been a catalyst for this book it has been the example of my oldest son, Paul, and his Company of Jesus, a group of men I look upon with awe and gratitude.

And of course a special word of thanks to the Holy Spirit, who guided me not only through the Long Retreat but during all those years before, the same Spirit who I pray guides me now, each day, wherever I am, heartbeat by heartbeat, breath by breath.

Montague, Massachusetts
June 1, 2001